Writing at Risk

INTERVIEWS

IN PARIS WITH

UNCOMMON

WRITERS

Writing at Risk

BY JASON WEISS

UNIVERSITY OF IOWA PRESS

IOWA CITY

University of Iowa Press,
Iowa City 52242
Copyright © 1991 by
the University of Iowa
All rights reserved
Printed in the
United States of America
First edition, 1991
Design by Richard Hendel

Printed on acid-free paper
Library of Congress Cataloging-in-
Publication Data
Weiss, Jason, 1955–
    Writing at risk: interviews in
    Paris with uncommon writers/by
    Jason Weiss.—1st ed.
        p.   cm.
    Includes bibliographical
    references.
    ISBN 0-87745-348-9 (alk.
paper).—ISBN 0-87745-349-7
(pbk.: alk. paper)
    1. Authors—20th century—
Interviews.   2. Paris (France)
in literature.   I. Title.
PN452.W47   1991   91-4787
809'.04—dc20   CIP

E. M. Cioran photo
by John Schults
Julio Cortázar photo
by Jacques Robert
Brion Gysin photo
by Jane Evelyn Atwood
Eugène Ionesco photo
by Jacques Robert
Carlos Fuentes photo
by Jacques Sassier
Jean-Claude Carrière photo
by Elizabeth Wajnberg
Milan Kundera photo
by Aaron Manheimer
Nathalie Sarraute photo
by Jacques Sassier
Edmond Jabès photo
by Elizabeth Wajnberg

FOR MY PARENTS

Contents

Acknowledgments

ACKNOWLEDGMENT IS MADE to the following publications in which much of this work first appeared: *Cineaste, City Lights Review, Conjunctions, Exquisite Corpse, Grand Street, International Herald Tribune, Invisible City, Jazz Magazine* (Paris), *The Kenyon Review, Los Angeles Times, Luna Park* (Paris), *New England Review, The Paris Review, Quilt, Reality Studios* (London), *The Times* (London).

I wish to thank all of the writers who agreed to be interviewed.

Also, thanks to David Meltzer, who first introduced me to the work of Jabès, which in turn led to Cioran.

Acknowledgments

Introduction

FEW PATHS ARE as uncertain as a career in literature. More than the other arts, the one which is centered on the written word lays itself open to a dizzying play of nuances which only the skill of the author—and a favorable wind—render coherent. As the principal medium for thought and narrative, speech and song, words bear a stricter relationship to meaning than image or gesture or sound and yet must encompass all of these if they are to seem alive. The plasticity of words, the wealth of their ambiguities, pose challenge enough to the conventional writer, but to one who seeks to go beyond, to reach new discoveries, the struggle is unrelenting.

Each of the writers interviewed in this book has changed the course of literary tradition. Probably they did not start out with that goal; or if it was part of their youthful ambition, they could not have imagined the forms it would take. The adventure they had embarked on was to wrestle with the verbal angel and to register occasional victories along the way in the form of insights or a finished product. But no sooner does one work end than another has already begun. In this, public approval placed a distant second for these artists compared to the stages of understanding achieved. It has been their wager with the world to make manifest the dreams and inner challenges that have occupied them.

In essence, they have put their lives at stake. What they knew was constantly confronted, provoked even, by what they did not know. The risk these writers courted was the investment of their entire effort, their very identity, in the chance they might be wrong. They were following their instincts into uncharted territory, where nothing was guaranteed and few previous models could serve as guideposts. Instead of fashioning the language to suit what they needed to find, redefining genres, they might have wasted the opportunity of their talents and gone astray.

Most of the writers here did not really publish much until they were well into their thirties. Even then, they had only begun to comprehend the particular challenge that stood before them. Where they venture to discuss literary theory in the interviews, they are quick to point out that it derives solely from their own practice, after a long experience of feeling their way along.

The nature of the risks assumed varies from writer to writer, according to their concerns. For E. M. Cioran, it involved a break with philosophy in order to address philosophical issues by way of his own discomforts. Eugène Ionesco in theater and Nathalie Sarraute in fiction had to make a comparable break, turning away from tradition to develop new rules. Julio Cortázar and Carlos Fuentes, in their short and long fiction, did not reject what was handed down to them quite so much as they had to reconstruct it to handle the realities of their emerging cultures. Milan Kundera had to redirect the novel to accommodate multiple registers, exploring some of the lost roads of its history as proposed by writers such as Laurence Sterne and Robert Musil. Edmond Jabès had to forge a new way of writing where a perpetual questioning and doubt itself were his strength. Brion Gysin often treated words for their abstract dimensions, diverting language through the lessons learned from other disciplines, especially painting. Jean-Claude Carrière is a special case: he started as a young novelist but soon changed course to abandon the author's supremacy in favor of a more collaborative process that was always putting him to the test, in film and also theater. Nonetheless, he remains a writer committed to the dictates of the imagination; whether devising an original script or adapting a literary work, he must navigate the pitfalls while trying to discern the order implicit in each story, to make it play.

It will be noted that all but one of these writers are foreign to France, where they were interviewed. Carrière, the exception, made his reputation working with foreign artists and is by far the most international of French screenwriters. Writing inherently requires some distance, if one is to put into words what others simply live. The experience of being an outsider is inescapable; it is both the writers' blessing and curse. Even the time of writing, the rhythm of the hours as the act unfolds, sets writers apart. So, when they have had to learn new local customs, to hear a different language in the streets and in their own work perhaps, how much more is their thought affected by the fertile confusions and mysterious resonances of being an outsider? Exile, whatever its reason or source, beyond the very real difficulties, accentuates the writers' condition. There they can find a kind of privilege. Their identity may flourish among greater contrasts; less subject to local cultural assumptions, they are at the same time separated from their original circumstances. This dislocation predisposes some to a feeling for risk, since they are already closer to the edge. By reaching out beyond what they know, they might find the secrets of a more expansive language.

THESE LITERARY INTERVIEWS began, after I moved to Paris in 1980, as an excuse for me to meet famous writers. What other reason would they have, I thought, for speaking with a young writer like me? It was a unique opportunity to ply them with questions, provided I could figure out what to ask. Little did I know that the entire pursuit would turn into an apprenticeship, a schooling unlike any other.

Sometimes, especially at first, the occasion for an interview was a newspaper profile I was preparing, for which I tried to read nearly every work of the writer. My research would result in pages upon pages of questions that inevitably would generate far more material than I needed for one article. I began to publish the full interviews in literary journals and then to contact the journals directly proposing other encounters.

There were a number of unwritten rules, I soon discovered. In some cases, the publication for which the full interview was intended turned it down when the piece was finished, even though they had printed a previous interview of mine. This in turn led to contact with other journals which eventually did publish the work; each time I promised myself that I was through with these time-consuming exercises in frustration.

Gradually I understood that I was on the trail of a book, not conceived but rather lived as such. That is, I was engaged in a practice that followed the twists and turns of my own literary curiosities, paying little heed to fashion or to external notions of form (there were, incidentally, several writers who refused to give interviews). Thus, both the interviews and the writers vary quite a bit here, yet throughout the discussions keep returning to certain cultural preoccupations that were not always planned.

Doubtless there is an art of the interview, which I may have learned a bit in spite of myself. But there is equally a sort of metaphysics. Just because a question is posed does not mean an answer will follow, at least not the one that was hoped for. Or the answer may appear later, scattered among other insights. A question may be a provocation to talk—of the friendly kind, in these instances—and it may also be a way to steer the conversation in an intended direction. It might work, it might not, opening a different door instead. However, there are numerous occasions for chance to enter in as well, depending on time, mood, or fruitful digressions. At any rate, the interviewer must remain ever alert to the possible questions that may arise through the course of the meeting and be ready to redefine the areas of inquiry that were originally planned. As much as anything, the interview is a process, relying on the ability to improvise, like writing itself.

Several conditions marked these interviews. The longest encounters tended to be with those writers who had been interviewed least, because the terrain was most open. On the other hand, one challenge with the more widely known writers was to avoid repeating questions that had been asked too often, which sometimes resulted in a shorter piece. Instinctively I was attracted to the foreigners there, being one myself; some wrote in French, some didn't. It was their sense of literary adventure that drew me in. My reason for including Carlos Fuentes in this book, since he was not living in Paris at the time, is that not only was the interview conducted there, but he had once been ambassador to France and was very aware of the longstanding relationship between Paris and Latin American culture. At every turn, my sense of Paris as *the* international crossroads was reinforced by these interviews.

Lastly, a technical note. All but two of the interviews were conducted in French; one of Gysin's first languages was English, and Fuentes too had learned English as a child. The rest of the pieces were translated by me at the same time that I transcribed them from the tapes. That is, I chose to translate their speech as I heard it, rather than the words on a page. In this way, I hope the flavor of their spoken language is better retained.

Writing at Risk

E. M. Cioran

A keen stylist and rigorous thinker, concerned with the most funda-
mental issues of being, E. M. Cioran has often been compared with
such writers as Beckett and Borges. Though he might have been better
known had he written fiction or plays rather than his very particular
essays and aphorisms, Cioran's books reach across great distances: those
within the self as well as those between people.

   Cioran insists that he's not a writer; his fifteen books would appear
to prove otherwise. Even his titles provoke a look inside: A Short History of Decay, The Temptation to Exist, The Fall into Time, The
New Gods, The Trouble with Being Born, Drawn and Quartered,
and History and Utopia. *Of this last, which was originally pub-*
lished in 1960, he says, "I wanted to make an apology of utopia, but
when I read different utopias, I said this isn't possible." Among the
other books in French, Syllogismes de l'amertume *(1952) bears spe-*
cial note; it was his second book, but the first of aphorisms. At the time
of the interview he was working on a new collection of aphorisms, pro-
visionally called Ce maudit moi *and later published as* Aveux et
anathèmes *(1987).*

   A native of Rumania, son of a priest, Cioran is not a systematic
thinker. Rather his mind advances with that "patience to go in circles,

in other words, to deepen," *as he described in* The New Gods. *At seventy-two he could almost be a survivor of himself, though his fatigue seems more existential than physical. Yet Cioran's ready humor pierces even the gravest considerations with the wit of the condemned. Or as he once wrote, "In the blood an inexhaustible drop of vinegar: to what fairy do I owe it?"*

Known to be very private, Cioran has never given an interview to the French literary press, being too close to home, or to the American press (except for some moments with a Time *magazine correspondent years ago). The following interview took place over two mornings in mid-August,* 1983, *in his Latin Quarter apartment where he has lived since the early* 1960s, *though he has been in Paris since before the Second World War.*

JW: You've said that Sartre and others, by using a German style of discourse, did some harm to philosophical language. Can you elaborate on this?

EMC: Well, first I'll tell you that when I was quite young I myself was affected by this German jargon. I thought that philosophy wasn't supposed to be accessible to others, that the circle was closed, and that at all costs one had to use this scholarly, laborious, complicated terminology. It was only little by little that I understood the impostor side of philosophical language. And I should say that the writer who helped me tremendously in this discovery is Valéry. Because Valéry, who wasn't a philosopher but who had a bearing on philosophy all the same, wrote a very pure language; he detested philosophical language. That jargon gives you a sense of superiority over everybody. And philosophical pride is the worst that exists, it's very contagious. At any rate, the German influence in France was disastrous on that whole level, I find. The French can't say things simply anymore.

JW: But what are the causes?

EMC: I don't know. Obviously Sartre, by the enormous influence he had, contributed to generating this style. And then it's the influence of Heidegger, who was very big in France. For example, when he's speaking about death, he uses such complicated language to say very simple things, and I understand how one could be tempted by that style. But the danger of philosophical style is that one loses complete contact with reality. Philosophical language leads to megalomania. One creates an artificial world where one is God. I was very proud as a young man and very pleased to know this jargon. But my stay in France totally cured me of that. I'm not a philosopher by profession, I'm not a philosopher at all, but my path was the reverse of Sartre's. That's why I turned to the French writers known as the moralists—La Rochefoucauld, Chamfort, and all that—who wrote for society ladies and whose style was simple but who said very profound things.

JW: Was it philosophy you were first interested in?

EMC: I studied philosophy almost exclusively from the age of seventeen to twenty-one, and only the great philosophical systems. I disregarded most poetry and other literature. But I was happy to break quite early with the university, which I consider a great intellectual misfortune and even a danger.

JW: Were you reading Nietzsche then?

EMC: When I was studying philosophy I wasn't reading Nietzsche. I read "serious" philosophers. It's when I finished studying it, at the point when I stopped believing in philosophy, that I began to read Nietzsche. Well, I realized that he wasn't a philosopher, he was more: a temperament. So, I read him but never systematically. Now and then I'd read things by him, but really I don't read him anymore. What I consider his most authentic work is his letters, because in them he's truthful, while in his other work he's a prisoner of his vision. In his letters one sees that he's just a poor guy, that he's ill, exactly the opposite of everything he claimed.

JW: You write in *The Trouble with Being Born* that you stopped reading him because you found him "too naïve."

EMC: That's a bit excessive, yes. It's because that whole vision, of the will to power and all that, he imposed that grandiose vision on himself because he was a pathetic invalid. Its whole basis was false, nonexistent. His work is an unspeakable megalomania. When one reads the letters he wrote at the same time, one sees that he's pitiful, it's very touching, like a character out of Chekhov. I was attached to him in my youth, but not later on. He's a great writer, though, a great stylist.

JW: Yet critics often compare you to him, saying you follow in his tracks.

EMC: No, that's a mistake, I think. But it is obvious that his way of writing made an impression on me. He had things that other Germans didn't, because he read a lot of the French writers. That's very important.

JW: You've said that you also read a lot of poetry in your youth.

EMC: That was later. It was, if you like, my disillusionment with philosophy that made me turn to literature. To tell the truth, it's from that point on that I realized that Dostoyevsky was much more important than a great philosopher. And that great poetry was something extraordinary.

JW: How did your severe insomnia affect this attitude at the time?

EMC: It was really the big reason for my break with philosophy. I realized that in moments of great despair philosophy is no help at all, that it holds absolutely no answers. And so I turned to poetry and literature, where I found no answers either but states that were analogous to my own. I can say that the white nights, the sleepless nights, brought about the break with my idolatry of philosophy.

JW: When did these sleepless nights begin?

EMC: They began in my youth, at about nineteen. It wasn't simply a medical problem, it was deeper than that. It was the fundamental period of my life, the most serious experience. All the rest is secondary. Those sleepless nights opened my eyes, everything changed for me because of that.

JW: Do you still suffer from it?

EMC: A lot less. But that was a precise period, about six or seven years, when my whole perspective on the world changed. I think it's a very important problem. It happens like this: normally someone who goes to bed and sleeps all night almost begins a new life the next day. It's not simply another day, it's another life. And so, he can undertake things, he can manifest himself, he has a present, a future, and so on. But for someone who doesn't sleep, from the time of going to bed at night to waking up in the morning it's all continuous, there's no interruption. Which means there is no suppression of consciousness. It all revolves around that. So, instead of starting a new life, at eight in the morning you're like you were at eight the evening before. The nightmare continues uninterrupted in a way, and in the morning, start what? Since there's no difference from the night before. That new life doesn't exist. The whole day is a trial, it's the continuity of the trial. Well, while everyone rushes toward the future, you are on the outside. So, when that's stretched out for months and years, it causes your sense of things, your conception of life, to be forcibly changed. You do not see what future to look toward, because you don't have any future. And I really consider that the most terrible, most unsettling, in short, the principal experience of my life. There's also the fact that you are alone with yourself. In the middle of the night, everyone's asleep, you are the only one who is awake. Right away I'm not a part of humanity, I live in another world. And it requires an extraordinary will to not succumb.

JW: Succumb to what, madness?

EMC: Yes. To the temptation of suicide. In my opinion, almost all suicides, about ninety percent, say, are due to insomnia. I can't prove that, but I'm convinced.

JW: How did it affect you physically?

EMC: I was very tense, in a feverish state, and ready to explode. Everything took on another intensity, no matter what it was. I was far more violent, I quarreled with everyone. I couldn't put up with anything. And I found everyone idiotic. Nobody understood what I understood. It was the feeling of not belonging. Then too, this feeling that everything is a comedy, that it all makes no sense. The future was meaningless for me, the present as well. And so, philosophically—because one is always a philosopher—it's a sort of exasperation, an intensification of the state of being conscious. Not self-conscious, conscious. The state of consciousness as the great misfortune, and in my case the permanent misfortune. Normally, it's the opposite, it's consciousness which is our advantage. I arrived at the conclusion that no, the fact of being conscious, of not being oblivious, that is the great catastrophe. Because I was conscious twenty-four hours a day. One can be conscious several hours a day, five minutes, but not all day, all night. People are conscious by intervals, but there it's a matter of acuteness, all the time.

JW: Have you met other insomniacs through the years who suffered like that?

EMC: Not to that degree, no. Perhaps in a lunatic asylum one might. But I wasn't crazy at all, that's what's interesting. What I often liked to do, I should say, was go for walks at night. Curiously enough, I did that in Paris as well, until about ten years ago. Very often, in the middle of the night, if I couldn't sleep, I'd get up and go walking through Paris for two or three hours. Now it's become too dangerous to just go out for a walk like that at four in the morning. I liked to go all over the place. I'd wait until people were going to work, and then I'd come home and sleep a little. But I was doing better by then.

JW: That helped calm you a little.

EMC: Yes. I'll tell you, speaking of that, this period of deep insomnia came to an end in France, and you know how? The bicycle. This is quite a curious phenomenon, I was a bit like someone suffering hallucinations; I'd been in Paris a few months, and one day on the boulevard Saint Michel someone offered to sell me a bicycle. It was a racing bicycle, not expensive at all. I said yes and bought it, which for me was a stroke of providence, unheard-of luck. I went all over France with that bicycle, I'd be gone for months. Because I had come here on a grant from the French government to do a thesis for several years, from 1937 until the war, until 1940. To do a thesis in philosophy . . . which I certainly did not do! I never went to the Sorbonne, I lied. But with that I'd cover kilometers and kilometers, for months, I went all through the Pyrenees. I'd do a hundred kilometers a day. And it's this physical effort that allowed me to sleep. I remember, France was very cheap before the war. I'd come into a village, I'd eat whatever I wanted, drink a bottle of wine, and then I'd go sleep in the fields. It was a very natural life, very healthy. Physical exercise morning till night. When you do a hundred kilometers a day, there's no way you're not going to sleep, it's out of the question. So, it wasn't thanks to medicine. Because, unfortunately for me, I had seen a lot of doctors in Rumania and in France, and they all gave me medications that messed up my stomach and everything, that was the big danger, and even with sleeping pills I only managed to sleep two or three hours at most. And then I'd have a headache all day, it was horrible. I was poisoned from sleeping pills. I don't take them anymore. And so, this providential bicycle saved me.

JW: Did other insomniacs recognize the cure you found?

EMC: Yes. You see, there is a gang of insomniacs, there is a sort of solidarity, right, like people who have the same illness. We understand each other right away, because we know that drama. The drama of insomnia is this: it's that time doesn't pass. You're stretched out in the middle of the night and you are no longer in time. You're not in eternity either. The time passes so slowly that it becomes agonizing. All of us, being alive, are drawn along by time because we are in time. When you lie awake like that, you are outside of time. So, time passes outside of you, you can't catch up with it.

JW: In *The Fall into Time* you wrote, "Other people fall into time; I have fallen out of it." Was that from insomnia?

EMC: No, but it does have a remote effect. I consider my best writing to be those few pages on time there in that book. That is, people fall into time and fall further down than time. I feel it to be one of my points of originality, if you like. It's that you also are conscious of time. Normally people are not. Someone who acts, who is involved in doing something, doesn't think about time, that's absurd. But the consciousness of time proves that you are outside of time, that you've been ejected. One could really call it a philosophical, a metaphysical, experience. Now I'll tell you, I recall the first occasion in my life when I had a revelation of time. I was a child, I was five, and I remember exactly, it was an afternoon, during the First World War. I can even say the hour, I remember it was three in the afternoon.

Abruptly I felt that I was watching time pass, that I wasn't a part of it, I was outside. And I consider this sensation that I had, which didn't last even ten minutes, to be my first conscious experience of ennui, of boredom. Ennui is also a sort of becoming conscious of time, because the time does not pass. So, I was destined a bit to that consciousness of time, insomnia only accelerated it.

JW: Were there other people around at that moment when you were five?

EMC: No, I was absolutely alone. I wasn't able to formulate it, obviously, but I know it was that. Because I've never forgotten it. I remember it like it was yesterday, yet it was a whole life away. I consider it was there that I ceased to be an animal. I had entered humanity, I'd begun to have the experience of being human. So I was predestined to lose sleep because what is sleep? It is the return to unconsciousness, to animality, the return to the before-life, to oblivion. Insomnia is the worst illness.

JW: What happened to you on the level of dreams during your most severe insomnia?

EMC: Because of the sleeping pills I did manage to sleep two or three hours at most, but I had horrifying nightmares, absolutely horrifying. And so strong that I woke up with my heart pounding.

JW: Have there been many responses to what you've written about this experience of feeling yourself outside of time?

EMC: I have met people who recognized themselves in what I said, they recognized these sensations, because I've received a lot of letters. They hadn't formulated it perhaps, but they said, "I lived the same thing," they have the same feeling of existence.

JW: Speaking of your insomnia, I noticed you wrote that you had a very happy childhood.

EMC: A wonderful childhood. I believe I was unhappy in my life as punishment for having had such an extraordinarily happy childhood. I'm talking about early childhood, until the age of seven or eight, no more. Later was a catastrophe. Because I was born in a mountain village, very primitive, I was always outside in the open air. I lived like I was out in the wilds. I have wonderful memories of that time.

JW: And you remained in that village until what age?

EMC: Until I was ten. And there we had a garden next to the cemetery, which also played a role in my life because I was a friend of the gravedigger. I was always around the cemetery, all the time I was seeing the disinterred, the skeletons, the cadavers. For me death was something so obvious that it was truly a part of my daily life. I didn't start acting like Hamlet, but it is true that after that I began to be obsessed with skeletons and even the phenomenon of death. And that had an effect on my insomnia. Which means that for someone to have an obsession with death, one already has a sense of the unreality of life. It's there, the process. It's not the obsession with death that makes you discover that life is unreal, it's when you discover that life is without substance, that it's nothing at all, illusion, that the obsession with death settles in.

I'll tell you an anecdote that played a role in my life. I was about twenty-two and one day I was in a terrible state. We were living in Sibiu, a city in the provinces where I spent my whole youth, and where my father was the priest of the city. That day only my mother and I were home, and—when I remember things, I remember them very precisely, I even remember the hour, it's very strange—I think it was around two in the afternoon, everyone else had gone out. All of a sudden, I had a fantastic fit of despair, I threw myself on the sofa and said, "I can't take it anymore." And my mother said this: "If I had known, I would have had an abortion." That made an extraordinary impression on me. It didn't hurt me, not at all. But later I said, "That was very important. I'm simply an accident. Why take it all so seriously?" Because, in effect, it's all without substance.

JW: Which is interesting too, considering that your father was a priest.

EMC: Yes, but this was said by my mother! At the time, abortion didn't exist. But that proves that individual life is an accident and it is. Well, you can say, "But everyone knows that." Everyone knows that, but only now and then. It's another thing to know it morning and night, that's why it's maddening. So when we speak of these things, we absolutely must speak of the frequency and the duration. It's the fact of having that feeling constantly.

JW: You've said a number of times, as in *Drawn and Quartered*, that "we should change our name after each important experience."

EMC: After *certain* experiences. We should change our names right away, but later there's no point. Because you feel that you're another individual, that in the end you've touched on something extraordinary, you're not yourself anymore. So, another life has to be started. But, that's an illusion too. It's an impression of the moment.

JW: Considering these experiences of yours, how much did you begin reading French writers like Baudelaire, who spoke of comparable states?

EMC: I sort of worshipped Baudelaire. He is a great poet, yet Mallarmé is greater, so is Rimbaud, they're more original than he is. But that's in the deep sentiments. I've written somewhere that there are two writers whom I always think about, and whom I don't often read: they are Pascal and Baudelaire. They have been constant companions. It's not a matter of pride, it's simply an inner affinity, as if we're part of the same family. In a book about his youth, Pascal's sister, Madame Perier—you know that Pascal was ill all his life, he died relatively young, at the age of thirty-nine—she said her brother told her one day that from the age of seventeen he knew not a single day without suffering. I was in a public library in Rumania, in Bucharest, and when I read that it made such an impression on me that I wanted to cry out, and I put my hand in my mouth so as not to. I told myself that's what's going to happen in my own life, it was a presentiment of a sort of disaster, but even outside of that, Pascal and Baudelaire were the two who spoke most profoundly about the crucial experience of ennui. My life is inconceivable without ennui. Though I get bored now less than before.

JW: Why's that?

EMC: Because of old age. With old age things lose their intensity. So, everything that's good and everything that's bad gain in depth but not on the surface, if you like.

JW: But don't you find there are things that gain in intensity with old age?

EMC: No. One doesn't become better on the moral plane with old age. Or wiser. Contrary to what people think. One gains nothing in getting old. But as one is more tired, one gives the impression of wisdom.

JW: In *The Trouble with Being Born* you wrote: "What I know at sixty, I knew as well at twenty. Forty years of a long, a superfluous, labor of verification." Which surprised me a little, perhaps because I didn't want to believe it.

EMC: There is no progress in life. There are small changes, above all it's a question of intensity, as I said.

JW: With the insomnia, were you able to use it in a way, to go deeper with your thinking?

EMC: Certainly. Whether or not everything I've thought was due to insomnia, it would have lacked a certain frenzy without it. That's undeniable. Through insomnia all these things took on another dimension.

JW: Did you write much through all those sleepless nights?

EMC: Yes, but not so much. You know, I've written very little, I never assumed it as a profession. I'm not a writer. I write these little books, that's nothing at all, it's not an oeuvre. I haven't done anything in my life. I only practiced a trade for a year, I was a high-school teacher in Rumania. But since then, I've never practiced a trade. I've lived just like that, like a sort of student and such. And that I consider the greatest success of my life. My life hasn't been a failure because I succeeded in doing nothing.

JW: And that's difficult.

EMC: It's extremely difficult, but I consider that an immense success. I'm proud of it. I always found one scheme or another, I had grants, things like that.

JW: But your books have gained a lot of attention, haven't they?

EMC: They've only been talking about my books for the last three years, really. To tell you quite simply, they talked about me for a few months in 1950, regarding *A Short History of De-*

cay, and then, for thirty years, hardly at all. Really. I wasn't known, a few people in literary circles knew me. But everything changed a few years ago with the paperback editions.

JW: Yes, you were explaining how when *Syllogismes de l'amertume* came out in paperback, it was a big success.

EMC: That's the one. In more than twenty years it sold only two thousand copies. So it was my good luck to have been able to spend almost thirty years in a sort of oblivion. For me the tragedy of a writer is being famous when you're young, that's extremely bad. It forces everything, because most writers, when they're known fairly young, they write for their public. In my opinion, a book should be written without thinking of others. You shouldn't write for anyone, only for yourself. And one should never write a book just to write a book. Because that has no reality, it's only a book. Everything I've written, I wrote to escape a sense of oppression, suffocation. It wasn't from inspiration, as they say. It was a sort of getting free, to be able to breathe.

JW: What then has been your relationship with the practice of writing? The act of thinking, of following through certain ideas, is one thing, but the writing remains something else.

EMC: Yes, but you see, even so, there is another aspect to all that in my life because I changed languages. And for me that was a very important event. Because I began writing in French at the age of thirty-six. One *can* change languages at fifteen or twenty . . .

JW: When did you start studying French?

EMC: I hadn't studied it. In Rumania everyone knew a little French, not that they studied it. There were people who knew French extremely well, but that wasn't my case because I was born in Austria-Hungary. My parents didn't know a word of French, they spoke Rumanian and Hungarian. We had absolutely no French culture. But in Bucharest, French was the second language in the intellectual circles. Everyone knew French, everyone read it. And it was very humiliating for me, I spoke French very poorly. My peers knew French quite well, especially among the bourgeoisie, of course. I read French, naturally, but I didn't speak it. And so I came to France in '37, I was twenty-six, and instead of setting about to write in French, I wrote in Rumanian up until '47, but without publishing anything. I wrote lots of things. Then I was in a village in Normandy in 1947 and I was translating Mallarmé into Rumanian. All of a sudden it struck me that this made no sense. I'm in France, I'm not a poet to begin with, I translate poorly, why am I doing this? I didn't want to go back to my own country. And that was a sort of illumination. I said, "You have to renounce your native tongue." I came back to Paris with the idea of writing in French and set right to it. But, it was much more difficult than I thought. It was even *very* difficult. I thought I'd just start writing like that. I wrote about a hundred or a hundred and fifty pages and showed them to a friend, who said, "That's not right, you'll have to do it all over." I was furious, but that made me get serious about it. And I threw myself into the French language like a crazy person, surrounded by dictionaries and everything. I did an enormous amount of work. I wrote the first book four times. Then, when I wrote the next one after that, I couldn't write anymore. Because the words disgusted me, why write? The *Syllogismes de l'amertume* are little odds and ends, fragments. And now it's the book of mine they read most in France.

JW: Did the first book change much, writing it four times?

EMC: Yes, the style, a lot. Really, I wanted revenge in a way on all those folks in Rumania who knew French, but it wasn't conscious. And also, I had a complex about being a foreigner.

JW: Did you know many people during your early years in Paris?

EMC: No. And especially not in intellectual circles. I didn't know writers at all, I didn't hang out with them. I was shy, I was totally unknown. I knew a lot of refugees who came to Paris, but not the French. I knew people who weren't in literature, which is more interesting. Some years ago there was a Rumanian who came to Paris, who said that he wanted to meet some writers. I said, "You shouldn't hang out with writers. It's more important when you come from abroad to speak with a cab driver or a whore than with a writer." He got mad, started insulting me. He didn't understand what I meant.

JW: There are certain passages in your books where you take up the cause of bums, as if they have the right attitude about things.

EMC: But that's due to the fact that I had a friend who was a bum, who was *very* interesting. He'd play his instruments in loads of cafés, he'd pass the hat. I saw him four or five times a year, or he'd come to visit me. He's the one who opened my eyes to the life of bums, because that's the life he led. Well, he wasn't a poor fellow, he did earn some money playing. But he was a fellow who thought about things, and everything he told me was amazing. A very original life. You know what he did one day? He went up to the Champs-Elysées to that big café, Fouquet's, he played on his clarinet and people didn't give him a thing. He said, "Since you're poor, I'll help you," and he put some money down on every table. So, they called the police. He was wearing slippers, and he left his slippers there and went across to the other sidewalk. And there, he did something really extraordinary. There was a very elegant young woman passing by and he said to her, "The police have been bothering me, and I left my slippers over on the other sidewalk. Would you mind going to get them for me?" And she went and got them. He was always doing things like that. I spoke about him in my last book, *Drawn and Quartered*.

JW: For this reason as well, comparing you with Beckett as Susan Sontag did seems inevitable.

EMC: I like Beckett a lot, he's charming, very refined. I know him well, though we haven't seen each other in a long time. I wrote an essay about him. But yes, I think there are certain affinities.

JW: So it was only after you'd published some books that you got to know writers much?

EMC: Yes. But the only writer I still see, really, is Michaux. I stopped frequenting literary circles. But there was a period when I did have a real social life, and for very specific reasons. It was a time when I liked to drink, whiskey and such, and I was very poor. I was invited by rich ladies who had parties. I could drink and eat, I was invited to dinners, I'd go three times a week to different people's places. I accepted practically any dinner, because I was dependent on that. And so, I was often at a salon where I met lots of people, but that's a long time ago, the mid-1950s. I can't go to parties anymore, it's absolutely impossible. And then too, I don't drink anymore.

JW: I read that. "Years now without coffee, without alcohol, without tobacco," you wrote. Was it because of your health?

EMC: Yes, health. I had to choose. I was drinking coffee all the time, I'd drink seven cups of coffee in the morning. It was one or the other. But tobacco was the most difficult. I was a big smoker. It took me five years to quit smoking. And I was absolutely desperate each time I tried, I'd cry, I'd say, "I'm the vilest of men." It was an extraordinary struggle. In the middle of the night I'd throw the cigarettes out the window, first thing in the morning I'd go buy some more. It was a comedy that lasted five years. When I stopped smoking, I felt like I'd lost my soul. I made the decision, it was a question of honor, "Even if I don't write another line, I'm going to stop." Tobacco was absolutely tied up with my life. I couldn't make a phone call without a cigarette, I couldn't answer a letter, I couldn't look at a landscape without it.

JW: You felt better afterward, I hope.

EMC: Yes. When I'm depressed, I tell myself, "You did succeed in conquering tobacco." It was a struggle to the death. And that's always made me think of a story Dostoyevsky speaks about. In Siberia there was an anarchist at the time who was sentenced to eighteen years in prison. And one day they cut off his tobacco. Right away he gave a declaration that he was renouncing all his ideas and everything at the feet of the tsar. When I read that in my youth, I hadn't understood it. And I remember *where* I smoked my last cigarette, about fourteen years ago. It was near Barcelona. It was seven in the morning, it was cold, the end of September, and there was a foolish German who dove into the water and started swimming. I said, "If this German can do that at his age, I'm going to show that I can too." So I went in like that and I had the flu that night!

JW: The first time we met, you were saying that a writer's education must remain incomplete.

EMC: Ah yes. A writer mustn't know things in depth. If he speaks of something, he shouldn't know everything about it, only the things that go with his temperament. He should not be objective. One can go into depth with a subject, but in a certain direction, not trying to cover the whole thing. For a writer the university is death.

JW: Could you speak about the evolution of your use of the aphorism? Where does it come from?

EMC: I'm not sure exactly. I think it was a phenomenon of laziness perhaps. You know, very often aphorisms have been the last sentence of a page. Aphorisms are conclusions, the development is suppressed, and they are what remains. It's a dubious genre, suspect, and it is rather French. The Germans, for example, only have Lichtenberg and Nietzsche, who got it from Chamfort and the moralists. For me it was mostly due to my dislike of developing things.

JW: But what made you decide to use the aphorism for certain books and not others? Your second book, *Syllogismes*, was all aphorisms, though the first wasn't; for the next twenty years you hardly use them in your books, and then *The Trouble with Being Born* is all aphorisms too, as is much of *Drawn and Quartered*.

EMC: Well, now I only write this kind of stuff, because explaining bores me terribly. That's why I say when I've written aphorisms it's because I've sunk back into fatigue—why bother? And so, the aphorism is scorned by "serious" people, professors look down upon it.

JW: Because professors can't do anything with an aphorist.

EMC: Absolutely not. When they read a book of aphorisms, they say, "Oh, look what this guy said ten pages back, now he's saying the contrary. He's not serious." I can put two aphorisms that are contradictory right next to each other. Aphorisms are also momentary truths. They're not decrees. And I could tell you in nearly every case why I wrote this or that phrase and when. It's always set in motion by an encounter, an incident, a fit of temper, but they all have a cause. It's not at all gratuitous.

JW: For a book like *Syllogismes*, did you select which aphorisms would go into each section?

EMC: I organized them into chapters more or less. It wasn't written like that, not systematically. But in the end all that does inevitably have a unity because it is the same vision of things.

JW: Because it seems that with each book the title is very appropriate.

EMC: Yes, it's justified. For *The Trouble with Being Born*, though, I wanted to write a whole book on that. It wasn't possible, that's true. But the starting point was that.

JW: Do you have particular writing habits or conditions when you work?

EMC: I've never been able to write in a normal state. Even banal things, I've never been able to say, "Now I want to write." I always had to be either depressed or angry, furious or disgusted, but never in a normal state. And preferably, I write in a state of semi-depression. There has to be something that's not right. Because I find that when one is neutral, why write? Why declare things? And so, perhaps as they've said, there is a bit of a morbid aspect to what I write. And it is true, I've noticed, that the people who react the best to what I've written are the neurotics, the half-crazy, those who act out of passion.

JW: Do you have the idea for your books before you write them?

EMC: Most of the books were written just like that, off the cuff. The only ones where I had the idea beforehand were *The Fall into Time* and *History and Utopia*, because they're all of a piece.

JW: What kind of responses have you had from readers?

EMC: I can give you a few examples, what I call singular encounters, people I've seen only once. When I published my first book, *A Short History of Decay*, it got a very passionate reaction, I received a lot of letters. But the most extraordinary was from a girl who was about twenty. I was living in a hotel on rue Monsieur Le Prince, I opened this letter, it drove me mad. I was completely unknown and suddenly I get this, where it says, "This book was written by me, not by you. It's our book," etcetera. So I said, "If this is what it's like, I won't write anymore." Because at any rate I would never try to be like that. Why continue? I didn't know what to do, because she wrote, "If you ever want to see me, I'll be coming to Paris for Easter." Finally I wrote her we could meet, I said, "I was very impressed by your letter. Tell me who you are." So, she told me an amazing story, which I can repeat because I'm not mentioning her name and she's a lot older by now. She said, "Well, my life isn't of much interest, except that I lived with my brother like man and wife for six months." He knew I was going to meet her and didn't want me to, at any rate I think that it was over by then. But I realized it's not worth seeing a girl like that again, it wouldn't make any sense. But I was really struck by this story.

All right, the second story. For two years I received letters from a woman who was absolutely crazy. It was more like a sort of mixture of madness and intelligence. This was about three years ago. She kept insisting that she wanted to meet me. I said I didn't want to. Well, one day, about two years ago, I was depressed. It was an afternoon, the middle of the summer. I was very depressed, feeling that I was worthless. I said, "I'd like to see someone who has a good opinion of me." Who liked me. I'd been receiving letters from this woman for more than a year, and I hadn't replied much to them. I call her up, it was six or seven in the evening, she answers the phone. I say, "Listen, I'd like to see you." She says, "Right away. I live in the suburbs, I'll take a taxi, be at your house in an hour." A very pretty voice, see. At eight o'clock, I had gotten all fixed up with a tie, I open the door, and when I open the door I explode with laughter. She was a monster! An old woman, seventy-five years old, nearly eighty, little and all twisted up, but horrible! Something unimaginable. I went "Ha!" I couldn't stop myself. I'd put on a tie . . . What could I do?

Because, really, I had invited her to dinner. I thought, "I'm not going to a restaurant with this woman."

JW: So what did you do?

EMC: I invited her in, "Have a seat." I thought, "I can't speak of dinner now." It was impossible, there was nothing in the house. So I said to her, "But who are you?" If I had had a tape recorder! I sat there, I said practically nothing. She set to telling me about her life. She told me everything, with details to make you vomit sometimes. She told me how when she was a young girl, she'd gone into a church to confess, and the priest had said to her, "But, Miss, this isn't where you should go. You should go to Saint Anne's." That was the lunatic asylum. And she was the one who was telling me this. She was rich, she had several homes in Paris. And she'd read a fair amount. She knew my books by heart, she kept quoting passages. At midnight I decided that four hours of entertainment was enough, and I saw her to the door.

JW: But you do consider these single encounters important. Are there others?

EMC: A few years ago, there was a friend of mine who told me that he'd met a twenty-five-year-old engineer who wanted to meet me. Finally, I said all right, we'll go stroll around the Luxembourg Gardens nearby. It was a summer evening. We spoke about one thing and another, literature and such, and finally he said to me, "Do you know why I wanted to meet you? It's because I read your books, and I saw that you're interested in suicide. I'd like to tell you about my case." And so he explained to me that he had a good job, he earned a lot. He said, "In the last two or three years, I've begun to be obsessed with suicide. I'm in the prime of life, and this idea has taken hold of me. I haven't been able to get rid of it." We talked for three hours about suicide, circling the Luxembourg Gardens. I explained to him how I was—I am still—obsessed by it, I consider suicide as the only solution, but, I told him, my theory is this: that suicide is the only idea that allows man to live. Suicide gives me the idea that I can leave this world when I want to, and that makes life bearable. Instead of destroying it. So for three hours we discussed every aspect of this problem, and then I suggested that we not see each other again, because there wouldn't be any point.

JW: In an encounter like that, have you had the feeling of saving him a little?

EMC: Yes, a little. That's happened to me several times, with young women particularly. I've always prevented them from committing suicide. I've always tried to tell them that, since you can kill yourself anytime, you should put it off. But you should not abandon this idea.

JW: But you do feel a certain responsibility to such people.

EMC: Yes, I can't avoid it. Because my theory of suicide is that one shouldn't kill oneself, one should make use of this idea in order to put up with life. So, it's something else, but they've attacked me, saying this fellow makes the argument for suicide and doesn't do it himself. But I haven't made such an argument. I say that we have only this recourse in life, that the only consolation is that we can quit this life when we want to. So, it's a positive idea. Christianity is guilty of leading a campaign against this idea. One should say to people, "If you find life unbearable, tell yourself, 'Well, I can give it up when I want to.'" One should *live* by way of this idea of suicide. It's in *Syllogismes* where I wrote that sentence: "Without the idea of suicide, I would have killed myself from the start."

JW: Even in your most recent writings you've written about suicide. In "Tares" (Flaws), the selection of aphorisms published in the review *La Délirante*, you were saying that the idea of suicide was natural and healthy for you, because you've lived with it nearly all your life, but that what was not healthy was "the furious appetite for existing, a serious flaw, a flaw par excellence, my flaw."

EMC: Yes, it's a sort of avowal, because I've always kept in mind what Baudelaire said, "the ecstasy and the horror of life." For me, everything that I've experienced in this life is contained in that phrase.

JW: But you were considering suicide when you yourself were quite young. What made you decide to go on?

EMC: Because I considered life as a delaying of suicide. I had thought I wasn't going to live past thirty. But it wasn't from cowardice, I was always postponing my suicide, see. I exploited this idea, I was the parasite of it. But at the same time this appetite for existing was very strong in me too.

JW: I wonder if there were people in whom you could see their impending suicide. I think of Paul Celan, for example, whom you knew quite well.

EMC: No, I couldn't see it in him. You know, he translated my first book into German. When he arrived in Paris, at the start, I saw him often, he lived nearby on the rue des Ecoles. But later, we saw each other a lot less, he had moved. With him it really was a very serious illness which hastened his end. At the time that I met him I could never have imagined that he would kill himself. Except that sometimes he was very violent, he put up with all life's troubles very poorly. In Germany, at the beginning, people didn't know if he was a great poet or not, the least attack made him ill. He took everything to heart. He suffered from an extraordinary vulnerability, and that's what aggravated his case. I believe that he really killed himself because it wasn't possible otherwise. It wasn't at all an accident. It was inevitable. One thing that moved me tremendously, one evening about eleven, it was raining a little, I was with a young man, we were talking, on the other side of the Luxembourg Gardens. It was November, there was nobody on the street, and I noticed someone coming in our direction who was looking at the ground and making gestures, talking with himself. It was Paul Celan. And when I saw him, I was startled, frightened. I stopped and watched him, he didn't even see me. He didn't see anyone, talking to himself. And it broke my heart because I understood, he's not well. He was a man who was profoundly wounded. He was too tormented to take refuge in skepticism.

JW: You, on the other hand, have always been a skeptic.

EMC: Skepticism has played an enormous role in my life. It has been therapeutic, an anodyne. I'm not a skeptic by temperament, if you like, because I'm a bit frenetic. Perhaps I'm a false skeptic. I'll tell you an unbelievable story, a bit of German silliness. They phone me from Munich one day, this was just a few years ago, "Monsieur, we have invited a number of scholars for a conference on the future of humanity. There are physicists, philosophers, and so on, but we need a skeptic and we can't find one. Would you be interested in participating?" I refused, I'm not a skeptic in the service of the Western world. But I found that unheard-of, by telephone, like one calls a doctor, a specialist. I could put that down as my profession: Skeptic. Besides, I'm not a skeptic all the time.

JW: At what point did you start reading Jonathan Swift?

EMC: After I came to France. I became profoundly interested in Swift, I read everything about him I could find. He fascinated me. During certain periods he was extremely important for me. At any rate I can say that I've read a lot in my life, precisely because I was a man without an occupation. What the French call an idler, someone who doesn't work. Being very poor, I lived like a rich man, without work. But in return I read. So I consider that I've done my duty all the same. But I read also in order not to think, to escape. To not be me. And too, I've always tried to find the defects in others, the flaws.

JW: At various times in your books you've expressed your interest in biographies.

EMC: Above all I like to see how people end. When you read about someone's life, anyone's, you see what illusions he started out with. It's very interesting to see how they fail him.

JW: You were also very taken with Shakespeare in your youth.

EMC: I've got a really crazy story about that. As I said, I only worked in a profession for one year in my life, I was a philosophy teacher in a high school when I was twenty-five. It was a period when I was going through a sort of religious crisis which resulted in nothing. I was reading a lot of mystics, but I was also reading a lot of Shakespeare. It's very odd because they have nothing in common. I was so caught up with Shakespeare I thought all the rest were imbeciles. And so I made the decision on my own, I said, "I'm not speaking with anyone but Shakespeare." That had a troublesome consequence, because it was a provincial city. I was in a café where I often went, and someone who was a teacher in the same school came up and asked, "Can I sit at your table?" I said, "Yes. But who are you?" I knew him. He said, "What do you mean? You know me! I'm the gym teacher at the school." I said, "Ah? You're not Shakespeare?" "What do you mean, of course I'm not Shakespeare. What an idea!" "Seriously? You're not Shakespeare? Then get out!" He went immediately to the school and declared that I'd gone mad.

JW: But you were completely conscious of what you were doing.

EMC: Naturally. Absolutely. Otherwise it would have been very serious, I would have been locked up. No, no, I was totally aware. It was an absurd decision and I carried it through. It lasted for two or three days, that was enough. But I wanted to show who Shakespeare was for me, I had such admiration for him. I think if I had had the genius, the work I would have liked to have written is *Macbeth*.

JW: Who were the poets you read? Wasn't it mainly English ones?

EMC: For me the English were the greatest poets. Emily Dickinson, too, in America, she's terrific. During the war here, I had had a sort of passion for Shelley, for the man, I read him a lot. Naturally, I read Keats, who is a greater poet. But also Blake. And then, I read the lesser poets. But the lesser poets in England would have been the great poets in another culture. In my opinion, the English have no philosophy, no metaphysics, because their poetry replaced metaphysics. They said everything in their poetry. Then I got very interested in the minor poets of the nineties, Ernest Dowson and others.

JW: What was your situation under the Occupation?

EMC: Very bad, because I was called up for the Rumanian army and I refused. They summoned me to the embassy and said, "If you don't go back to Rumania, you'll be sent under German escort." I said, "If you do that, I'll kill myself." It was the Rumanians with the Germans against Russia. I said, "I don't want to be a soldier." There was a guy who drove me crazy, he was a military attaché who looked like a character out of Dostoyevsky. He'd summon me and say, "You'll be sent under German escort!" I said, "You're a colonel. *You* go there, not me. I am incapable of holding a rifle! This war is lost, you don't need me." He made me sick, he kept threatening me with summonses until the end of the war. And then I discovered something amazing. Someone told me, "One of your friends demanded that you be sent to the Russian front." Because he was jealous of me. He was an intellectual who was doing a thesis at the Sorbonne, and he was the one who had done everything! I'd thought he was a friend. And it was his best friend who came to tell me. That's what life is. The fundamental human sentiment is envy. Especially people who are the closest to you. You see, the whole history of humanity is really in the Bible, in the fall from paradise and then the two brothers, Cain and Abel. It's all there. So that every success automatically gains the jealousy of people who know you. One sees envy right away, it expresses itself like admiration, the eyes light up.

jw: Did your experiences during the war enter into your first book much?

emc: Oh yes, inevitably, a lot. The book begins with a denunciation of fanaticism. Before the war, I wasn't concerned with history. The phenomenon of history is only comprehensible if one admits the idea of original sin. I'm not a believer, I have no religious conviction, but I yield to certain religious explanations for things. History can only be interpreted if one admits that man has been marked by evil since the beginning. He is condemned, he's cursed. The profoundest book that was ever written is the first book of the Old Testament, Genesis. Everything is said there. The whole vision of human destiny, of man. The very fact that God is afraid of man, that's what is so fantastic. He realized that this guy is dangerous, that man is a monster, and history has proved it. Man is a being apart, extremely gifted, but harmful. There is an amazing thing in the Koran, that when man made his appearance on earth a fish came up out of the water and a vulture came down from the sky, and they said, "The danger has come," the catastrophe. And the fish dove down to the bottom of the water and the vulture flew away into the sky. Man is accursed. History is at once demonic and tragic, the whole history of the world. Naturally, we know the events that we've lived through, but one has only to look at what's been going on up until now. That's why I'm against ideologies: they're either too silly or too generous. Because ideologies construct history, and history isn't constructed, it's there. All these moral concepts have no reality in history.

JW: But you don't seem to deny morality either.

EMC: No, I don't, but that has nothing to do with history. And it's even characteristic that history speaks only of monsters. Why? Morality is a sort of criticism. In fact, take the case of Christianity: Christian morality is rather a good one. But Christianity has launched wars without precedent, unheard-of massacres. The Christian wars are the most terrible, the most intolerant, the most atrocious, and all in the name of God. So, that's why I opened that book with a denunciation of fanaticism and what I call the temptation of fanaticism. Because it is very tempting, especially in one's youth. And one of the profound reasons why I consider skepticism a truly interesting attitude, and perhaps the only valid one, is the spectacle of world history. The only conclusion from that is skepticism, so anti-fanaticism. But fanaticism is no accident, because it's an emanation of man, of his instincts, of his will, his pride, everything. That's in the Bible as well. Why did the angels revolt? Lucifer was ambitious, he didn't want a chief, a God. Well, one could say that the whole history of the world is him. You know, in Christianity they say that until the Last Judgment it's Satan who is the chief, who rules over the earth. That Christ will not be able to do anything here, that he has no influence. That Satan is their king.

JW: How did you get interested in Spain? There are many references to Spain in your books.

EMC: The interest goes deep. It's the country in Europe that has most attracted me. I'd originally applied for a grant to go there—I wanted to study with Ortega y Gasset—before coming to Paris, but then the Civil War broke out. How did it begin for me? For personal reasons, because I've always been attracted by countries that had grandiose dreams and then failed. Well, I consider the example of Spain the most terrific failure, the illustrious failure. As a student I had read a book about the Spanish national character, and I came upon something that really struck me. A fellow is telling about his travels through Spain, in third class, and all of a sudden he sees a campesino, a peasant, who is carrying a sack and who throws it on the ground, saying, "¡Qué lejos está todo!" How far everything is! I was so struck by this phrase that it became the title of a chapter in my first book in Rumanian, which was never translated. Of course I read the work of Unamuno, his commentary on *Don Quixote* and the rest. Then I was very impressed by the fact that around 1900 he learned Danish in order to read Kierkegaard in the original. Unamuno would call him "my brother," and I too was captivated by Kierkegaard.

JW: Was there any romantic or exotic image in this for you, being rather far from Spain?

EMC: A little, inevitably. But it's not that, I don't think. It's the whole psychology apart. A people which is really quite different and is conscious of its difference. And then, the *conquista*, I've read a lot about that folly.

JW: Were you interested much in previous epochs of Spain, in the Moorish presence there?

EMC: Enormously. The whole origins of the Arabic invasion and everything and also the tragedy of the Jews in Spain. For example, one of the things that moved me the most was what happened in Segovia when they were beginning to leave and they went to bow over their parents' graves to say good-bye. The Dominicans came into this cemetery, with their cross, saying, "Convert!" The people were crying, because they loved Spain, it had been one of the most beautiful periods in Judaism. And the priests with their cross coming in there to make them convert to Christianity immediately, it's heartbreaking. Moreover, Spain fell apart chasing out the Jews. It was suicide. That's exactly what

Germany did, that sort of madness. It is the Jews' tragedy that they have been chased from countries they were particularly attached to. They paid very dearly for considering Spain and later Germany a home. To be punished by what one loves, that's the mystery of Jewish destiny.

JW: The Jews have always mixed in to some degree with the dominant culture, they've both given and taken a lot.

EMC: Yes, but the Jews took things deeper. For example, in Germany they gave a livelier turn to things. They didn't have that German heaviness. They had the same depth, but with a lot of spirit and humor. It was a fruitful encounter, in every domain. But that itself was an ominous sign. Yet in spite of it all, there is an extraordinary Jewish optimism. They are the only tragic people who are optimists.

JW: In *Drawn and Quartered* you say, "A self-respecting man is a man without a country." Elsewhere you've written, "I have no nationality—the best possible status for an intellectual." But most people say one has to have roots, for a writer too.

EMC: For a writer maybe, but I'm not a writer. For a novelist, yes, in a certain sense. Even for a poet as well, because he's rooted in his language. But for me the fact of having lost my roots went with my conception of the intellectual without a country. In coming to Paris I became denationalized. What is so beautiful about Paris is that it's a city of uprooted people, and I felt extremely good in this environment. I always hated what was intellectually provincial.

JW: What was the cultural orientation for you in Rumania?

EMC: The Rumanians, in the Austro-Hungarian empire, were a population kept in darkness. But I'm not anti-Hungarian, I have a lot of admiration for the Magyars. And as for folk music, it's Hungarian gypsy music that I prefer from that part of the world, I like it a lot. For example, one of the composers I love is Brahms, for his gypsy side.

JW: How did the folklore, the native character of the Rumanians affect you?

EMC: What I inherited from the Rumanian people, the peasants, is fatalism. The Rumanians, I think, are the most fatalistic people in the world. I learned it as a child, because people would always say things like "There's nothing one can do" and "There's only destiny" and so on. That vision of life marked me, I can't deny it, a sort of philosophy of surrender. And these peasants are closer to Greek tragedy than those in the West, it's the same vision: that man is a sort of plaything of destiny.

JW: Among the various people that you came to know here in Paris, were there many Rumanians? I think, particularly the writers, of Ionesco and Isidore Isou.

EMC: I know Isou very well, I see him often. He lives near here, he goes to the Luxembourg Gardens every day. I used to see Ionesco a lot, he's a very good friend. He is as interesting a man as he is a writer. He has loads of humor in life and is never banal. And it's funny, we're more friends here than we were in Rumania.

JW: You knew him well there?

EMC: Since we were students together in Bucharest, except he was in French and I was in philosophy. He's a profoundly unhappy man, success has only aggravated it. Which is what I like about him. Instead of coming to terms with life, he's never been in so much despair as since he's been famous. He was very poor in Paris before getting known as a writer. For years we'd talk on the phone almost every day. You can die laughing with him, even when he's in despair. He's a man who is haunted by the idea of death, much more than I am. Because with age, for me, that obsession has grown weaker. But with him, it's the contrary. It's not that he's afraid to die. He has the sense of the ephemeral, of things not lasting, and his work is an expression of that. One could even say that his humor is somewhat the disconsolation of dying. That obsession with death pushes him quite far, he travels a great deal. He's been all over the world. It's an escape.

JW: Is it true that Ionesco is obsessed with Russia?

EMC: Like all people from the East.

JW: But you write that the future is Russia's.

EMC: The immediate future, that's all.

JW: In *History and Utopia* you wrote that Russia's future will depend on "the bearing with which it spends its reserves of utopia."

EMC: Listen, I've always been very taken with Russian culture. It goes back to when I was about fifteen. My parents had settled in Sibiu, my father had become the priest for the city and also a counselor to a very important fellow in the church hierarchy. This man was very cultivated, had a huge library, and he had everything on Russia. So, as a teenager I was able to read an enormous amount on Russia. And since I was very passionate about Dostoyevsky, I became very taken with it. At the same time I conceived a great admiration for Russia and a great fear. To such a degree that I consider there is a Russian inevitability.

JW: Historically.

EMC: Yes. I believe in a Russian destiny which we cannot escape. It's obvious that all the peoples in the West have exhausted their sense of a mission. The English, the French, the Germans—it doesn't interest them to play a role anymore, they all know it's not worth the trouble to get caught up in history now. Each nation has a mission to carry out and that's over for them. The Russians have only to wait, while looking toward the West.

JW: But you feel that Russia will take over all of Europe.

EMC: Yes, but not even by war. By a sort of pressure. One feels Russia is weighing on Europe. And the Russians are doing something stupid, because the Russian dream was to compete with the West, obviously, to take its place, but that was when the West was still powerful. There is no danger for the Russians now, but their dream continues—instead of leaving the West in peace. They're afraid of Germany, that's ridiculous, the Germans have become a nation of tourists.

JW: But it's between Russia and the United States now.

EMC: Naturally. The United States has not exhausted its historical role, but at the same time its mission has arisen because it's been provoked from abroad, I believe. America was brought in by the West, the West having given up. Someone had to take over for them, America was forced by Europe's weakness. Russia has always been carried away by a dream of universal domination. And it will burst one day from this dream, but as the result of a catastrophe beyond words.

JW: Is there a political regime that you prefer?

EMC: I believe the ideal regime is a left without rigid dogmas, a left exempt from fanaticism.

JW: Is it all the same to you, for example, that the Socialists won in Spain?

EMC: In Spain a leftist government is absolutely indispensable. For an intellectual it's obvious that, at the stage in history we've arrived at, the ideal is an intelligent leftist government, but on the condition that it doesn't run aground. Freedom is an ideal, but still, freedom must be dominated. Man is a diabolical animal, and he tends to make poor use of freedom, that's undeniable. And Socialist governments don't know that. Freedom has to be controlled, unfortunately, because man can't stop himself.

JW: In *A Short History of Decay*, you defined freedom as "an *ethical* principle of *demonic* essence."

EMC: The best governments in the world have been ruined by uncontrolled freedom, because man abuses it. Why was England one of the rare countries to have known freedom for so long? Because there were prejudices. English prejudices were very strong, they contained the people. They were stupid prejudices but that doesn't matter. They gave a sort of consistence to society, they provided limits that one was not to go beyond. So, the problem of freedom is at once philosophical and political: to what point can the human animal be free without perishing?

JW: In *Syllogismes* as well you had written: "History, in effect, amounts to a classification of police; because what is the historian dealing with, if not the conception that men have had of the policeman through the ages?" Which seems even more so now.

EMC: That's unhappily true.

JW: About Christianity, then. First of all, having a father who was a Greek Orthodox priest, at what point did you begin to sense "the lugubrious stupidity of the Cross," as you put it in *A Short History of Decay*?

EMC: Rather early. I was terribly anti-Christian when I was young. My father, for example, was not intolerant at all. He was very humane. He concerned himself with people—because he wanted to be a lawyer and he couldn't in Austria-Hungary. He took his profession seriously; he had the habit for instance of saying a prayer before eating. And every time, I'd disappear; I'd go to the bathroom and wait until he finished. From about the age of thirteen or fourteen, when I started to read, I was against it, I thought it too stupid. I had a sort of repulsion against it. My philosophical awakening was an anti-Christian one. Then something happened anyway, a little later: I was about eighteen, I began to get interested not in religion itself but in the mystics. Not because of their religious faith but for their excess, their passion, for their inner violence. So, I began to read the great mystics, and I understood early on that I could not have faith. But it interested me because the mystics lived a more intense life than others. And also the fact of a sort of extraordinary pride: me and God, God and me.

JW: You yourself weren't tempted to follow the mystic's path, though?

EMC: No. But I had my insomnia, which gives you amazingly ecstatic states. You see, when you're under a great deal of nervous tension, there are moments—which Dostoyevsky speaks about in *The Possessed*, with Kirilov—when you're suddenly seized with the feeling of truly being God, the whole universe is centered on you. What is called ecstasy has diverse forms, according to the conceptions you have. I knew these states, which are frequent for epileptics. I was never epileptic, but because of this amazing nervous tension I knew what is called ecstasy. It manifests itself by a sort of sensation of extraordinary light, inside and outside. And it's at that point that I really understood the mystics.

JW: You're speaking of the Christian mystics particularly.

EMC: Yes, inevitably. Saint Teresa of Avila, Saint John of the Cross, all of them. So, my interest in the mystics wasn't abstract, intellectual, it came from my own experiences.

JW: But what did you do with the Christian side of them?

EMC: That didn't interest me, because I've always considered the

mystics were practically outside of that. They were all persecuted, because the Church considered them dangerous,
heretics—they were often thrown in prison. Mysticism is
the extreme state of religion.

JW: Which religion lends a language to.

EMC: That's right. The Church doesn't know what to do with
them. It accepts them finally, but while they are alive they're
persecuted.

JW: You also wrote in *A Short History of Decay* that you loved
all the women saints very much.

EMC: Yes, that passion had a morbid aspect too. I was about
twenty-five then.

JW: But why did you stop loving them?

EMC: It was like a passing bit of madness. I read them all. It was
a form of perverse eroticism. Certainly, there was a bit of a
sick side to it.

JW: You seem hardly to speak at all, though, about atheism.

EMC: But I've always been attacked as being an atheist. I'm a false
believer and a false atheist. I can't abide by religions, they're
institutions, but religion has interested me solely because
of the mystics, these extreme cases.

JW: Though atheism is perhaps too much a certainty.

EMC: It's always very suspect. It's absurd to say that God doesn't
exist, because one can't define the concept of God. But I
should explain why I speak so often of God—it's true for
these last twenty years. Each person, obviously, knows extreme states of solitude, where nothing exists anymore, especially at night when one is absolutely alone, thus there is
the difficulty of speaking with oneself all the time. So, I've
defined God like that, as the partner in moments of extreme
solitude. One thinks of God when one can think of nothing
else anymore, of no other person. So, it has nothing to do
with faith, in my case, it's solely a pretext for dialogue. It's
a monologue, but because everything else has vanished,
one clashes with God, the last companion in solitude.

JW: Though for many people that question of certainty is a big
problem. They can't really believe in God, but they're not
sure either that God doesn't exist.

EMC: The existence of God doesn't even interest me. The function he plays for us who don't believe is that when one doesn't know whom to speak with anymore, one speaks with him. It's a sort of survival.

JW: You've studied the history of Christianity rather thoroughly, but you've also studied other religions a lot.

EMC: Buddhism, above all. I was very interested in Buddhism— less now that I'm old. But Buddhism has played a big role in my life, since my youth.

JW: When did that interest start?

EMC: I was about twenty-four or twenty-five. If I had ever adopted a religion, it would have been Buddhism, I think. And for a long time I even boasted of being a Buddhist until I realized that was absurd.

JW: You hadn't actually taken on all the precepts.

EMC: No. You know, the Buddhist considers anger as that which most hinders salvation. Well, I'm very irritable, it's stronger than me, I'll get into a fit of anger. And then there's detachment. I'm incapable of attaining it, so I realized that I was a dubious Buddhist. What attracted me to Buddhism is the statement that everything is illusion, that nothing is real. It's perhaps the negative aspect of Buddhism that I liked, the statements on life that it makes. But not the solutions, because if I know that nothing is real, I still react like other men: I love people, I hate them, and so on.

JW: Well, in your writings you also seem to deny the possibility for Westerners to really even be Buddhists.

EMC: Absolutely. Because it's not possible for most people. My temperament hasn't changed, I wasn't made to be set free. What people don't realize is that it's one thing to like that form of wisdom and it's another to live it. That's where my fatalist side comes in, that we do not escape ourselves.

JW: Yet you often advise detachment in your books.

EMC: All the time.

JW: But in *The Fall into Time* you write, "Our sole recourse: to renounce not only the fruit of action, but action itself, to make a rule of nonproduction." Which brings up the old problem then: why write?

EMC: I try to be what I should be, see. I wrap myself up in those things because all my life I've had the feeling of nothingness; it's also done me a lot of good. It's helped me to put up with a lot of things and also to understand Buddhism, but at bottom I'm much closer to certain Romantics. Finally I reached the conclusion that I was not to be saved and that I was destined to torture myself! The rest was desire.

JW: Though, as you've written, it was also a paradox for the mystics, that they wrote books.

EMC: Yes, why do they write, since they're writing for God? God doesn't read. So, one can't dwell on the ultimate consequences of an attitude, one would have to either become a monk or commit suicide. At bottom one has to admit that life is made of these contradictions, that's what's interesting. If I identified completely with what I've written, for example, I wouldn't have written. There's the whole problem. What should I have done? I should have been a sage, but I couldn't. I wanted to be one, but I didn't manage to, so I wrote books. Everything I've done has been the result of a spiritual failure. But for me that is not necessarily a negative concept.

JW: In *The Trouble with Being Born*, you speak of "the man I would have liked to be," which is a phrase found elsewhere in your work as well. But who is that?

EMC: You know, in my youth I was extremely ambitious or, rather, arrogant. Inevitably, in becoming much more lucid one sees how one was undeserving of precisely the image one had of oneself. All my life I've had the feeling of this unworthiness, of having stopped short of what I could have been, though that too is an illusion. I've suffered from that, and then in the end it's all over and what does it matter, whether one produces a body of work or not. What's important, finally, is having said certain things that can count, not only for oneself but for others. But I should say this, that in everything I've written I never thought of others. I wrote for myself. But "the man I would have liked to be" is not at all who I could have been. What I wanted is to have comprehended things, to have understood, to not be fooled. My fear has always been of being a dupe, and so

I tried to be less so than others. It's the fear of believing—in whatever it might be. For me every belief is trickery.

JW: You've said that Christianity's career is over. Yet a lot of new evangelical sects keep springing up, in the United States, for example.

EMC: Listen, the religion won't disappear overnight. But my idea is this: that Christianity is like a cadaver that drags on, it no longer has any spiritual force. It can try, obviously, but Christianity can't renew itself from within anymore. It has given all it can. It's a sort of survivor now, that could last a long time yet. However, I don't believe that the religious foundation that exists in man can ever disappear. Because it makes up part of his essence.

JW: In your books you return quite often to the idea that we cannot cry enough. Where does that come from?

EMC: From personal experience. I've suffered, like all melancholics, from a sort of need to cry without being able to. I've experienced that very often in my life, because the only thing that could liberate you in these states is to cry, and I can't then. It may be neo-Romantic or something, but it's real. It's the need to cry as liberation. It comes too from that feeling of not belonging to the world. You're thrown into the world, but . . . what is it you're looking for here?

JW: Where do you situate yourself with respect to the whole movement of existentialism and the absurd in France?

EMC: Normally I would say I'm quite close to it. It's a way of thinking that is not foreign to me. But, with Sartre all that became a sort of fashionable philosophy, very unpleasant. Sartre was an extremely gifted fellow. He was *too* gifted. I think that if he had had less ambition, it would have been a lot better. He was fascinated by world fame. To his misfortune, he became world-famous relatively young, almost immediately.

JW: Did you ever speak with him much?

EMC: No, no. I was right next to him quite often at the Café de Flore, for whole days at a time. I never spoke with him, it was very strange. I ask myself why. It wasn't from shyness either, even though he was very famous and I was completely unknown. But the Flore was the only heated café, at the time of the Liberation, for example, when it was freezing outside.

JW: But he probably knew your books later.

EMC: I don't think so, frankly. Or else he would have mistrusted them, I'm nearly sure. I wrote a portrait of him in *A Short History of Decay*, without mentioning his name, called "On an Entrepreneur of Ideas." It was kind of sympathetic in spite of everything. What I would most reproach Sartre for is his total lack of humor. He had a Germanic, an Alsatian irony, very heavy, very insistent. But I don't want to speak ill of him, absolutely not.

JW: Let's get around to talking about music, finally. It seems that music would be capable of replacing philosophy for you.

EMC: Not only philosophy. Everything!

JW: In "Tares," you write: "Outside of music, everything is a lie, even solitude, even ecstasy. It is precisely one and the other but *better*."

EMC: I'll tell you my view of music in taking up that formula again. If everything is a lie, is illusory, then music itself is a lie, but the *superb* lie. That's how I would define music. Obviously, it's very difficult to speak about it. As long as you listen to it, you have the feeling that it is the whole universe, that everything ceases to exist, there is only music. But then, when you stop listening, you fall back into time and wonder, "Well, what is it? What state was I in?" You had felt it was everything, and then it all disappeared. So, that is why I say music is the superb illusion.

JW: You said that you've listened to Brahms a lot, his chamber works. What other composers did you listen to?

EMC: My big passion in the beginning was Bach, which brought about something very curious. Until the age of twenty, I had a profound contempt for my mother. I thought she was superficial. One day she told me, "You know, the only thing in the world that deeply moves me is Bach." And from that moment on, I completely changed my opinion of her. I understood that my image of her was false. Because of Bach. And two beings communicate extraordinarily when they listen to music together.

JW: You've also written that you scorn a person who has no taste for music.

EMC: I'll tell you, I never wanted to meet André Breton. Because Breton was totally impervious to music and to Dostoyevsky.

JW: Yes, you wrote that but without any name!

EMC: I would have conceded one of the two, but both of them, that's unpardonable. It doesn't matter what he might have done, why meet him?

JW: Have you ever written while listening to music?

EMC: No, but I'm starting to now a little. There are people, for example, Lévi-Strauss writes while listening to music, nearly all his work.

JW: Are there certain periods of music that you listen to? Do you like contemporary music at all?

EMC: Yes, for ten years I followed the concerts of the Domaine Musical here, which was directed by Pierre Boulez before he was very famous, from about 1955. So, I was interested in contemporary music a lot. But later I abandoned it for rather specific reasons. I didn't want to meet people anymore, I was tired of society, of receptions, and with that I stopped going to the concerts. But I like the music of Schönberg a lot and his contemporaries. And I know Stockhausen's work. But I'm not a specialist, and I've never been systematic about it. And then I fell back into Romantic music, such as Schumann.

JW: On the other side of that, you speak quite often of the loss of silence.

EMC: It's an obsession, I think. I consider the loss of silence extremely serious. For twenty-five years I lived in hotels in Paris, and the noise! I could have killed someone. I consider the disappearance of silence as one of the symptoms of the end of humanity.

JW: Are there certain of your books that remain closest to you now?

EMC: Yes, *The Trouble with Being Born* and *Syllogismes de l'amertume*, because they are fragments.

JW: In *The Trouble with Being Born* you wrote, "I have followed only one idea all the way—the idea that everything man achieves necessarily turns against him . . . I have *lived* it with a power of conviction." But your books are achievements; have they turned against you?

EMC: I'm thinking of man in general there, the destiny of man. That everything we do we end up by being punished for it. If we want to know happiness in life, it's to not do anything, to not accomplish anything, to live and nothing more. I feel that man should not have thrown himself into this amazing adventure that is history. Everything that he does turns against him because he wasn't made to do something, he was made solely to look and to live as the animals and the trees do. And I'll go even further, man should not have existed, he should have remained a species like any other and not have separated from the whole creation.

JW: In the same book there was a line concluding a certain passage that touched me a lot, where you write, "I ask those I love to be kind enough to grow old."

EMC: That came about because of an old friend of mine who suffers from a youngish optimism and who had just reproached me saying that I hadn't realized my potential in life. But we all fail to realize our full potential, and this failure is not only inevitable but desirable.

Julio Cortázar

When Julio Cortázar died of cancer in February 1984 at the age of sixty-nine, the Madrid newspaper El País *hailed him as one of the Hispanic world's great writers and over two days carried eleven full pages of tributes, reminiscences, and farewells.*

Though Cortázar had lived in Paris since 1951, he visited his native Argentina regularly until he was officially exiled in the early 1970s by the military junta, which had taken exception to several of his short stories. With the victory in late 1983 of the democratically elected Alfonsín government, Cortázar was able to make one last visit to his home country and to see his mother. Alfonsín's minister of culture chose to give him no official welcome, afraid that his political views were too far to the left, but the writer was nonetheless greeted as a returning hero. One night in Buenos Aires, coming out of a movie theater after seeing the new film based on Osvaldo Soriano's novel, No habrá más pena ni olvido *(A Funny, Dirty Little War), Cortázar and his friends ran into a student demonstration coming toward them, which instantly broke file on glimpsing the writer and crowded around him. The bookstores on the boulevards still being open, the students hurriedly bought up copies of Cortázar's books so that he could sign them. A kiosk salesman, apologizing that he had no more of Cortázar's books, held out a Carlos Fuentes novel for him to sign.*

Cortázar was born in Brussels in 1914. When his family returned to Argentina after the war, he grew up in Banfield, not far from Buenos Aires. He earned a degree as a schoolteacher and went to work in a town in the province of Buenos Aires until the early 1940s, writing for himself on the side. One of his first published stories, "House Taken Over," which came to him in a dream, appeared in 1946 in a magazine edited by Jorge Luis Borges, though they seldom met thereafter. It wasn't until after Cortázar moved to Paris in 1951, however, that he began publishing in earnest. In Paris, he worked as a translator and interpreter for UNESCO and other organizations. Writers he translated included Poe, Defoe, and Marguerite Yourcenar. In 1963, his second novel, Hopscotch, *about an Argentine's existential and metaphysical searches in Paris and Buenos Aires through jazz-filled nights, really established Cortázar's name.*

Though he is known above all as a modern master of the short story, Cortázar's four novels demonstrated a ready innovation of form while exploring basic questions about the individual in society. At the same time, his indomitable playfulness reached its highest expression in the novels. These include The Winners *(1960),* 62: A Model Kit *(1968), based in part on his experience as an interpreter, and* A Manual for Manuel *(1973), about the kidnapping of a Latin American diplomat. Whatever propels him in the different novels, the life within them is a dizzy enchantment.*

But it was Cortázar's many stories that most directly claimed his fascination with the fantastic. His most well known story was the starting point for Antonioni's film "Blow Up." Just before he died, a travel journal was published, Los autonautas de la cosmopista, *on which he collaborated with his wife, Carol Dunlop, during a voyage from Paris to Marseilles in a camping van. Cortázar signed over all author's rights and royalties for the book, which was published simultaneously in Spanish and French, to the Sandinista government in Nicaragua; the book has since become a best-seller. Two posthumous collections of his political articles on Nicaragua and on Argentina have also been published.*

Throughout his years in Paris, Cortázar lived in various neighborhoods. In the last decade of his life, royalties from his books enabled him to buy his own apartment. It might have been the setting for one of his stories. The building, in a district of wholesalers and chinaware shops, stands removed from the street by several rows of similar buildings, which have residences only on the top floors. Successions of light and shadow, in and out of the several archways, led to his staircase. Somehow the apartment seemed unexpectedly spacious, despite the thousands upon thousands of books spilling from every wall. A short, winding corridor led to other book-filled rooms, the walls lined with paintings by friends, each room suggesting a greater depth than its walls would allow.

Cortázar was a tall man, six foot four, though he had grown thinner than photographs revealed. The months before this interview had been particularly difficult for him, since his last wife, Carol, thirty years his junior, had recently died of cancer. In addition, his extensive travels, especially to Latin America where his political commitments took up much of his time, had obviously exhausted him. This interview took place on July 8, 1983, while he was home for barely a week. He was sitting in his favorite chair, smoking his pipe, near the thousands of records that filled the shelves from floor to ceiling.

JW: In some of the stories in your most recent book, *Deshoras*, it seems the fantastic is entering into the real world more than ever. Have you yourself felt that? As if the fantastic and the commonplace are becoming one almost?

JC: Yes, in these recent stories I have the feeling that there is less distance between what we call the fantastic and what we call the real. In my older stories the distance was greater because the fantastic was really very fantastic, and sometimes it touched on the supernatural. Well, I am glad to have written those older stories, because I think the fantastic has that quality to always take on metamorphoses, it changes, it can change with time. The notion of the fantastic we had in the epoch of the gothic novels in England, for example, has absolutely nothing to do with our notion of it today. Now we laugh when we read about *The Castle of Otranto*—the ghosts dressed in white, the skeletons that walk around making noises with their chains. And yet that was the notion of the fantastic at the time. It's changed a lot. I think my notion of the fantastic, now, more and more approaches what we call reality. Perhaps because for me reality also approaches the fantastic more and more.

JW: Much more of your time in recent years has gone to the support of various liberation struggles in Latin America. Hasn't that also helped bring the real and the fantastic closer for you? As if it's made you more serious?

JC: Well, I don't like the idea of "serious." Because I don't think I am serious, in that sense at any rate, where one speaks of a serious man or a serious woman. These last few years all my efforts concerning certain Latin American regimes—Argentina, Chile, Uruguay, and now above all Nicaragua—have absorbed me to such a point that even the fantastic in certain stories dealing with this subject is a fantastic that's very close to reality, in my opinion. So, I feel less free than before. That is, thirty years ago I was writing things that came into my head and I judged them only by aesthetic criteria. Now, I continue to judge them by aesthetic criteria, because first of all I'm a writer, but I'm a writer who is very tormented, preoccupied by the situation in Latin America. Very often that slips into my writing, in a conscious or in an unconscious way. But in *Deshoras*, despite the stories where there are very precise references to ideological and political questions, I think my stories haven't changed. They're still stories of the fantastic.

The problem for an engagé writer, as they call it now, is to continue being a writer. If what he writes becomes simply literature with a political content, it can be very mediocre. That's what has happened to a number of writers. So, the problem is one of balance. For me, what I do must always be literature, the highest I can do. To go beyond the possible, even. But, at the same time, very often to try to put in a charge of contemporary reality. And that's a very difficult balance.

JW: But are you looking to mix the two?

JC: No. Before, the ideas that came to me for stories were purely fantastic, while now many ideas are based on the reality of Latin America. In *Deshoras*, for example, the story about the rats, "Satarsa," is an episode based on the reality of the fight against the Argentine guerrilleros. The problem is to put it in writing, because one is tempted all the time to let oneself keep going on the political level alone.

JW: What has been the response to such stories? Was there much difference in the response you got from literary people as from political people?

JC: Of course. The bourgeois readers in Latin America who are indifferent to politics or else who even align themselves with the right wing, well, they don't worry about the problems that worry me—the problems of exploitation, of oppression, and so on. Those people regret that my stories often take a political turn. Other readers—above all the young, who share these feelings with me, this need to struggle, and who love literature—love these stories. For example, "Apocalypse at Solentiname" is a story that Nicaraguans read and reread with great pleasure. And the Cubans read "Meeting" with lots of pleasure as well.

JW: What has determined your increased political involvement in recent years?

JC: The military in Latin America, they're the ones who make me work harder. If they get out, if there were a change, then I could rest a little and work on poems and stories that are exclusively literary. But they're the ones who give me work to do. The more they are there, the more I must be against them.

JW: You have said many times that for you literature is like a game. In what ways?

JC: For me literature is a form of play. It makes up part of what they call the ludic side of man, *Homo ludens*. But I've always added that one must be careful, because there are two forms of play. There's soccer, for example, which is a game. And there are games that are very profound and very serious, while still being games. You must consider that when children play, you only have to look at them, they take it very seriously. They're having fun, but playing is important for them, it's their main activity. Just as when they're older, for example, it will be their erotic activity. When they're little, playing is as serious as love will be ten years later. I remember when I was little, when my parents came to say, "Okay, you've played enough, come take a bath now," I found that completely idiotic, because for me the bath was a silly matter. It had no importance whatsoever, while playing with my friends, that was something serious. And for me literature is like that, it's a game but a game where one can stake one's life, one can do everything for that game.

JW: What interested you about the fantastic in the beginning? Were you very young?

JC: Oh yes. It began with my childhood. I was very surprised, when I was going to grade school, that most of my young classmates had no sense of the fantastic. They were very realistic. They took things as they were . . . that's a plant, that's an armchair. And I was already seeing the world in a way that was very changeable. For me things were not so well defined in that way, there were no labels. My mother, who is a very imaginative woman, helped me a lot. Instead of telling me, "No, no, you should be serious," she was pleased that I was very imaginative, and when I turned toward the world of the fantastic, she helped me because she gave me books to read. That's how at the age of nine I read Edgar Allan Poe for the first time. That book I stole to read because my mother didn't want me to read it, she thought I was too young and she was right. The book scared me and I was ill for three months, because I believed in it . . . *dur comme fer*, as the French say. For me the fantastic was perfectly natural. When I read a story of the fantastic, I had no doubts at all. That's the way things were. When I gave them to my friends, they'd say, "No thanks, I prefer to read cowboy stories." Cowboys especially at the time. I didn't understand that. I preferred the world of the supernatural, of the fantastic.

JW: When you translated Poe's complete works many years later, did you discover new things for yourself from such a close reading?

JC: Many, many things. To begin with, I explored his language, which is highly criticized by the English and the Americans because they find it too baroque, in short they've found all sorts of things wrong with it. Well, since I'm neither English nor American, I see it with another perspective. I know there are aspects which have aged a lot, that are exaggerated, but that hasn't the slightest importance next to his genius. To write, in those times, "The Fall of the House of Usher"— that takes an extraordinary genius. To write "Ligeia" or "Berenice" or "The Black Cat," any of them, shows a true genius for the fantastic and the supernatural. I should say, in passing, that yesterday I went to a friend's house on the rue Edgar Allan Poe. There is a plaque where it says, "Edgar Poe, English writer." He wasn't English at all! I wanted to point that out because they should change the plaque. We'll both protest!

JW: In your own writing, besides the fantastic, there is a real warmth and affection for your characters as well.

JC: Certain readers and certain critics have told me that too. That when my characters are children and adolescents, I have a lot of tenderness for them, which is true. I treat them with a lot of love. I think they are very alive in my novels and stories. When I write a story where the character is an adolescent, I am the adolescent while I write it.

JW: Are many of your characters based on people whom you've known?

JC: I wouldn't say many, but there are a few. Very often there are characters who are a mixture of two or three people. I have put together female characters from two women I had known. It gave the character in the story or the book a personality that was more complex, more difficult, because she had different ways of being that came from two women.

JW: As with La Maga in *Hopscotch*?

JC: Well, she is based on one woman, with a lot of psychological characteristics that are completely imaginary. I don't need to depend on reality to write real things. I invent them, and they become real in the writing. Very often I'm amused because literary critics, especially those who are a bit academic, think that writers don't have any imagination. They think a writer has always been influenced by this, this, and this. They retrace the whole chain of influences. Influences do exist, but these critics forget one thing: the pleasure of inventing, pure invention. I know my influences. Edgar Allan Poe is an influence that is very present in certain of my stories. But the rest, I'm the one who invents it.

JW: Is it when you feel the need to give a character more substance that you mix two together? How does that happen?

JC: Things don't work like that. It's the characters who direct me. That is, I see a character, he's there, and I recognize someone I knew or occasionally two who are a bit mixed together, but that stops there. After that, the character acts on his own account. He says things . . . I never know what they're going to say when I'm writing dialogues. Really, it's all between them. I'm just typing out what they're saying. And sometimes I burst out laughing, or I throw out a page because I say, "There you've said silly things. Out." And I put in another page and start again with the dialogue, but there is no fabrication on my part. Really, I don't fabricate anything.

JW: So it's not the characters you've known who impel you to write?

JC: Not at all, no. Often I have the idea for a story where there aren't any characters yet. I'll have a strange idea: something's going to happen in a house in the country. I'm very visual when I write, I see everything. So, I see this house in the country and then abruptly I begin to situate the characters. It's at that point that one of the characters might be someone I knew. But it's not for sure. In the end, most of my characters are invented. Well, there is myself, there are many autobiographical references in the character of Oliveira in *Hopscotch*. It's not me, but there's a lot of me. Of me here in Paris, in my bohemian days, my first years here. But the readers who read Oliveira as Cortázar in Paris would be mistaken. No, no, I was very different.

JW: Does what you write ever get too close to being autobiographical?

JC: I don't like autobiography. I will never write my memoirs. Autobiographies of others interest me, but not my own. Very often, though, when I have ideas for a novel or a story, there are moments of my life, situations, that come very naturally to place themselves there. In the story "Deshoras," the boy who is in love with his pal's sister who is older than him, I lived that. There is a small part of it that's autobiographical, but from there on, it's the fantastic or the imaginary which dominates.

JW: You have even written of the need for memoirs by Latin American writers. Why is it you don't want to write your own?

JC: If I wrote my autobiography, I would have to be truthful and honest. I can't tell an imaginary autobiography. And so, I would be doing a historian's job, self-historian, and that *bores* me. Because I prefer to invent, to imagine.

JW: José Lezama Lima in *Paradiso* has Cemí saying that "the baroque . . . is what has real interest in Spain and Hispanic America." Why do you think that is so?

JC: I cannot reply as an expert. The baroque has been very important in Latin America, in the arts and in literature as well. The baroque can offer a great richness; it lets the imagination soar in all its spiraling directions, as in a baroque church with its decorative angels and all that or in baroque music. But I distrust the baroque a little in Latin America. Very often the baroque writers let themselves go too easily in writing. They write in five pages what one could very well write in one page, which would be better. I too must have fallen into the baroque because I am Latin American, but I have always had a mistrust of it. I don't like turgid, voluminous sentences, full of adjectives and descriptions, purring and purring into the reader's ear. I know it's very charming, of course, very beautiful, but it's not me. I'm more on the side of Jorge Luis Borges in that sense. He has always been an enemy of the baroque; he tightened his writing, as though he used pliers. Well, I write in a very different way from Borges, but the great lesson he gave me is one of economy. He taught me when I began to read him, being very young, that it wasn't necessary to write these long sentences at the end of which there was some vague thought. That one had to try to say what one wanted to with economy, but with a beautiful economy. It's the difference perhaps between a plant, which would be the baroque with its multiplicity of leaves, it's very beautiful, and a precious stone, a crystal—*that* for me is more beautiful still.

JW: The lines are very musical in your writing. Do you usually hear the words as you're writing them?

JC: Oh yes, I hear them, and I know that in writing—if I'm launched on a story, I write very quickly, because I can revise later—I will never put down a word that is disagreeable to me. There are words I don't like—not just crude words, those I use when I have to—the sound, the structure of the word displeases me. For example, all the words in juridical and administrative language, they are frequently present in literature. And I hardly ever use those words because I don't like them.

JW: No, I can't imagine them in the spirit of your writing.

JC: It's a question of music, finally. I like music more than literature, I've said it many times, I repeat it again, and for me writing corresponds to a rhythm, a heartbeat, a musical pulsation. That's my problem with translations, because translators of my books sometimes don't realize that there is a rhythm, they translate the meaning of the words. And I need this swing, this movement that my lines have. Otherwise, the story doesn't sound right. Above all certain moments in the stories must be directed musically, because that's how they give their true meaning. It's not what they say but how they say it.

JW: But it's difficult to be at the same time rhythmically musical and economical like a crystal.

JC: Yes, it's very difficult, of course. But then I think especially of certain musics that have succeeded in being like that. The best works of Johann Sebastian Bach have economy with the greatest musical richness. And in a jazz solo, a real jazz solo, a Lester Young solo, for example, at that point there is all the freedom, all the invention, but there is the precise economy that starts and finishes. Not like the mediocre jazz musicians who play for three-quarters of an hour because they have nothing to say. That's why I'm very critical of certain forms of contemporary jazz. Because they have nothing more to say, they keep filling up the space. Armstrong, or Ellington, or Charlie Parker only needed two or three minutes to do like Bach, exactly like Johann Sebastian Bach, and Mozart. Writing must be like that for me, a moment from a story must be a beautiful solo. It's an improvisation, but improvisation involves invention and beauty.

JW: How do you start with your stories? At any particular point of entry? An image?

JC: With me stories and novels can start anywhere. But on the level of writing, when I begin to write, the story has been turning around in me a long time, sometimes for weeks. But not in a way that's clear; it's a sort of general idea of the story. A house where there's a red plant in one corner, and then I know that there's an old man who walks around in this house, and that's all I know. It happens like that. And then there are the dreams, because during that time my dreams are full of references and allusions to what is going to be in the story. Sometimes the whole story is in a dream. One of my first stories—it's been very popular, "House Taken Over"— that was a nightmare I had. I got up like that and wrote it. But in general they are fragments of references. That is, my subconscious is in the process of working through a story. The story is being written inside there. So when I say that I begin anywhere, it's because I don't know what is the beginning or the end. I start to write and that is the beginning, finally, but I haven't decided that the story has to start like that. It starts there and it continues. Very often I have no clear idea of the ending, I don't know what's going to happen. It's only gradually, as the story goes on, that things become clearer and abruptly I see the ending.

JW: So you are discovering the story *while* you are writing it?

JC: That's right. I discover it a bit while I am writing. There too is an analogy, I think, with improvisation in jazz. You don't ask a jazz musician, "But what are you going to play?" He'll laugh at you. He simply has a theme, a series of chords he has to respect, and then he takes his trumpet or his saxophone and he begins. But he hasn't the slightest idea . . . it's not a question of an *idea*. They're different internal pulsations. Sometimes it comes out well, sometimes it doesn't. Me, I'm a bit embarrassed to sign my stories. The novels, no, because the novels I worked on a lot; there's a whole architecture. My stories, it's as if they were dictated to me a little, by something that is in me, but it's not me who's responsible. But then it appears they are mine after all, I should accept them!

JW: Are there certain aspects of writing a story that always pose a problem for you?

JC: In general, no, because as I was explaining, the story is already made somewhere inside me. So, it has its dimension, its structure, it's going to be a very short story or a fairly long story, all that seems to be decided in advance. But in recent years I've started to sense some problems. I reflect more in front of the page. I write more slowly. And I write in a way that's more spare. Certain critics have reproached me for that, they've told me that little by little I'm losing that suppleness in my stories. I say what I want to, but with a greater economy of means. I don't know if it's for better or worse. In any case, it's my way of writing now.

JW: You were saying that with the novels there is a whole architecture. Does that mean working very differently?

JC: The first thing I wrote in *Hopscotch* was a chapter that is found in the middle now. It's the chapter where the characters put out a board to get from one window to another. Well, I wrote that without knowing why I was writing it. I saw the characters, I saw the situation, it was in Buenos Aires. It was very hot, I remember, and I was next to the window with my typewriter. I saw this situation of a guy who's trying to make his wife go across, because he's not going himself, to go get some silly thing, some nails. It was totally ridiculous in appearance. I wrote all that, which is long, forty pages, and when I finished I said to myself, "All right, but what have I done? Because that's not a story. What is it?" And then I understood that I was launched on a novel but couldn't continue. I had to stop there and write the whole section in Paris before. That is, the whole background of Oliveira, because when I wrote the chapter with the board, I was thinking of myself a little at that point. I saw myself as the character, Oliveira was very much me at that point. But to do a novel with that, I had to go backward before I could continue.

JW: You were in Buenos Aires at that point.

JC: At that point, because afterward the whole book was written here. That chapter I wrote in Buenos Aires.

JW: And you sensed right away that it was a novel.

JC: I sensed right away that it would be the novel of a city. I wanted to put in the Paris I knew and loved there, in the first part. It would also be a novel about the relations among several characters, but above all the problems, the metaphysical searches of Oliveira, which were mine at the time. Because at that period I was totally immersed in aesthetics, philosophy, and metaphysics. I was completely outside of history and politics. In *Hopscotch* there is no reference to questions of Latin America and its problems. It's later that I discovered that.

JW: You've often said it was the Cuban revolution that awakened you to that.

JC: And I say it again.

JW: Do you revise much when you write?

JC: Very little. That comes from the fact that the thing has already been at work inside me. When I see the rough drafts of some of my friends, where everything is revised, everything's changed, moved around, there are arrows all over the place . . . no no no. My manuscripts are very clean.

JW: What are your writing habits? Have certain things changed?

JC: There's one thing that hasn't changed, that will never change, that is the total anarchy and the disorder. I have absolutely no method. When I feel like writing a story I let everything drop, I write the story. And sometimes when I write a story, in the month or two that follows I will write two or three stories. In general, it comes in series. Writing one leaves me in a receptive state, and then I catch another story. You see the sort of image I use, but it's like that, where the story drops inside of me. But later, a year can go by where I write nothing literary, nothing. I should say too that these last few years I have spent a good deal of my time at the typewriter writing political articles. The texts I've written about Nicaragua that are distributed through the syndicated press agencies, everything I've written about Argentina, they have nothing to do with literature, they're militant things.

JW: Do you have preferred places for writing?

JC: In fact, no. At the beginning, when I was younger and physically more resistant, here in Paris for example a large part of *Hopscotch* I wrote in cafés. Because the noise didn't bother me and, on the contrary, it was a congenial place. I worked a lot there, I read or I wrote. But with age I've become more complicated. I write when I'm sure of having some silence. I can't write if there's music, that's absolutely out of the question. Music is one thing and writing is another. I need a certain calm; but, this said, a hotel, an airplane sometimes, a friend's house, and here at home are places where I can write.

JW: About Paris. What gave you the courage to pick up and move off to Paris when you did, more than thirty years ago?

JC: Courage? No, it didn't take much courage. I simply had to accept the idea that coming to Paris, and cutting ties with Argentina at that time, meant being very poor and having problems making a living. But that didn't worry me. I knew in one way or another I was going to manage. Primarily I came because Paris, French culture on the whole, held a lot of attraction for me. I had read French literature with a passion in Argentina. So, I wanted to be here and get to know the streets and the places one finds in the books, in the novels. To go through the streets of Balzac or of Baudelaire. It was a very romantic journey. I was, I am, very romantic. I have to be rather careful when I write, because very often I could let myself fall into . . . I wouldn't say bad taste, perhaps not, but a bit in the direction of an exaggerated romanticism. So, there's a necessary control there, but in my private life I don't need to control myself. I really am very sentimental, very romantic. I'm a tender person, I have a lot of tenderness to give. What I give now to Nicaragua is tenderness. It is also the political conviction that the Sandinistas are right in what they're doing and that they're leading an admirable struggle. But it's not only the political idea. There's an enormous tenderness because it's a people I love. As I love the Cubans, and I love the Argentines. Well, all that makes up part of my character, and in my writing I have had to watch myself. Above all when I was young, I wrote things that were tearjerkers. That was really romanticism, the *roman rose*. My mother would read them and cry.

JW: Nearly all your writing that people know dates from your arrival in Paris. But you were writing a lot before that, weren't you? A few things had already been published.

JC: I've been writing since the age of nine, right up through my whole adolescence and early youth. In my early youth I was already capable of writing stories and novels, which showed me that I was on the right path. But I didn't want to publish. I was very severe with myself, and I continue to be. I remember that my peers, when they had written some poems or a small novel, searched for a publisher right away. And it was bad, mediocre stuff, because it lacked maturity. I would tell myself, "No, you're not publishing. You hang onto that." I kept certain things, and others I threw out. When I did publish for the first time I was over thirty years old; it was a little before my departure for France. That was my first book of stories, *Bestiario*, which came out in '51, the same month I took the boat to come here. Before, I had published a little text called *Los reyes*, which is a dialogue. A friend who had a lot of money, who did small editions for himself and his friends, had done a private edition. And that's all. No, there's another thing—a sin of youth—a book of sonnets. I published it myself, but with a pseudonym.

JW: You are the lyricist of a recent album of tangos, "Trottoirs de Buenos Aires." What got you started writing tangos?

JC: Well, I am a good Argentine and above all a *porteño*—that is, a resident of Buenos Aires, because it's the port. The tango was our music, I grew up in an atmosphere of tangos. We listened to them on the radio, because the radio started when I was little, and right away it was tangos and tangos. There were people in my family, my mother and an aunt, who played tangos on the piano and sang them. Through the radio we began to listen to Carlos Gardel and the great singers of the time. The tango became like a part of my consciousness and it's the music that sends me back to my youth again and to Buenos Aires. So, I'm quite caught up in the tango. At the same time being very critical, because I'm not one of those Argentines who believe the tango is the wonder of wonders. I think that the tango on the whole, especially next to jazz, is very poor music. It is poor but it is beautiful. It's like those plants that are very simple, that one can't compare to an orchid or a rosebush, but that have an extraordinary beauty in themselves. In recent years, as I have friends who play tangos here—the Cuarteto Cedrón are great friends, and a fine bandoneón player named Juan José Mosalini—we've listened to tangos, talked about tangos. Then one day a poem came to me like that, which perhaps could be set to music, I didn't really know. And then, looking among unpublished poems—most of my poems are unpublished—I found some short poems which those fellows could set to music, and they did. But we've done the opposite experience as well. Cedrón gave me a musical theme, I listened to it, and I wrote the words. So I've done it both ways.

JW: In the biographical notes in your books, it says you are also an amateur trumpet player. Did you play with any groups?

JC: No. That's a bit of a legend that was invented by my very dear friend Paul Blackburn, who died quite young, unfortunately. He knew that I played the trumpet a little, for myself at home. So he would always tell me, "But you should meet some musicians to play with." I'd say, "No," as the Americans say, "I lack equipment." I didn't have the abilities; I was playing for myself. I would put on a Jelly Roll Morton record, or Armstrong, or early Ellington, where the melody is easier to follow, especially the blues which has a given scheme. I would have fun hearing them play and adding my trumpet. I played along with them . . . but it sure wasn't *with* them! I never dared approach jazz musicians; now my trumpet is lost somewhere in the other room there. Blackburn put that in one of the blurbs. And because there is a photo of me playing the trumpet, people thought I really could play well. Just as I didn't want to publish without being sure, it was the same thing with the trumpet. And that day never arrived.

JW: Have you worked on any novels since *A Manual for Manuel*?

JC: Alas no, for reasons that are very clear: it's because of political work. For me a novel requires a concentration and a quantity of time, at least a year, to work tranquilly and not abandon it. And now, I cannot. A week ago I didn't know I would be leaving for Nicaragua in three days. When I return I won't know what's going to happen next. But this novel is already written. It's there, it's in my dreams. I dream all the time of this novel. I don't know what happens in the novel, but I have an idea. As in the stories, I know that it will be something fairly long that will have elements of the fantastic, but not so much. It will be, say, in the genre of *A Manual for*

Manuel, where the fantastic elements are mixed in, but it won't be a political book either. It will be a book of pure literature. I hope that life will give me a sort of desert island, even if the desert island is this room, and a year, I ask for a year. But when these bastards—the Hondurans, the Somocistas and Reagan— are in the act of destroying Nicaragua, I don't have my island. I couldn't begin to write, because I would be obsessed by that all the time. That demands top priority.

JW: And it can be difficult enough as it is with the priorities of life versus literature.

JC: Yes and no. It depends on what kind of priorities. If the priorities are like those I just spoke about, touching on the moral responsibility of an individual, I would agree. But I know many people who are always crying, "Oh, I'd like to write my novel, but I have to sell the house, and then there are the taxes, what am I going to do?" Reasons like, "I work in the office all day, how do you expect me to write?" Me, I worked all day at UNESCO and then I came home and wrote *Hopscotch*. When one wants to write, one writes. If one is condemned to write, one writes.

JW: Do you work anymore as a translator or interpreter?

JC: No, that's over. I lead a very simple life. I don't need much money for the things I like: records, books, tobacco. So now I can live from my royalties. They've translated me into so many languages that I receive enough money to live on. I have to be a little careful; I can't go out and buy myself a yacht, but since I have absolutely no intention of buying a yacht . . .

JW: Have you enjoyed your fame and success?

JC: Ah, listen, I'll say something I shouldn't say because no one will believe it, but success is not a pleasure for me. I'm glad to be able to live from what I write, so I have to put up with the popular and critical side of success. But I was happier as a man when I was unknown, much happier. Now I can't go to Latin America or to Spain without being recognized every ten yards, and the autographs, the embraces . . . It's very moving, because they're readers who are frequently quite young. I'm happy they like what I do, but it's terribly distressing for me on the level of privacy. I can't go to a beach in Europe; in five minutes there's a photographer. I have a physical appearance that I can't disguise; if I were small I could shave and put on sunglasses, but with my height, my long arms and all that, they recognize me from afar.

On the other hand, there are very beautiful things: I was in Barcelona a month ago, walking around the gothic quarter one evening, and there was an American girl, very pretty, playing the guitar very well and singing. She was seated on the ground earning her living. She sang a bit like Joan Baez, a very pure, clear voice. There was a group of young people from Barcelona listening. I stopped to listen to her, but I stayed in the shadows. At a certain point, one of these young men who was about twenty, very young, very handsome, approached me. He had a cake in his hand. He said, "Julio, take a piece." So I took a piece and ate it, and I told him, "Thanks a lot for coming up and giving that to me." And he said to me, "Listen, I'm giving you so little compared to what you've given me." I said, "Don't say that, don't say that," and we embraced and he went away. Well, things like that, that's the best compensation for my work as a writer. That a boy or a girl come up to speak to you and to offer you a piece of cake, it's wonderful. It's worth the trouble of writing.

Brion Gysin

I.

Painter, poet, inventor is how Brion Gysin described himself. Add historian, novelist, songwriter, raconteur, and all-around instigator, and you begin to take in the picture. From his early book, To Master—A Long Goodnight, *including a history of slavery in Canada which won him one of the first Fulbright fellowships in 1949, to his discovery of the cut-up technique of writing, which his pal William S. Burroughs put to good use (their collaborations were finally published in 1978 as* The Third Mind), *through his invention of the Dreamachine and becoming one of the fathers of sound poetry with his permutation poems, Gysin was a multimedia visionary. This seems especially evident in his two novels,* The Process (1969), *drawn from his years of experience living in Morocco, and* The Last Museum (1986), *based in part on the Bardo Thodol of the Tibetan Book of the Dead as well as on his extended residence at the Beat Hotel in Paris, where many of the beat generation stayed during the late 1950s and early 1960s.*

Gysin was an artist who made things happen. For a man who could handle seven languages, his true métier was language in all forms.

Writing and painting crossed paths repeatedly throughout his life; his écritures or writing paintings—the most abundant period in his visual work, starting in the late 1950s—juxtaposed Japanese calligraphic lines, read vertically, with a modified Arabic line, read right to left. Together the two strands formed a textured grid that had the magic of a written language.

Perhaps it was inevitable that he should be constantly translating his ideas from one form to another. Born in London of Swiss-Scottish parents, Gysin grew up in western Canada, until he was sent to school in England. At the age of eighteen he left for Paris, where he soon showed his artwork in the famous Surrealist Drawings show of 1935, only to have it taken down on opening day by André Breton because of Gysin's insubordination. As the war approached he traveled to Greece and then to America, living mostly in New York; in 1949 he returned to Europe and eventually, at the invitation of Paul Bowles, he went to Tangier in Morocco.

For twenty-three years he was a regular visitor to Tangier. Through Bowles he heard the Master Musicians of Jajouka, whom he much later introduced to Brian Jones of the Rolling Stones and also to Ornette Coleman. Gysin was so enchanted with their music that for several years he ran a restaurant called the Thousand and One Nights, which enabled him to employ the musicians and to hear them every night.

Through the years Paris remained his most constant home. The first part of this interview took place in August 1980 at his apartment directly across from the Centre Pompidou, the museum more commonly known as Beaubourg. At the time he had renewed hopes of at last making some money from the Dreamachine, which he co-invented twenty years earlier. The five-foot-high contraption was not a complicated device; it consisted of a transparent cylinder encasing another slotted cylinder that turned by a motor around a light bulb, flashing stroboscopic pulses of light. It was the first artwork to be experienced with the eyes closed.

Gysin died of a heart attack at his home in Paris, at the age of seventy, in July 1986. Late the preceding year he had been named a Commander of Arts and Letters by the French minister of culture.

JW: How does the Dreamachine work? Can it be described specifically?

BG: Oh yes, very scientifically. I had the actual experience, in the back of a bus, driving along a row of trees that was spaced exactly as was necessary to produce the effect with the sun setting behind the trees. I closed my eyes and had what I thought was a spiritual experience. Like Mr. Saul on his way to Damascus about to become Saint Paul, same thing happened to him and presumably for the very same reason. He must have been riding on the back buckboard of the chariot like that and gone down a row of trees, horses going at just the right speed, and he closed his eyes and saw all those crosses.

The present version of the machine, which is being made by the Swiss in a limited edition of twenty, is a sort of optimum pattern of an open cylinder. What we had done originally was a cylinder with just the exact slots. Then I made one like a coliseum where each row was a different speed. Later, I developed the current one whereby the incidence of curves produced every one of those gradations between eight and thirteen flickers a second, because that's where it is, in the alpha band. In fact it is a complete exposition of the alpha band. You see so many things in there, after the hundreds of hours that I have looked, that you get to a place which is real dreaming, where apparently it affects the very back part of the original bottom brain or somewhere like that. The only person it ever happened to the first time around was old Helena Rubinstein, with whom I had a long romance about the Dreamachine. Madame would say, "Oh yes, I had a boat trip. Oh yes, I'm in a speed boat between Venice and the airport. Oh, I'm taking the train in Venice." And so on. She's the only person I've known who really just saw them all like movies.

But I would go even so far as to think it's possible that everything that can be seen is seen only in the alpha band. Because you see all the religious symbols, you see like dreams, like movies. Maybe that's really all that we can see and that's where it's stored in our brains, within that range of the alpha waves.

JW: What brought on the realization that this dreaming might lie within the alpha band?

BG: In the late forties and early fifties, when they first had an electroencephalograph, scientists discovered the alpha band of brain activity. They showed that it changed between eight and thirteen pulses, or interruptions of light, per second. Below eight, for example, you're down into deltas and thetas, which give you a very logy, unpleasant feeling, maybe like these ultrasound effects that people are talking about. We read that out of a book by Gray Walter, an American from Saint Louis who happened to work and spend his life in the Bristol neurological center in the west of England. He was the man who invented the thinking mouse, the toy mouse that could learn. He made the thing electronically in such a way that it could not just run to a certain number and back again, it could make a mistake and then correct the mistake. William Burroughs went to a lecture of his. He never had any other effect on me except that one thing he said, just in half a sentence, that people who are subjected to interruptions of light between eight and thirteen times per second reported experiences of color and pattern. I said, "Oh, wow, that's it!" Ian Sommerville was back studying mathematics at Cambridge and I wrote him and said, "This is the problem. How can we make it at home? How can we do it with just what we've got?" So, when he came back to Paris the next holidays to the Beat Hotel where we were staying, we didn't have enough watts. We had three rooms, Burroughs in one room, Ian in another, and me in a third. We sort of ran wires loose out the windows and everything so we could get enough. That's where it first started, we made some very beautiful machines that got lost. Ian was very good with all that sort of cutting and handling, very expert.

JW: So that has evolved up to the current version of the machine.

BG: It's gone much further than anything he ever saw. The last things he saw were more like the one that's over in the Pompidou museum. They bought one and I agreed to call it a prototype.

JW: Did all the earlier versions work along the same lines?

BG: They all produce the same effect, but this is the ultimate artifact, or pre-ultimate. It's being handled by Karl Lazlo, a big private art dealer and enthusiast. He wanted to do something with me, and we came to the idea that he would just occupy himself with the Dreamachine. Because it takes quite a bit of doing, to get all those pieces made and all. Nobody wants to do it anymore, bending plastics and such, it's very difficult to find anyone.

JW: What about mass production?

BG: Mass production has always been the question, even in the 1960s. First Phillips was interested in the idea, and some people in America, and toymakers. When they looked into it they found that the least they could begin with—that was 1965, a long time ago—should be fifty thousand units. Where were you going to get fifty thousand little motors? What size was it going to be? How were you going to package it? Above all, how much shelf space was it going to take up? Because then you imagine fifty thousand boxes that big. Well, you could put so many diamond bracelets in that space and make so much more money. Those are the sorts of things that held it up for all these years. I have all those problems stored away in the back of my head. So, the first real breakthrough was Lazlo saying, "Yes, I will do it, I will make this number." Because naturally one would like to make a smaller model, like a sort of bedside lamp, for example. And I'm not at all sure that I'm necessarily going to profit much from this. But I'm sure that it's going to happen at some point or another, I've known this for twenty years.

JW: Did you have one in Tangier?

BG: I never had one working there. Because by the time I got back to Tangier from all these hassles and wrassles . . . I was ten months meeting all those people, everybody from sort of ethical culture toymakers to real crocodiles in the slue of the swamp type toymakers. I mean, they're a horrendous lot and weirdo people, really very strange. I got to know their problems, at least they explained what it was. It wasn't a question of selling them on the idea. They got the idea right away. But then how do you actually do it? Whew!

JW: Have you had any retrospectives of your paintings in Paris?

BG: No, only one small one that was put together by some friends of mine. Because I swore I wasn't going to come back here, this is foolishness too. That's why my situation is like it is. You're supposed to be here all the time, you're not supposed to go running away for twenty-three years in Morocco. Or if you're in New York, you're supposed to be in the New York scene and be part of the show, in a way. That's what you're getting paid for, to be there to be part of the show. And I have sinned against all these things. Stupidly, in some ways. I realize it's a hang-up. But these things are sort of getting ironed out just very late in life. It's lucky they're being ironed out at all.

JW: But wasn't it your own interest that took you to other places?

BG: Yeah. It was also that whole Beat Hotel thing, from which the Dreamachine came and from which the cut-ups came. William managed to get his ass out of there. Then we went to America and put together *The Third Mind* in 1964–65. And then both of us decided we couldn't make it in New York, and so we came back to Europe and William set up in London. I said, "Oh, I'd sooner die than live in London," and I went back to Morocco. I really left Morocco again only in '73. I left because friends of mine with whom I had left all of the *écriture* canvases, which were all done at the Beat Hotel between 1959 and 1963, and lots more, they put together a show—like an homage—in a gallery on the same street next door to where the Beat Hotel was, on the rue Git-le-Coeur. It was really from their hearts that they'd done it, so I was very impressed. I said, "Oh, I've just got to come back and take care of the store," that's all. I came back and then I got sort of mowed down by cancer and knocked out of the scene for a while. So now I'm just scrabbling again. Things are definitely coming together, but they've been hung up for twenty years.

JW: Are you still painting?

BG: It's almost ground to a halt, I must say. First of all, because I started writing more. Also, because it just wasn't working. I didn't have a gallery, I didn't have an income from it. Then, oddly enough, my work slipped off into photography.

JW: How did you arrive at doing your *écriture* paintings?

BG: Well, it turned out that everybody got this sort of message of calligraphy. It came to me through the war, because I was a translator of Japanese. That's how I got interested, it wasn't from the point of view of painting at all. After the war, I came back here as a Fulbright fellow—not as a painter Fulbright, I mean as a writer, historian. During the war I met a cat who was the great-grandson of Uncle Tom, the man who told his life story to Harriet Beecher Stowe. And so, I wrote a book about Josiah Henson. From there, because the escaped slaves went to Canada and founded agricultural colonies there, I wrote the history of slavery in Canada. It was on the basis of that that I got my Fulbright. Later, about the same time I was doing the repetitive poems, I was looking for something that would repeat graphically. In Rome in 1960, I found a housepainter's roller which I then recut to produce this (shows a print which bears a curious resemblance to the exposed structure repetitions of the Centre Pompidou or Beaubourg). When I saw the plan for this museum, I said, "Well, it seems to me that back in about . . ." So I became very interested in this place across the road.

JW: Had you been living in this apartment since before Beaubourg was built?

BG: No. The frame was up when I moved in here. So, I started photographing Beaubourg. The whole idea dates back to 1960. Then I realized that the camera is also a roller, that what is inside it there is also a roller. I began in black and white, and then I moved into color. Then I decided that I would jump inside the camera and count, just like the roller counts. The series of photos begins by being taken out of this window here. I got the idea in this room, what I can see from here. And then I put it together again (Beaubourg, section by section, or shot by shot, to re-form the whole picture or view). And then, just studying the elevators, using it the way I used the roller, as blocks of ink or whatever. And then I go around the building, take the escalator from behind.

JW: How was it you came to learn Japanese?

BG: First of all, I started out in the American army and it wasn't working out very well. I saw that I could easily be shipped out into some fucking Pacific island or something. So I made great efforts to try and do something. I joined the paratroopers and then I broke my wrist on the very first training jump.

JW: Why did you join the paratroopers?

BG: It was a gas, man. Everybody worthwhile was there, it was a great gang of people. Real crazy, every hothead insane person from the East coast was there, and the South. Anyhow, that didn't last very long. So I went off and got myself a transfer to the Canadian army, by all sorts of finagling around. It was they who started me on the Japanese. I said, "Oh no, what have I stepped into? I have great respect for these charming people, but I'm not learning it all." Really, the only thing I got out of it was the way of holding a brush and the use of a brush, the language of a brush. The whole business of running ink on the paper.

JW: Did you study painting in school?

BG: No! I wasn't allowed to have any painting lessons. In fact, to this day I can't imagine what anybody learns in an art school. I'm sure there are very useful short cuts and stuff like that perhaps, handicrafts. And it is a bitch to have to teach yourself, that's a fact.

JW: How did you come upon the idea for your *écriture* paintings?

BG: I had had a very unfortunate experience with magic. Somebody had done me a black magic thing, and I'd actually had the cabalistic square of paper where you write across this way and then you turn the paper and you write across the other way, and then you've got the thing locked in and it *happens*. I thought, yeah, how about using Japanese calligraphy in this direction, without turning the paper, and then just running an Arab line across it, and so I had a grid. That's how it all came into being for me.

JW: You can look at those paintings from any direction.

BG: That's right. And then I ran into the idea of the permutations in poetry. So I carried that over to painting, where I had a grid and then I cut and permutated it to make a big picture.

JW: Is it all actual writing in the *écritures*?

BG: You mean, can I read it and it says so and so? No. But it has most of the sort of magic elements of writing in it. The attack of the brush to the paper.

JW: Jackson Pollock was also doing a sort of writing, *écriture*, in dripping the paint.

BG: Sure enough. This was very much in the whole line of what was happening to painting itself. Painting as image was being eaten up by Picasso, let's say, he was the last cannibal. He ate up all the images, he chopped them all up and did what he did. Then people began to be interested in the matter—what the French had always been talking about, *la matière*, the stuff—and would say, "Well, let's play with the stuff. What does the stuff do?" It was very much in the air.

JW: Do you know how to write Arabic too?

BG: Yeah, but I never learned properly. As with Japanese, the real reason there was because I thought, "Oh, if I really learn this properly, then I will be writing sacred texts." I didn't think it was a very good idea. It's funny, in that book of Dizzy Gillespie's (*To Be or Not to Bop*), he says, "There's only one thing I really regret in my whole life: somebody once got me to put on a funny turban and pretend that I was praying to Mecca. Because I realize that I was making fun of these cats and it isn't at all what I meant. I think a lot of the trouble I had came from that." Of course he's right, a lot of the trouble came from the image as it went out, his whole public image changed. They were going, "Ah, he's one of those Muslim cats," and so he got less work.

I've always been at least partially inventive as well. It doesn't please me unless that's involved. So, in a way getting into photography became a bit of a dead end for me, as far as the visual work was concerned. That's why I jumped on all the writing stuff I had hanging up.

JW: What got you into jazz?

BG: Gee, it's kind of a sad story. I've been thinking about that recently. In those great 52nd Street days I was always on the wrong side of the street. I was always at the Cloop or Tony's or whatever, which was exactly the opposite. I'd just go dashing over like that to ask Billie Holiday where to score and I remember, John Latouche and me, she gave us the key to her flat. We took a cab wa-a-ay uptown, you let yourself in, and on the piano there's this great big lamp. You unscrew the lamp and reach in, and you find a couple of joints. And instead of sitting at her number, really, 'Touche would drag me back to listen to something he had written for a Broadway show that he was going to be doing. He couldn't read music, but he could really hammer away and imitate everybody else. I spent all of my musical time in New York on Broadway, because I worked on Broadway the first two years I got there. I was Irene Sharaff's assistant on a whole bunch of musicals: *By Jupiter, Lady in the Dark, Banjo Eyes.*

JW: How long were you in New York?

BG: From '40 to '49, with time away in the army. And naturally, because of the way it turned out for me, I heard less of bebop starting. And I heard of William S. Burroughs only over the telephone. Because John Latouche had a German secretary, who was William's first wife. She wore a monocle and sort of mannish tweeds. William had married her in Athens, as a matter of fact, just to get her entry into the States. By this time she was working for John Latouche. John had made a whole lot of money from *Taking a Chance on Love,* and *Cabin in the Sky,* and those sorts of things. He'd say, "I'm making more money than the President of the United States," and "If you don't throw your money out the window, it won't come in the door anymore," things like that. He really lived like that, zoom! And he wouldn't be bothered, dig, with bebop. One day I was at 'Touche's house and the telephone rang, she goes to answer it. And 'Touche says, "If that is your husband William Burroughs, don't let him up here because he's got a gun!" And I thought, "Wh-who's this William Burroughs? I mean, she's married to the man. Come on, he must be kidding." He says, "Yeah, yeah, she's married to this dangerous lunatic and I don't want him up here." I said, "Ooh."

JW: That was the first time you'd heard of him?

BG: First time I ever heard of him.

JW: With your permutations and the other work using repetition, had you been influenced by any of Gertrude Stein's work?

BG: Well, it was considered anti-surrealist to frequent Gertrude Stein or Cocteau or Gide or any of those people, dig? Maybe that's how I got thrown out of the surrealist group. I mean, what were the terms? It would have been some kind of court-martial for bad attitude, something like that.

JW: Because your interest was more eclectic.

BG: Right. I never did dig those autocrats setting themselves up like that. Any more than Virgil Thomson in New York, where I got to know all the classical composers, everybody in that whole gang. Except Henry Cowell, who was the most interesting, he was away. He got a seven-year rap for advances to a sailor in a toilet in San Francisco. Seven years!

JW: How close was your novel, *The Process*, to life in Tangier? Do you remain in touch with the people you knew there?

BG: Hamri, who is the hero, villain, and mainspring of my novel, he really exists. In fact, he exists so strongly that just this very morning he came bouncing through the mail. In the book he's just called Hamid, but everything in the book is true. Everything! (Reads:) "Dear Brion, I look for mail from you, please! Ali is complaining too. I don't want God to complain also. Regards, greetings, and my finest salutations, from Hamri, the painter of Morocco." And this is coming from Santa Monica to me. So, we're all still in business together, it looks like. The musicians are all his cousins and uncles and everybody like that. They are one family of the Al-Serif tribe and they live in the village of Jajouka. It's a village that must have once been an important military post, say, in Byzantine times, inasmuch as from it you can see Larache, the first good port of any size on the Atlantic, and was the site of Lixus, the Roman town and the Greek city. The golden apples of Hercules were there, growing presumably on an island in the harbor, attended by a group of prostitute-priestesses, a traditional thing that had come all the way from the Phoenicians through the Carthaginians. From that village you control the pass up into the mountains, which dominate that whole valley, that whole seaboard, of the Rif Mountains. So, these people remember exactly who was related to whom in the year 800 when the first prophet of Islam came there and they all became Muslims. He is buried in the village and so they call themselves his children; they are the Al-Serif, the sons of Serif, who was buried in the tomb there. And around him they do musical therapy. They cure mental disease and anxiety through a musical experience where the patient has the sensation that he smells a very beautiful smell. The musicians produced this for Ornette (Coleman). A real wipe-out session occurred where *twice* this sensation was produced, everybody had this overpowering sense of the perfume. William Burroughs wrote a nice little piece about it for *Penthouse*.

JW: How did you first come upon the Jajouka musicians?

BG: I heard them in 1950, thanks to Paul Bowles who was a key figure in all of that Moroccan experience. He's got his Morocco like Somerset Maugham has his Java or whatever. It has nothing to do with my Morocco personally, at all.

JW: Were the foreigners all part of one scene when you were there?

BG: Well, it was a colonial world, a real holdover. You were living in and breathing the past. The further inland you went, you were breathing even medieval times, in Fez still. I mean, I've lived in the time of Chaucer. I've actually lived morning, noon, and night, with everybody around me dressed and looking like they were doing things out of Chaucer, in Fez. In Tangier, it was an atmosphere that nobody has ever really caught yet.

JW: How did you come upon the permutations idea in the late fifties?

BG: Well, mine was a knockout discovery for me. In *The Doors of Perception* Huxley quotes the famous divine tautology, "I am that I am," which is supposed to be what Jehovah said. If you've read Velikowski on the subject, he thinks there was an actual event that took place over a period maybe as long as twenty-five years in the third millennium when the whole Sinai desert did say, "I am that I am I am that I am" (speeds it up into abstract sound). That it had the sort of vibrations that were happening in this idea. Velikowski thinks that what we now consider Venus was a comet that entered the galaxy and then got caught into our system, but as recently as that, and that there is a folk memory of that time.

I have carpets hanging up that do bear him out, the starry serpent runs through them. This pattern comes from the Berber mountains in the south of Morocco, and it goes to Mexico and so on. Well, he says there was actually an event when Venus did the zigzag followed by a trail of zigzag meteorites and everything, for a period of about twenty-five years in the third or fourth millennium, and that people really remember it. And that at that time indeed, the desert, you could hear it saying, "I am that I am I am that I am" (speeds it up), and that's where the whole idea came from. So, I saw the phrase on paper and I thought, "Ah, it looks a bit like the front of a Greek temple," only on the condition that I put the biggest word in the middle. So, I'll just change these others around, "am I," in the corner of the architrave. And then I realized as soon as I did this, it asked a question. "I am that, am I?" And I said, "Wow, I've touched the oracle!" So then I turned the next one, and I said, "Oh, all the way along it has to do this." Then I did those two versions on tape with the BBC in 1960. One is like this, it goes around, around, and it goes out, out, out, further out, out, and ends quiet. The other one has a voice that begins very slow and comes in, and then two voices come and fight, and then go out.

JW: Are there recorded copies of this work?

BG: That work is scattered and not united at all now. "The Permutated Poems" was a twenty-three-minute program and I don't have the whole tape of that. Because that has the very important pistol poem in there. I came to the BBC with a beautiful shot of a cannon that I had recorded in Morocco. And they said it was too long, which of course it was, we had to get something sharp on the tape. They said, "We have a pistol here that we use for haunted houses, murder scenes, and things like that. Would you like to hear it?" I listened to all of their pistols and I picked one. I said, "Record it for me at one meter away, at two meters away, three, four, five. And then we just play them and we permutate that. Then we take the whole thing and double it back on itself like that." And it was, "Oh . . . wow . . . there . . . ah." So it took quite a while to do, as you can imagine. That whole piece was unfortunately cut up and the whole thing as it's supposed to be doesn't exist anymore at all.

JW: I'm surprised that all that isn't together.

BG: I haven't been minding the store!

JW: Around 1960 you invented the cut-up technique of writing. While cutting a mount for a drawing, as you described it, you sliced through a pile of newspapers. You picked up the raw words and began to piece together the texts. At the time you said that "writing is fifty years behind painting." Has it caught up at all since then?

BG: Well, I also said, "Should writing try to catch up?" But look at what's happened to painting even since I said that, some twenty years ago. Poor painting herself is just tottering on the edge of the precipice or maybe has already fallen in, where it's all become deceptual art. Anybody can do it because there's nothing to be done except just sit there, for example, or wear a certain kind of clothes and do these public performances. So, art as painting has really disappeared. Nobody wants to see paint properly applied to canvas anymore, that's considered very old-fashioned.

JW: How do the cut-ups differ from what Tristan Tzara did?

BG: Particularly because there's an actual treatment of the material as if it were a piece of cloth. The sentence, even the word, becomes a real piece of plastic material that you can cut into. You're not just juggling them around, or putting them into . . . Tzara's words out of a hat were simply aleatory, chance.

JW: Doesn't the personality of the writer become diminished in the cut-ups?

BG: Oh no, I think it becomes multiplied. There's a long interesting piece that Burroughs wrote, where he speaks of plagiarism, simply sort of taking on the spirit of the person whose work you're handling. Becoming a Rimbaud, or becoming a Shakespeare, partially so. Obviously, those are roles which are given to the writer. He has all the rights to those roles, after all.

JW: Were the sound poets working now hearing what you did back in the Beat Hotel days, with the permutation poems and your use of tape recorders?

BG: Oh, sure. And all the repetitive musicians too heard those things. The only one who's ever come up on stage and said so to me is Phil Glass. But I'm sure the others heard it too.

JW: What pieces of yours were they hearing?

BG: They heard "I Am That I Am," and "Calling All Reactive Agents," and "Pistol Poem." Because "Pistol Poem" was played a lot on the radio. When the permutations were laid one over the other like that, it goes off into 4/4 time and then becomes a crazy little waltz. By itself! So, the whole point of it, and anybody who listens to it sees, is the idea that you just put the material into a certain risk situation and give it a creative push. Then the thing makes itself. That's always been my principle.

JW: Were you writing at an early age?

BG: Yeah, everybody was writing around my house. But I've always found that it's impossible to do two things at once. If you're really into one thing, you have to get into that a while. Sometimes it's only because your household isn't laid out right. Because if you're living in such a small space, if you've got to write and cook and eat on that same table, you live one way. And if you've got three rooms in which these three different things happen, then you do it another way. If I had my setup here, *plus* a studio room, then I could be very different. There are reasons for investing more of one's energy in an ongoing enterprise than in one that seems to be standing still for a while. *The Third Mind* had begun to happen in 1959–1960, and it had actually been in the form of a book since 1965, though not as it is today. It appeared in French two years previous to the English-language edition, and the big help came from Gérard-Georges Lemaire here in France. On the other hand, some enterprises are presumably hopeless right now, like *Naked Lunch* as a film.

JW: What ever happened to your screenplay of the book?

BG: At the time, William said it couldn't be done. Anthony Balch wanted to make the film. As it turned out, with the kind of money we could put together, we would have to do it in England. The script is still very funny. It was written with the idea that Mick Jagger could do it, or anybody, David Bowie could play it. I discussed it with Milos Forman, over dinner at La Coupole, and he said, "I will never have anything to do with sex and drugs!" I said, "Well, what are you going to do?" He said, "I'm going to do *Hair.*" You can imagine the script anywhere, as a kind of nostalgic Hammer film, like those English horror films that were so great. It begins in an English country house where William is really kind of old J. Paul Getty, and it gets funnier and funnier.

II.

As a song lyricist, Brion Gysin worked on several projects. His most abiding collaboration was with soprano saxophonist Steve Lacy, whose sextet recorded the album Songs *(1981). Lacy's group also toured another set of Gysin songs as a ballet, playing in France and Italy, but the music was never recorded: the lyrics were part of Gysin's screenplay of* Naked Lunch. *Gysin did record his own solo album, performing most of that material,* Orgy Boys *(1982). He already had sung on the Lacy record, with the bawdy "Luvzya," in duet with drummer Oliver Johnson. Later he recast some of his songs and wrote new ones with the guitarist Ramuntcho Matta. On a single they recorded "Junk" and "Kick That Habit," among his original permutation poems, playing with trumpeter Don Cherry, plus a bassist and drummer. Then they recorded one side of an album under Gysin's name (1985), performing in several Paris concerts. At the time he liked to refer to himself as the oldest living rock star.*

The following interview with Gysin and Lacy, on the occasion of the release of their album, took place in May 1981.

JW: Steve, you were setting painters' texts to music and through that you found Brion. How did you know of him?

SL: I guess I knew he was a poet-painter.

BG: We met through Victor Herbert and then again at the American Center in '73.

SL: In '65 in London, I had heard recordings—at that time they called it electronic poetry—and some of Brion's stuff was on there.

JW: His permutation poems?

BG: It must have been Henri Chopin's record, *OU.*

SL: I thought it was amazing, I really liked it. I had been think-ing in . . . not with electronics, but some of the results achieved.

JW: Did that tie up with any jazz roots for you?

SL: Well, jazz is speech rhythms. It's like *parlando* music. And it all comes from phraseology anyway, it's just a language. So, when I heard that stuff, I found it exciting.

BG: My opinion is that Dizzy Gillespie hasn't been recognized as a great sound poet.

SL: Absolutely. No question about it.

JW: Your whole interest in that seems unique for a jazz musician.

SL: Well, you could find little snippets of that in many people, back to Louis Armstrong. You can think of Fats Waller and Billy Strayhorn and Ellington and then to people like Red Allen and Roy Eldridge. Well, many. I think what I did was dig a certain vein a little bit wider or deeper than is custom-ary, but it was nothing new on the scene really.

JW: Brion, when did you first know of Steve?

BG: I'd heard his music and heard records, it must have been about '59 or '60. That was the moment jazz and poetry had suddenly arrived and been talked about in New York in 1959. There were a couple of efforts at this made by Greg-ory Corso and others. I didn't think it worked at all. Then in Paris I met a group of poets called the Domaine Poétique. We had possibilities to do anything we wanted. That went on 1961–64.

JW: What was your first collaboration?

SL: The first thing was "Dreams." The music was written in '69, and I asked him to give me the lyrics in about '73 or '74. By that time I knew he was the inventor of the Dreamachine. And that really struck me. I had this piece called "Dreams," and it was a melody that came to me in a dream in Rome. It was written to Italian lyrics by Falzoni, but it never got off the ground. But the melody was haunting. So I thought Brion, being an expert on dreams, might be able to supply me with the necessary lyrics, in English. And he agreed. He came up with the most fantastic thing, really, the lyrics are out of sight.

JW: The music was what it is now?

SL: The melody was identical. But the bass line and some of the inner voices took a while to work out, quite a few years.

JW: Brion, when did you first start noticing jazz?

BG: Oh, I always noticed it. I used to be very snooty about it too. I remember saying, "Well, it's all very well, but they're improvising on tunes that don't interest me in the first place." That's where I stood, on the wrong side of the street. But I knew I was hearing both sides of the street.

Later, in Morocco, Paul Bowles and I were sharing an Arab house with a high tower where you could get very good reception. He had a good radio and we used to play nightlong games of listening to German jazz, Japanese jazz, Australian jazz, and all sorts of things you could get on short wave.

Also, in New York, Latouche did a rather disastrous show together with Duke Ellington, *Twilight Alley*. I went to Duke Ellington's house and *saw* how that whole music machine worked.

JW: Was there a musical imprint that you intended on your new record together, *Songs*? It seems on the edge of various styles. There are strains of Kurt Weill, for instance.

SL: Well, I'm aware of all these people and what they've done, and Weill was a big influence in my own work. But one thing that's been a strong factor in this is my own desire to insert serious lyrics into the jazz fabric. It's like a search for quality. To raise the level of the lyric, so you have something good to play on. Because we play with those words. When we play those tunes based on Brion's words, all the music comes out of the words. I've been lucky to have Brion's stuff to work with. For me it was a miracle finding stuff already made of that quality. Like when he gave me the words to "Dreams," it came out perfect. Then I wanted to see what he had already done. He showed me this stuff and read it for me, and I thought it was great. Because it seemed like it was already set. Just the way he would read it, I could hear it in a certain way that it was already pitched. So I just had the fun part of mulling it over, listening to tapes of him reading it, and finally fixing the pitches and everything myself. And then to getting them realized is a long step and that involved, well, learning them.

BG: That's right, I was just knocked out. In this photograph taken by Hart Leroy Bibbs during the recording session I'm just in a state of sheer ecstasy. And it's because, when it was all put together like that with the sextet, I heard my own voice coming right through there in the whole thing.

JW: How far back does the earliest song date from?

BG: Well, in the forties, I had a project for making a musical out of the biography that I wrote of the man who was the original Uncle Tom, Josiah Henson (*To Master—A Long Goodnight*). And the only one from that period is "Nowhere Street."

JW: What had you written of that project?

BG: I wrote the story and the lyrics. The story was as it really happened, not the way Harriet Beecher Stowe saw it. In other words, how it led him on to all that and how he got kicked in the ass in the end by his name becoming the most pejorative one of all. He never thought this shit was going to fall on him like that. That was the way the musical was supposed to go. And "Nowhere Street" was . . . there's a separation with his great love, he's decided to make it north and she's left in a kind of deserted town like Cincinnati, a suburb of Cincinnati in 1850, where "Nowhere Street" was. She comes on stage and the leaves are falling and lights are coming on in the houses and going off in others. Mysterious—a kind of haunted house sort of thing, and frogs croaking.

JW: How much of that did you see when setting the music?

SL: I never heard this part about Cincinnati before. But Bobby Few (piano player in Lacy's group) is from Cincinnati.

BG: No shit!

SL: But it's apparent in the lyrics. They're so vivid in their painterly abilities that the whole thing is right there for you.

JW: Do the Jajouka musicians of Morocco seem to be any point of contact between you?

SL: Yes. Brion hipped me to that whole thing—the music I've heard, meeting some of the people, and playing with the

BG: president. It's been sort of a good glue between us, reinforcing other things. I've gotten into it as far as I could in the time. But it's a trip. I would have to go there and give up everything else . . .

BG: Like me. Like I did.

SL: . . . and get to it. And I'm not about to do that.

BG: He's scared.

SL: I'd like to go in a helicopter, stay for a few days and get out of there, you know, when I could.

BG: Like me. I stayed all the time there because of that.

SL: It would have been wild to hear Trane play with them. But maybe in another life or something, in another world.

JW: When the two of you perform together, what establishes the time?

SL: Well, what we do is like when the songwriters do a demo of their tune. The lyricist sort of says it and the other guy sort of plays the melody, but shifting a little. So it's not strict time. Sort of collapsed here and stretched out there, so it gives you an idea of how it might sound.

BG: Here's the poor author standing in the crook of the piano.

SL: Like an *art pauvre*. No, sometimes it really comes out perfect, where it's not exactly sung but heard. A kind of delivery.

BG: This is where you're standing out there in front of twenty prospective backers and their girlfriends.

SL: Yeah, they got the singer next to them and the money in their pockets. "These guys wrote this song. Honey, you think you'd like to sing this? I'll buy it for you." . . . But where we usually do it is poetry festivals, where any kind of a musical phenomenon takes it out of the level of the ordinary there.

JW: What is the role of improvisation between the two of you?

SL: In his work, I found it to be very jazzlike, in that he was living it. When he delivers it, he's playing. It's different each time. It's delivered in a free, improvisational manner, and that leeway is written right into it.

BG: And things that I've written *sur commande*, like "Hey Gay Paree Bop," I sort of commanded myself into song. So in those, there are all kinds of points written where you can go off, do anything you like, but come back to them.

SL: Yeah. The more we do that, the freer it's getting. And I imagine if we do it for a while, then somebody else'll pick it up there and do it another way. And that's got to be.

BG: I would certainly hope so. Because if we're all going to space, what's going to space with us will be music.

SL: Especially little tunes you can remember.

III.

In late 1985 Gysin finished his second novel, The Last Museum, *excerpts of which had been published in various literary reviews over the years. The book turned out quite different from what he originally imagined it would be and was his main project in his last years. However, other books also appeared during that time. Once again, young friends and supporters brought this work to light. Terry Wilson's book of interviews with Gysin,* Here to Go *(1982), was published by Re/Search Publications in San Francisco and subsequently by Quartet Books in London, which also reissued Gysin's long-out-of-print first novel.* Légendes de Brion Gysin *(1983), a short book of childhood memoirs with photos, came out in translation in France. Two older manuscripts were printed by Inkblot Press in California:* Stories *(1984), mostly written in Morocco in the 1950s, and* Morocco Two *(1986), his updated film script version of the Dietrich-Cooper classic. Also, in August 1985, in barely a week, Gysin painted a last major work, the ten-canvas series called "Calligraffiti of Fire," commissioned by the Academia Foundation.*

The following interview took place over two afternoons nearly a year apart, in the fall of 1984 and the fall of 1985. During the interim Gysin arrived at the final version of his novel by cutting it drastically. The excised bits were due to appear in a limited edition as The Faultline.*

JW: Why did your new novel, *The Last Museum*, take you over fifteen years to write?

BG: I wonder how I got it done so quickly, really. It was meant to last me a lifetime.

JW: You went through two or three main periods of writing the book?

BG: At least. One whole manuscript was submitted to my editor at Doubleday because I had signed my first contract with them in 1968. And they refused it. I remember the phrase my editor added, "What was Mr. Gysin thinking about, writing this?" I'd spent about a year writing that big, thick, woolly manuscript in Tangier.

JW: The final version is the shortest, isn't it?

BG: Oh yeah, by far. The original version was tied to all the events of 1968 in Paris as well, which went quickly out of fashion. None of the novels written about that worked.

JW: There was also a change before you reached the final version, I believe, from the third person to the first.

BG: Yes, back and forth actually. But essentially the decision was made most recently to go right back to the same sort of first person that I had used in *The Process*, with many different voices, each one speaking in his or her own voice. Writing it in such a way that the voices actually sound back up off the page, that they stand out and are recognizable, without saying "he said," "she said," and that sort of thing. If there's any confusion it just sounds like a crowd talking but with different tones of voice.

JW: As all the things you do are interrelated, the way you describe it sounds like the effect of looking at your Moroccan marketplace paintings.

BG: Yes, that's absolutely true.

JW: But it's also connected to the aspect of flicker that one encounters with your Dreamachine.

BG: As being a further dimension of human experience that isn't usually referred to and that most people haven't been in touch with, except momentarily in their lives. Because the Dreamachine is now available to anybody who can sit in front of one with eyes shut for a while and get to know more about himself, know more about vision. Vision isn't just limited to seeing what's out there, it also involves seeing what's going on inside your own head.

JW: The Dreamachine experience is very central to *The Last Museum*. It's even more brought out here than in *The Process*. It's faster, more intense, and moves more places. The flicker is quicker, in a sense.

BG: Yes, I think so too. But I think very much of the Dreamachine as being an absolute watermark in the history of art. First of all, it's the first object in the history of the world that you look at with your eyes closed. It's much more like a religious experience in that sense. Which is what I thought immediately when I first had the flash of it riding in this car in the south of France in 1958.

JW: How do you see that experience working in the fact of writing?

BG: Well, in *The Process* it was really completely based on cannabis, on kif and smoking hash—or grass at any rate—in Morocco, the whole scene, and the music of Jajouka high in the mountains. Everybody up there was on this sort of level of the emotion, the vibration of grass goes all the way through life there. So, in *The Last Museum* I'm putting it into a deeper region, that of death and after-death experience. I put it into a much more spiritual level, which is that of the flicker, the alpha band experience between eight and thirteen flickers a second. Hence all that interest in time, too, and smaller and smaller increments of its measure.

JW: Are all those terms such as pico- and femtoseconds real?

BG: Oh absolutely, yes. Those are real entities with which modern science is dealing all the time now, within the last ten years.

JW: The way it was tucked in there every now and then almost seemed like a joke.

BG: Well, it *is* a joke to be dealing with fractions of seconds, with one three-hundredth of a second or whatever.

JW: Each time they're kind of tossed off like that, and then eventually they start coming back a little, getting larger.

BG: First of all it's to progress you down into the very low level where the trintoseconds are now talked about, one to the minus thirtieth. They're not much in use yet because that's on the molecular level. Well, one could imagine a sestosecond, which is just a fraction of that, sixty zeros strung across the page, one to the minus sixtieth. These are obviously the areas in which we're going to be working.

JW: Virtually everything in this book is working that fast, in a way. All the regular preoccupations in a novel are brought along at that speed of consciousness.

BG: The principal problem in the novel itself is time, time in which these events occur. I treated it one way in *The Process*, and I treated it in a much more advanced way in *The Last Museum*.

JW: You set both books some time in the future. Why?

BG: I've always been tempted to do that. For instance, *The Process* was predicated on the fact that the dollar had fallen, whereas in actual fact the present state of the dollar now is much more likely to allow someone to buy the Sahara than it was then. Nevertheless, I put that book into the future at a time when any good full-blooded American thought the dollar could *never* fall.

JW: The main importance of setting it then is a historical function.

BG: Yes, but it's also to set the reader's mind at a place where he doesn't quite expect it to be set. He knows that the mind-space, the time-space, is something that he has been used to reading as: I am, I was, I will be. Now it's much more complex than just that. It circles around Present Time, the precise time you are reading it in.

JW: The new book?

BG: Yes. Both novels talk about Present Time a great deal. Present Time is the exact time in which you are completely concentrated on what you are reading. I mean, the words are slipping over the razor's edge of the seconds as you read.

JW: When did you come upon the Bardo Thodol structure of *The Last Museum*? Wasn't the book at one point somewhat of a history of the Beat Hotel, or did the different elements come in at different times?

BG: Now that I think of it, yes. The very first manuscript was really written very quickly, with the idea of satisfying Doubleday and getting out of the contract. Because they'd behaved so badly over *The Process*, they'd hated it and ordered it scrapped. I thought, "My God, if I go through with this again . . ." The new contract was signed and I was already getting a monthly allowance, I thought I better write just what comes off the top of my head and center it around 1968. I'd been in Paris in 1968 and so a lot of things fell into place quite easily. I thought I'd write that kind of easy novel.

JW: But what was there already in that first version?

BG: Well, the hotel was always there, and it always had seven floors and seven rooms on each floor, like the days in the week for example. The forty-nine days of the Bardo Thodol of the Tibetan unreal estate firm.

JW: Were both the Beat and the Bardo in your mind at that point?

BG: I've forgotten, really. And that manuscript I destroyed, not too long ago as a matter of fact, it was completely superfluous. I abandoned it without rereading it even. I've done that often in my life. Shoals of manuscripts I've just . . . Burroughs too, I mean, really—the amount that he's thrown away, just lost or forgotten or . . . The first book that I wrote, in the 1940s, has disappeared completely, called *Memoirs of a Mythomaniac*. *Town and Country* published two chapters of it, so that's still available someplace. But all the rest of it is gone forever, as far as I know. There were three copies, I remember, and I destroyed only one. The other one was with an agent, who died I think. The third, where is it?

JW: Was that book more autobiographical?

BG: Yeah, it was *détourné* autobiography, more so than this.

JW: Well, I see more autobiography in this book than in *The Process*.

BG: Oh yeah, lots more. *The Process* had everything in it that I knew about Islam and Morocco, all the fun I had. That was partly because of Paul Bowles' position in regard to Morocco, his monstrous Morocco, which I've only occasionally visited in the twenty-three years I lived there.

JW: Did you use the cut-up much in *The Last Museum*?

BG: Sure, absolutely. Also in *The Process*, long ago. But I smoothed them out so that they don't look jagged anymore. Whereas William used them raw and it had an impressive force, sheer poetry with his own brand burned into it.

JW: You make very special use of repetitions in this book, particularly you repeat facts and anecdotes. Is it like the same image seen coming back again?

BG: That's one part of it, yeah, and it trails everything else along with it as it comes. It pulls back that previous experience right up into the present again. And it's very like my permutated poems, all the repetition with slight variants all the way as the same words turn over. On rereading it recently, correcting the manuscript for the thousandth time, I thought that worked very well. First of all, it's a bit of a surprise to anybody who's reading it, "Oh, is this on purpose?" And then you say, "Yes, it *is* on purpose." And it works through that. So, what I mean to do is for it to be happening in Present Time, the most Present Time possible situations, conversations as quick as a flash back and forth. Now you realize that several different levels of time are being suggested simultaneously.

JW: Another device in the book that works similarly to the repetitions is when you write "(see illustration)" during certain passages.

BG: It pulls up a picture, doesn't it? First, you're teased; then you're a little annoyed; and then you start making your own. But the illustrations are there, I have them in my notebooks.

JW: In the Tibetans' Bardo there are seven floors. Why did you end your book at the fourth floor?

BG: It ended itself at the fourth floor. From there on you are precipitated into an area of doubt, but with some knowledge of what is ahead upstairs. You know there's an animal floor and maybe a bird floor above that filled with holy ghosts, like the sacred pigeons on the very roof. But then again, as we don't know the facts, maybe the roof blew off a long time ago. You can see how the underpinnings of Present Time have been torn out by the bottom floor having been ripped out, so that you've got the whole Bardo structure apparently suspended in midair. The floors below are disappearing up to that level, but then the others above do seem to exist.

JW: And you hear possible news from upstairs. Did you take a lot of notes in relation to this novel?

BG: Oh God, books and books and books, yearbooks of notes and clippings.

JW: Are the place-names in California true, as they spread out into Death Valley?

BG: That's all taken off the map. I went around by car to all those places in 1978, Apollo County and Mirage Lake.

JW: You have a lot of fun with names in this book.

BG: I've always enjoyed well-chosen names in literature. It's an extra little pleasure to give people some amusement, the fact that you're implying character by the sort of name you use or your vision of that character. You're letting them in on this private information which is a sort of joke.

JW: You have a fondness for historical resonances, reminding us how some things haven't changed nearly as much as we think.

BG: I try to put things together in a place where you can see them. Like in the Middle Ages there were indeed outlandishly dressed guitar players with long hair and pointy shoes who were going around everywhere like hippies, and the fact that they're out there today in front of the Pompidou Center, you start to say, "Ooh, wow." A whole pinch of time is taken right under your fingers, you can just feel it. And when I say that they always had trouble with the students in May wine time, just at the time of their examinations, well, you say, "Ooh, wow, that explains May 1968 and many another May."

JW: How strictly was the whole book mapped out?

BG: Oh, *very*. To the millimeter, to the femtosecond. *The Process* too, *The Process* is a machine after all. I chose the persons of speech—I, thou, etcetera, I used them all—and then found out how they worked together, how they could talk to each other. A good deal of *The Last Museum* had to do with the geography of the hotel, it becomes clearer and clearer. Right from the very beginning, you should have moved from

Room One to Two, Three, Four, but those rooms had already gone to the museum in California. That really kept guiding me all the time. The form that I had decided upon made it at the time a more stringent control but therefore all the easier. I believe in discipline. In my painting too, in everything I do, I always invent a problem, invent the rules for a game which doesn't exist yet and then I do what I can except that I must keep to my own rules. I don't go outside the square of the page or the canvas, or I *do* continually run out through all the edges but I make the rule and stick to it. It's man as a maker of things. You have the right to do whatever you like with the material. Nobody can say no to that, can they?

JW: But you have continued to make changes in *The Last Museum*, haven't you?

BG: Sometimes I can't even say no to good advice from a publisher or two. Everyone told me my manuscript was too long, so I cut it. I cut about one hundred pages out of it, eventually. Some fifty short excerpts of that will be published with fifty illustrations by Keith Haring. They will be brought out as an art book with text and drawings on facing pages so that a really surprising tension is set up between the words and the pictures. I find it sensational and so will you, I think.

Eugène Ionesco

It was with his first play, La cantatrice chauve *(The Bald Soprano), in 1950, that Eugène Ionesco became famous. One of the leading dramatists in the "theater of the absurd," as critics billed it, Ionesco followed with* The Lesson, The Chairs, Rhinoceros, Exit the King, *and other plays, short stories, theater criticism, journals, polemics, and a novel. His last play,* Journeys among the Dead, *was written in 1980.*

Since then, he has also returned to painting, which he first took up over ten years earlier. "Painting retaught me the taste for writing by hand," he says. In 1988 he published La quête intermittente, *which he describes as "autobiographical reflections, flashes, thoughts, meditations, different things, and the quest is intermittent because it is the quest for the absolute."*

Born in Rumania in 1912 of a French mother, Ionesco spent his childhood there and in Brittany; he has lived in Paris since 1939. His work traces an ongoing metaphysical inquiry, sparked by a dark humor amid the ruins of language. Life is a death sentence, his characters are constantly reminded, and yet there is light. A strange order reigns in the world of his theater, subverting the social order with the faithfulness of dreams.

The following interview took place over several afternoons at Ionesco's Montparnasse apartment in late March 1987. The Théâtre de la Huchette in Paris had recently celebrated the thirtieth consecutive year of its productions of The Bald Soprano *and* The Lesson, *just as Joseph Chaikin was preparing a new production of Ionesco's first play in New York.*

JW: It seems that through all your work, except for the polemical writings, you show little interest in realism.

EI: Realism is a school, after all, like romanticism and expressionism, and it is not the expression of reality. Because reality does not exist. We don't know what it is. No man of science, no physicist, can tell you what is real. So, like Mircea Eliade, I say that the real is the sacred. And I give much more importance to the imaginary world than to realism, as we call it. The realist writer, novelist, or playwright is never honest. He is honest but at a certain level he is not. Because he is engaged, because he always has a tendency to express his ideology, the realist writer is biased. But the poet is not biased; the poet does not invent, he imagines. So one lets the imagination billow forth, and in the imagination the poet carries along all sorts of symbols which are the profound truths of our soul. Of our unconscious, as it is called now, but I call it the extraconscious.

JW: Were you never tempted to take, for example, a story or an episode from your lived life and transform that into writing?

EI: Oh, it's transformed in such a way that it is unrecognizable. Because I use my dreams a lot in writing, and the dream is a drama. When we dream we are always in character. As Jung said, the dream is a drama in which the dreamer is at once author, actor, and spectator. And dreams are much more profound than what we call reality. The truth of the soul, our truth, the human truth, is found more in dreams. That's something the German poets, whom I don't know very well, were well acquainted with, that is, Hölderlin, Novalis, Hoffmann, Jean-Paul (Johann Paul Friedrich Richter). Among the French it's Nerval.

JW: Regarding dreams, do you often remember them? Do you write them down much?

EI: I've had a number of experiences concerning them. Many of my plays come out of dreams, like *The Killer* or *Journeys among the Dead*, the last play I wrote. And even *The Bald Soprano*. *Amédée* is the dream I had of a cadaver that I saw in a large dark hallway of an apartment where I lived. In other plays, too, there were apparitions from dreams but, as in *Amédée*, the language was more or less rational, conscious. In my last plays, though, especially the last one, the language tries to stay close to the language of dreams and correspond to the image, so that the language is deteriorated, invented, assonant—an oneiric language. The characters change: one moment they're this and another they're that, as in a dream. And that hasn't always been understood. At the start I used images from dreams that I put in a play which was more or less realistic. Later I tried to use both the oneiric image and the oneiric language. My last play is in full oneiricism, a language that isn't a rational language. At the start I used images from dreams because they were images that came back to me from dreams. Later I learned to remember things I had dreamed. Apparently Novalis knew how to remember his dreams. I learned how from a professor in Zurich. But since then I've forgotten a bit how to remember my dreams because I haven't applied that method anymore. All the same, I think that dreams do come through, especially in the painting I do.

JW: They come through unconsciously.

EI: Yes. When I see the image that I have written, I recognize the dream, the phantasms.

JW: How did you learn to remember your dreams?

EI: At the clinic in Zurich when the machine showed I was dreaming they would wake me up and say, "What did you dream?" After that, I got into the habit of remembering. You can remember your dreams if you are trained to.

JW: Were you writing down your dreams?

EI: No. I dictated my plays to a typist. I was in an armchair, and I let the unconscious or preconscious or half-conscious images from the dreams rise up.

JW: During the writing itself.

EI: During the writing itself. I dictated my dreams. And since many of my plays spring from dreams, then if I am doing autobiography, it's a dreamed autobiography. That is, I remembered my old friends, my old enemies, especially people who were dead. I made them live again and I lived along with them. An action was realized that had been inspired on contact with my dreams. That is not at all French. Because the French write lucidly, and Beckett, too. He writes lucidly and doesn't leave the way open to the irrational. But I did.

JW: So one must have confidence in the irrational.

EI: Yes. I've always thought that dreams are not silly. In dreams are solitude and contemplation. We can reflect more truly there than in real life. There is a lucidity of dreams that is, we can't say superior or inferior, but more penetrating.

I emerge from the dream when I write, so the work appears fresh with the water of the dream, if I can say that, mingled with reality. Reality surprises it and snatches it up.

JW: Yet it is dreams that tend to subvert reality.

EI: Literary critics imagined with *The Bald Soprano*, for example, that I had written it to scare the bourgeoisie, to parody bourgeois theater, to make a sort of politics. In reality, especially with my first plays, they have no political application whatsoever. I didn't write *The Bald Soprano* while dreaming; I wrote it in a fully lucid state, but taking special care to designify, to remove all meaning from things, words, characters, action. So, in removing all meaning, one returned to a dream state, we could say. And to a sort of contemplation in spite of oneself.

JW: On various occasions you have spoken of your sense of amazement before the world.

EI: I have felt that since childhood. My course, if we can call it such, has been the following. First, I'm born into the world, born consciously. I look at the world and my first question is: why the world? What is all this which surrounds me and why is there something rather than nothing? This something appears absolutely miraculous to me. We have difficulty accepting the world's presence, but we accept it. It's there, the world is there, and still we don't know for sure if it is there, because it could collapse from one moment to the next, it could deteriorate, it could not be. I am not sure that there is something, but finally it seems there may be. Once we admit the world's existence, the world's presence, we ask the second question: why is there more evil than good? In plays like *The Bald Soprano*, everything is designified. It's a piece that has the structure of a play, with a slow moment, a faster one, then a great movement that is very dramatic. The people argue, quarrel, fight, we don't know why. There is no action, there are no characters. Later, with *The Killer*, the second question was asked: why evil sooner than good? Those then are the two directions, the two great questions that are the source of my dreams, of myself.

JW: Before *The Bald Soprano*, which you wrote in your mid-thirties, you'd written two earlier books in Rumanian: the book of criticism, *Nou* (No), and the study of Victor Hugo. Had you always wanted to be a writer?

EI: From the age of nine I said I was going to write, that I could do nothing else but write. But all the same, art leads to contemplation. And that's what brings us closest to God, to divinity, to the extent that we can in a certain manner approach it. Especially when we do not have a religious vocation. I make literature and I write plays to ask myself these questions in a state of wonder. Wonder is the philosopher's first sensation, moreover, and wonder is also the beginning of contemplation, perhaps even contemplation itself. But I've written all my life, and I have done only that, from lack of a religious vocation, regretting my lack of a religious vocation and perhaps my lack of grace. But God knows whether or not I have grace. Do you believe in God?

JW: More or less, I suppose.

EI: Like me. So you have the sense of the sacred. And the sacred is the only reality, as Eliade said. Like everyone, I have been afraid of death, of the deaths of my friends, and of putrefaction. And we know that the sacred always subsists, it does not putrefy. I think it's odd that the French do not have a sense of death. Apart from Pascal, perhaps Claudel, perhaps Péguy—but Péguy had too much literature and too much politics—the French do not have the feeling of death. They have the feeling of aging and putrefaction. One of the most beautiful French poems is "Une charogne" by Baudelaire, where it's putrefaction. And what is the most beautiful in Zola is not the descriptions of society, it's not his militancy for Dreyfus. What's most beautiful, most profound, and what he does not realize himself, is the death of Nana. Or the death of Thérèse Raquin, where we see a woman who was very beautiful, full of gifts and full of talent, rot away and become a cadaver. They have a sense of putrefaction, but they have neither a sense of death nor a sense of resurrection.

JW: What brought about your first book, *Nou*, which you wrote in your early twenties?

EI: That book is very difficult to describe, because it is a mixture of literary politics, scandals, vanities, characters that no one knows outside of Rumania. First, I realize that literature is worthless. Just as nothing is of value in the world, literature is worthless. Literature and culture are not worth anything. That is the foundation of the book, and in that book are my complaints, my regrets for a lost paradise, and the permanent search for a paradise by way of a certain literary meanness. All of that is very mixed together. But above all there is a question that dominates and that I posed to the most important literary critic in Bucharest, because that's where I was: if God exists, there is not any reason to write literature. If God does not exist, there is not any reason to write literature. I've always wavered there my whole life until now, and that's why there is derision in my work. Why write, if there is God? Why write, if there is no God? So that is the basis; that has undermined my whole literary life, my entire existence. Everything I've written is, "Why write?" That's why I have done plays where there is this question, where the characters are ridiculous, they're derisory. My characters are not tragic because they have no transcendence—they are far from that. They are laughable. That's why one critic called our theater "the theater of derision," but he didn't know exactly why there was derision. The derision was due to my metaphysics.

JW: It's as if the writing exists within that ambiguity.

EI: Yes, mine does. The others, no. They're poets who speak of love, of social life, of war, of politics. But even without realizing it, Brecht wrote *Mother Courage*, and in *Mother Courage* what do we see, what is most important? It's not the war, but the presence of the canteen woman. They said it was an anti-war play, but I think it was a criticism of life. The canteen woman's children die, she gets older and older; it's decrepitude, old age, and that is what the truth is. He speaks of the Thirty Years' War, but he's speaking of something other than the Thirty Years' War. Unintentionally. That's why I've said that the great poets wanted to make propaganda, lots of great poets. Arthur Miller, but Arthur Miller does not reach the level of metaphysics. Lots of writers think they are speaking of one thing; in reality it's something else they are thinking. Consciously or unconsciously.

JW: In the United States a certain realism forms the main literary tradition, which of course includes Arthur Miller. But there are others, such as Robert Wilson in theater, whom you've expressed an interest in.

EI: I've seen two or three of his plays: *Deafman's Glance*, another in Berlin, and another in Paris which I've forgotten the name of. It lasts twenty-four hours: the audience comes for two, three, four hours, then they leave, they come back. The actors barely move, they barely move. It's a derision of theater, but it's a derision of life, of man. Above all it's a derision of action. That's why I really like the book by Jan Kott, *Shakespeare Our Contemporary*, where he shows the following. A mean, corrupt, vicious prince is in power; another young prince, to make the world just, kills the mean prince; he in his turn ages, grows corrupt, vicious, criminal; so another young prince comes to take his place; he becomes in his turn vicious, corrupt, etcetera; so another young prince, and so on. And for him it's both a criticism and an explanation of Shakespeare's theater. We see the kings killing each other off, and he compares that with Stalin.

What has been going on in history for the last two centuries? There was the rule of the nobles, which was based on inequality and privilege. They kill the nobles and install the bourgeoisie; a society where the child works fourteen hours a day, where people die in misery much more than in the time of the nobles. Later, man is exploited. They say that man must not be exploited, so the revolutionaries make a new regime, which is the Stalinist regime, where the privileges are greater still. Not only that, but what is serious about man is that justice truly signifies injustice, punishment. Freedom means privilege. And so the meaning is now known to us, but it took us some time to know it. This immense chaos that I try to interpret, to speak of a bit, Shakespeare had spoken of it long before me: life "is a tale told by an idiot, full of sound and fury, signifying nothing." If I write a theater of the absurd, I can say that my grandfather was Shakespeare.

JW: In *Notes and Counter Notes*, speaking of the avant-garde, you said that the avant-gardists "finally merged into the theatrical tradition and that is what must happen to every good avant-gardist." The same thing has happened with you. Has that bothered you in any way?

EI: I think I've become a classic: they study me in schools. But I think that people can recognize the truth of what I said initially and be moved. Besides, the young people who come to the theater now don't laugh anymore. Twenty years ago they laughed a lot, but now they're a bit frightened by these words that don't say anything, that do not signify, that don't want to signify.

JW: In 1970 you entered the Académie Française. Did that change your work as a writer in any way?

EI: Not at all. That had no importance. It had only an external importance, and that was entirely temporary. I saw people at the Académie who came in wheelchairs or who limped, and I told myself, that's what the truth is, and that is what will happen to me, too. Sure enough, now I have a cane. But it does help, since we live on several levels of consciousness. In the least lucid consciousness, we are glad to have a nice house, and we are glad that other people give us their respect. Entering the Académie is the respect that people have for you. So why refuse it? In the end, we don't refuse, we accept, as we accept living, as we accept earning a little money. As one accepts living, because one does not commit suicide every day. So we continue to live in a world that is our own and that is absolutely infernal. Swedenborg said that we already live in hell. And I believe that we already live in hell. Not only because there is war on every side, not only because there are earthquakes, but even if there weren't, we already live in hell, at the furthest gate from paradise, if one believes in that. I wonder how I would live if I didn't have the hope, even uncertain, of paradise. I'm still living, I don't kill myself, because God forbids me to, because one hopes in spite of everything, one hopes without hoping, a mixture of belief and disbelief, one hopes for the hereafter, the resurrection of the dead. And the glorified body that never grows old. But it's hard to put up with life.

JW: How do you regard the development of your theater career?

EI: There have been several periods in what I've written. There was the period of *The Bald Soprano*, in which I shattered language joyfully. That gave me a feeling of enormous freedom, I could do whatever I wanted with words. Through the middle period, *Exit the King*, there was hope, there was still God. But later, with time, the disintegration of language grew heavier, it became tragic. That's what we see in my last play, *Journeys among the Dead*, where there are a lot of ghosts, dead people with whom I speak. In the end, the theatrical game disappears and there is a return to a certain metaphysics. Perhaps with God, perhaps without God, I myself don't know.

JW: Do you feel that your plays have become more and more oriented toward the spiritual?

EI: *The Bald Soprano* is a spiritual play, because it is my wonder before the world. In my first play I am amazed by the fact that there are people who exist, who speak, and I don't understand what they're saying, I don't know. In the second play, *The Lesson*, there is a play on words with death at the end. In *The Chairs* it's metaphysics—there was that mixture of metaphysics and moral ideology. All the time there was this mixture, and the critics didn't understand. In *Exit the King* you have an end that was inspired by the Tibetan dialogue of the dead. At the end the king dies, he loves life, he doesn't want to die. Then comes resignation, and after that, a spiritual guide who is the queen leads him toward the hereafter, according to the Tibetan rite. "Don't touch the flower, let your saber drop from your hand, do not fear the old woman who will ask you" I don't know what. Go up, go up, go up. In the Tibetan rite of death, women surround the dying man or even the recently dead, and they tell him, "Rise, rise, rise," so that he doesn't fall into the lower regions, the infernal regions. So the king's end was inspired by that.

JW: Has the audience become increasingly open to your theater?

EI: At first they were for me. There were the critics at *Le Figaro* who were opposed, the latecomers, the imbeciles. And then the young critics were for me, but they were Marxists. So when they understood that I was not a Marxist—I said so, I shouted it—at that point they turned away from me. And the backward critics who had attacked me, they said, "He's not a leftist, so he's one of us!" At the start they had said, "Dirty theater, bad theater, detestable theater"; now they said, "Good theater, admirable theater, *Exit the King* is like Shakespeare," and other foolishness. Now there's a return toward me of those who were and are no longer Marxist.

JW: Does it seem that audiences are less confused by your work than they used to be?

EI: With *The Bald Soprano*, which for me was a tragedy of language, they did not understand. With other plays they understood, but poorly. They understood politically. At first they were very favorable toward *Rhinoceros*, because they said, "Now there's a fine criticism of Nazism." I had considerable success in Germany. Later, when Barrault's theater did a revival of *Rhinoceros* some years ago, it became suspect again, because the people of the left who had said that it's a criticism of Nazism said, "But what if it's a criticism of us?" Because it is an antitotalitarian criticism.

JW: So people insisted on being very simplistic about it.

EI: You know, *Rhinoceros* was a great success the world over. It was played in Spain during Franco's time, because they said the rhinoceroses are the communists. It was played to great success in Argentina. Perón had fallen and they said it's an anti-Peronist play. The play was able to be performed in the countries of the Eastern bloc, because they said it is an anti-Nazi play. In Germany they said it's an anti-Nazi play and that was true, they felt it. But the play was performed in England. At the time England was a tranquil country—it is no longer a tranquil country. I said to my producer, "The English will have a hard time understanding this play because there was no civil war in England." In France there were Nazis and patriots, there was the Dreyfus case, with the Dreyfusards and the anti-Dreyfusards. So my producer told me, "Listen, I managed to get you Laurence Olivier as the leading actor, I managed to get you a great director," which was Orson Welles, "I got you a great theater. Excuse me if I couldn't get you the civil war in England."

JW: It seems that everyone wanted only to see their own story in it.

EI: I had asked some young people who hadn't known Nazism and who hadn't known communism, the Austrians, for example. The theater there was more than full, many many people came in Vienna, and I asked, "Here it is, this is a play in my antitotalitarian spirit. What do you understand now, what is it for you?" And they said, "But it's clear: for us it's an anticonformist play," against conformism. So, the play continues to exist.

JW: Has writing changed much for you over the years?

EI: Oh, I think my plays are very different from each other. Perhaps this sounds like boasting, but my plays, most of which have not been inspired by any other play, always change, it's always something else. I went to England recently with my play *Journeys among the Dead*, at the Riverside Theatre, and the English were very surprised. Apart from nonprofessional companies, my plays had not been performed in England in a long time, because I was against Brecht. The public came en masse; the first nights were full. Then after that, the other nights were empty. Because they thought they were going to find an Ionesco who would make them laugh, like the Ionesco of *The Bald Soprano*, for example. I came on at the end and explained my new play to them. So they came back to the theater. But except for the *Sunday Times* and the *Observer*, the reviews were bad. They didn't recognize me anymore.

JW: What about the act of writing itself? Your earliest plays are often dated at the end with the month they were written. That means you wrote the whole thing in a month?

EI: Yes. Three weeks or a month.

JW: Did you have to do several drafts?

EI: No. They came out very quickly. A few tiny details I changed, but I wrote them like that. Then I read them over. And when I had a secretary, I dictated to her at the typewriter. I hardly ever change it.

JW: You've always worked like that?

EI: Always.

JW: Even the longer plays?

EI: Even the longer plays, I never change them.

JW: So what brings you to the point of writing? Do you prepare much, do you take notes?

EI: No. I think about a dream, or else I sit down and wait for the characters to speak. And when I've heard an exchange of replies between two characters, then I continue.

JW: Do you sense from the start that it will be one act or two or three acts, do you feel the scope of it?

EI: Yes, more or less. I have no preliminary idea when I write, but as I write my imagination completes it. So the second half or more of the play takes shape in my head. Then I know how I'm going to end it. Though I must say that spontaneous creation does not exclude the pursuit and consciousness of style.

JW: Have you ever been tempted to act in one of your plays?

EI: I acted in a film, *La vase* (The Mire). I was the only and main character.

JW: Do you work much with the directors of your plays?

EI: Usually when it's in Paris I work with my directors. The play is developed with the director, by way of squabbling. I take the play away, I give it back again, I take it away, and so on. Especially with Jean-Marie Serreau it happened like that, and with Sylvain Dhomme as well, with *The Chairs*. I hate it when they ignore my stage directions. But when I do the play myself, be it *Exit the King* or *Victims of Duty*, which I like a lot, then I myself don't respect my own stage directions.

JW: Have you learned certain things now and then from the actors?

EI: I have never written for actors. And you must pardon my pride but actors have not affected my plays. The actors are characters that come out of my mind and who must conform to what I have seen in my mind.

JW: I've heard that you travel a lot.

EI: Yes, more and more. California, the United States, the East Coast, Canada, Argentina, Brazil, Uruguay, Colombia, China, Taiwan, Japan, Senegal, and a lot to Israel. Because I adore Israel. And perhaps sometimes I've been such a fan of Israel that now, when I see Arafat, the leader of the Palestinians, now I wonder if I shouldn't have been a bit more balanced. Because he is unhappy, his people are being killed. But I didn't want the Jews to be killed. Because if we hadn't supported them they would have been destroyed by forty Arab countries. So it was necessary to be on their side, and now it's necessary to think of the others, too, a bit. But I do not understand this rage that exists in Lebanon, in Syria, in Iran, in Iraq, in Thailand, in Vietnam, in the entire world. When I think that it goes back not a hundred years but a thousand years, and not a thousand but ten thousand years, and that it has always been like this, I am absolutely terrified. I tell myself, this world is hell, but hell has no end! Everyone is killing each other. Jesus said, "Love one another," and it's as if he had said, "Kill one another."

JW: Are you superstitious?

EI: Yes, very. I believe, for example, that in my last play I mistreated some dead people, some ghosts. My father, who is dead, my stepmother, my grandmother. And I believe that some rather terrible things happened to me because of that. I have other reasons to believe in the immediate unreality because those dead people, in my opinion, are there for some time, and at the end of several centuries they go away. I've had strange dreams. For example, I was in England at a friend's house. I slept in a room there and at night I dreamed that I was surrounded by doctors with white coats who told me, "We're going to operate on your brain. It's not fun, but it'll be all right, it'll pass." And then the doctors leave, only one remains, and I say to him, "Tell me the truth, doctor. I have a brain tumor, don't I? It's incurable, and that's why you don't want to operate on me anymore?" And he tells me, "Yes, go back home to the country." The country meaning a friend's house there. So I woke up, it was dawn, and I walked about from one room to another to see if I knew where I was, because I had been told that in many cases, those who have a malignant brain tumor lose their sense of direction. My wife wakes up and says to me, "What's wrong with you? You're crazy. Why are you running around the house like that?" I tell her my dream and she says, "It's nothing, just a story." Morning comes, we go to breakfast in the dining room. My daughter slept in the room next to us; she comes in and says, "Oh, Papa, you snored last night, a lot." I tell my daughter, "No, that's not true, I wasn't snoring." Our hostess is frightened, and she says, "Yes, yes, my little girl, it's your father who was snoring." All right. My daughter goes out to play, and our hostess says, "Excuse me, it's not you who was snoring. It's my grandfather. My grandfather died eight years ago; today is the anniversary. Each year on his anniversary we hear his death-rattle." So I say to our friend who was putting us up, "I know what he died from, your grandfather. He died from a malignant brain tumor. They wanted to operate; as it was incurable they sent him home." "How do you know?" "I dreamed it." But I've had a lot of other experiences.

JW: There is also a prophetic aspect to dreams.

EI: Yes, the night before my mother's death—I'm in the process of writing about her death at the moment—that night I saw her amid flames. I wanted to pull her away; I wasn't able to. The next day she was dead, from a stroke. And then I've had premonitions. During the war I went to Bucharest one year to arrange my military situation. One night I wake up, I say, "Earthquake!" My wife wakes up, completely terrified. There was no earthquake, there wasn't anything. So we go back to sleep. The next night I wake up. "Earthquake!" My wife says, "You're crazy!" and then she feels that everything's moving. It was true.

JW: What else do you know of ghosts?

EI: There are ghosts in Brittany, but very few. There were a lot in my childhood, because I grew up near Brittany, in the Mayenne region, to be exact. There were ghosts. There aren't any now. They've all taken refuge in England.

JW: How do you know?

EI: From the dream I had. And our friend there, in Maidenhead, told us other stories of ghosts as well. Apparently there are still some in Gascony, very few.

JW: I wonder how people can follow their route.

EI: I don't know, especially how they manage to cross the channel. Because apparently ghosts don't travel through water. Perhaps on a boat.

JW: In *Fragments of a Journal* you noted at one point, which you come back to several times, "Once again the dream that explains everything, this dream of the absolute truth, has escaped me." Do you think that such a dream, or the substance of such a dream, could ever be apprehended?

EI: It's a hope that is chimerical, metaphysical. It's a hope for illumination. But it's not a psychological hope, not realistic.

JW: You also like to cite the example of what the Zen monks discovered, when after a long search for illumination they end up reaching a sort of divine laughter in the face of the illusion of the world.

EI: But I hoped to have this illumination in a dream. I felt that perhaps there would be one of these dreams that could explain everything, everything. It's a mythical way, an absolutely unreal way to explain.

JW: Various people have spoken about guiding their own dreams.

EI: Yes, that exists. With the romantic poets, Jean-Paul, Novalis, Hoffmann, I think. But I'm not able to control my dreams. I never knew how.

JW: You've spoken of the crisis of contemporary language, saying that it doesn't exist.

EI: No, the crisis of language, so-called, does not exist. We can express ourselves scientifically or literarily; we have enough definitions for psychology, sociology, etcetera. It's sooner a crisis of communication between people. Or that's what I think now. There is a crisis in communication that is above all emotional. I don't know why. I think it goes way back, as with the Tower of Babel in Kafka. Men could not understand each other because first they said they wanted to reach God, and in reality from the first or second floor up they set to squabbling, for a better position or whatever. The crisis of language comes from that moment there, that mythic moment.

JW: As if people cannot really manage to understand what is important.

EI: Yes, that's right. Man does not understand the essential. Not only does he not understand: he could at least feel it, and he does not feel it either. He does not know at all, not in any way, neither emotionally nor intellectually. Intellectually is impossible because we cannot understand God. Since then, I think we've been bent on ... I've been especially bent on conceiving the inconceivable, comprehending the incomprehensible, the infinitely small, the infinitely large, comprehending what is limited and what is unlimited. That is, the great mysteries in which we live cannot be understood by ourselves, with our powers. We can understand them only thanks to mystical intuitions. Saint John of the Cross, identifying himself in a certain way with God, Saint Thérèse of Lisieux, Saint Teresa of Avila understood. But we cannot understand; ordinary language cannot understand. We must resign ourselves to not understanding. And that is the hardest thing.

JW: Your last play, *Journeys among the Dead*, seems to end by way of this resignation.

EI: At the end of the play there is a sort of desperate attempt to understand or make oneself understood beyond words, in another language, in a sort of metalanguage, to find meaning where there is no meaning. Where words have lost their meaning.

JW: The last words of that play are "I don't know." That recalls the words of certain writers who, after having lived their entire lives, their entire careers, arrive at this "I don't know."

EI: But that is another "I don't know." I know. I know what the radiator is, what this or that thing is, a logical or ordinary thing. It has to do with another kind of "I don't know," with a sort of spiritual incomprehension, metaphysical or divine.

JW: Does one have to live an entire life to arrive at this "I don't know"?

EI: I knew from the beginning. I knew it, or rather I suspected as much.

JW: Earlier you were speaking of arriving at something mystically, in discussing certain aspects of *The Bald Soprano*. Were you thinking in those terms at the time?

EI: Yes, but in a way that was less clear. Because I was much younger. Then to the degree that I didn't understand things, I asked myself why I didn't understand. And then seeing that whatever I do, I would never understand, I was beset with a sort of despair. I'm like that man who said, "My God, make me believe in you."

JW: You've often said that symbols have counted a lot for you. You believe profoundly in symbols. Even in *Fragments of a Journal* you wrote that you believe too much in the myths of psychoanalysis.

EI: Yes, because psychoanalysis is limited. It's a scientific language like any other scientific language. It's not a language that is metascientific, it's not a metalanguage, it's not something that goes beyond language.

JW: In a more recent book, you mention having seen a lot of "psychoanalysts, priests, and rabbis." Considering the plays and the dreams written down in your journals, what is your experience of psychoanalysis?

EI: Not too wide. I know psychoanalysis from books and from a bit of experience. An experience with Jungian psychoanalysis where one speaks, one discusses. Where one has waking dreams. But at any rate, without God one cannot begin to grasp whatever it may be. Any psychoanalysis goes a little farther than the usual language but not a lot farther. It remains more or less on the same plane.

JW: Did your discussions with "the priests and rabbis" ever bring you much?

EI: No, they didn't teach me anything. Nothing can make a person know, only prayer. But if I knew how to pray . . . I don't know how to pray. And they, the professional rabbis and priests, are moralists much more than anything else, much more than mystics. Saint Augustine, for example, seems to me much more a moralist than a mystic. I feel closer to Saint John of the Cross.

JW: You've made occasional mention of the gnostics. Have you read them much?

EI: Yes, and I've been tempted several times by gnostic thought. I was tempted by that heresy, as it is called, thinking that there is evil in the world and that God could not have been the author of this evil. So it was, as Cioran says, the evil demiurge who created this world.

JW: The gnostics spoke of the hidden God. Did that appeal to you?

EI: If one believes the gnostics, God is hidden. But I don't always believe that. Sometimes I believe it; other times I feel that he reveals himself in the plenitude of his light. The plenitude of light that I do not have, but I have vaguely felt something. I speak of it in *Fragments of a Journal* and in the first part of *The Killer*, where I say I felt happy one day, infinitely happy, blissful, because suddenly—it was a spring day—I felt that I was enveloped in a light greater than the sun, and yet the sun was at its zenith. The world seemed miraculous to me. That is, the handkerchiefs and the pants hanging on the clothesline suddenly seemed dazzlingly beautiful to me. Everything was made beautiful by God's presence; I felt myself protected by him. But that instant was very brief, really very brief, and after fifteen minutes, or ten minutes, or five—time is not measurable in such an instant—I felt as in a dizzy fall, as if I had lost something that was the most important thing of all.

JW: Early on you wrote that you would remember that moment for a long time afterward.

EI: Yes, but I also wrote many years later that it did not have the power to reconcile me. That is, what I had learned at that moment was very little, a tiny bit that God had deigned to give me, and I had lost it, I no longer had anything but the memory of a memory of a memory. The thing was as if it had dried up, and this memory no longer warmed my existence.

JW: What about *Hunger and Thirst*? That play seemed to mark a new step in your metaphysical path.

EI: I thought so, too.

JW: Did you feel it as such at the time?

EI: Yes and no. It was sincere, insincere, it was true, untrue, it was an innocent game, it was an overrated game. It was truth, or it was literature, I don't know myself. It was a search for the essential that was perhaps sincere, but this search was not entirely honest. Unwillingly, because there was all the literature, theological and literary, that was swallowed up in there. "Hunger and thirst": calling it that denotes their falsity. That is, these are words—from philosophy, from morality, from literature. I don't think that it's totally true, but where it was true is the vision my wife had: the character Madeleine, who sees the landscape, the garden she had seen as a six-year-old child. And I put that on the stage. And then it was a sort of confession like the others: I'm bad, here is paradise, here is hell.

JW: The vision you were speaking of, do you mean the vision at the end, of the garden with the silver ladder suspended in the air?

EI: Yes, it's a bit true and a bit untrue. I had that dream. I dreamed of a thicket and of a silver ladder. Later, when I talked to my friends about it, they told me that this archetypal dream exists. It exists in Jung and in the Bible. But I didn't know it existed. Perhaps it was the collective unconscious that I had penetrated, that I had rummaged in, and from which I had brought back certain things.

JW: That vision reappears at the end of your novel *The Hermit* as well.

EI: Well, there I think it's on purpose. What is true in there is the nonsense of all action, the stupidity, the absurdity of politics, of war. And the end was laid right over that. But I have often wondered how it is that for thousands and thousands of years it continues, always the same; it's war that continues. And I've wondered, perhaps committing heresy, how it is that God has not tired of this very long story without end. Endlessly ending. And it's always the same thing, the same consuming hate between people. Or the same need for love that is always betrayed and that has never really existed when you get right down to it. Because do people truly love each other?

JW: That corresponds a little with an aspect of *Hunger and Thirst*. Several times there you play with the idea of pity. For example, in the second act, "The Rendez-Vous," the Second Guard says, "Each person demands it for himself, none is able to give it to others."

EI: Yes, that's true. It does exist, as in the story of Father Kolbe.

He was a Polish Catholic priest who had been at Auschwitz in a concentration camp. A prisoner had escaped, so they chose a group who would live without food or drink for fifteen days if the prisoner did not return, to die of hunger and thirst. Father Kolbe was not among them; he was in the camp because he was Catholic and because he irritated the Nazis. Among those who were designated, one was crying. Father Kolbe asked the commander of the camp, "I want to go in his place." He went in his place, and there he lived among them for fifteen days, and after fifteen days he died. But he died after all the others, he helped the others die for fifteen days, and at the end he stretched out his arm for them to give him an injection, because in spite of his weakness he still didn't die. Now there is someone who loved others more than himself. But I know of no other case. Or yes, Jesus of course. But apart from Jesus and a few saints, I don't think so. I think that some old folks, to live a few days longer, would sacrifice the lives of children.

But in the end I am a man like all men and less courageous than many other men. Much more cowardly, as intellectuals often are; much more bourgeois. I would not make Kolbe's sacrifice. And at the same time I'm thirsty for glory. So everything in me is absolutely imperfect.

JW: Has there been a certain disappointment for you in becoming famous?

EI: No. I wanted fame, I wanted to escape anonymity. Existence in anonymity seemed inadmissible to me. I did not want to live in anonymity because I told myself that if I cannot live in God—living in God means to live in silence, in monastic life—then to live at least shining among men. I know that is an error, but I can't help it.

JW: At what point did you realize you wanted fame?

EI: Right away. When I started writing. When I was a child, when I was ten, eleven, twelve, I told myself, "I would like to be a saint." But one should not want to be a saint, one should be a saint. To want to be a saint is to want glory. Then I wanted to be a general. But being a general is first to brave danger, and it is also to want glory. So, not able to be a saint, not able to be a general, at least be a writer. I have the desire for and a mistrust of glory.

The problem for me was choosing between God and humanity. Not in order to love people really, but above all to shine among them. Which Saint Augustine condemned. So I chose humanity. And when one chooses humanity, one is often against God. It is a titan's attitude. But when one chooses God, one loves humanity as well. Like Saint Thérèse of Lisieux, who cried thinking of the unfortunate ones in hell.

JW: You worked for quite a while as a teacher. Have you sometimes felt as a writer that you are still a teacher?

EI: No. I don't want to teach anything. I don't propose a message. I propose, in the least ignoble part of me, in the noble part of me, I pose questions, problems, and I have no solutions. The solutions are automatic, political, ideological; the solutions are not each person's quest. Whereas if one poses the problem to each one of thousands or hundreds of spectators, each one of the spectators, though there be hundreds, becomes one again, a character, alone, like Bérenger in *Rhinoceros*. Bérenger was written to try to teach even so . . . you see, I'm contradicting myself. But it's the only play with a message, to try to give people the belief that they can think for themselves, the power to think for themselves outside of others, but I did not say who the others were. They were the Nazis, the conformists, the communists, I don't know who else. To make people understand that they could live alone, in solitude. As I myself managed to when I was young, in Rumania, where I was neither communist nor Iron Guard. So it is and it isn't a didactic message. It's not didactic because I'm telling about my experience. I expose the problem not so much for people to respond to each other about it but so they can respond to me and give me a voice.

JW: That image at the end of your novel *The Hermit*, with the garden and the silver ladder, which is more or less the same image at the end of *Hunger and Thirst*, it seems to give a bit more hope in the novel.

EI: Yes; that isn't hope, it's the desire to have hope. It's between literature and truth. But it is the sincere desire to have hope, the regret of not having had it, and I would have liked to give hope to this imaginary hero who is the hermit.

JW: In your later plays was it sometimes difficult to show images that were too deeply linked to your own life?

EI: No, I have no presumptions, I have no shame. Literature is without shame. It is "the heart laid bare" of Baudelaire. On the contrary, what I look for in literature is to be more and more true, more and more close to myself, and so more and more immodest.

JW: What was the response to your play *Man with Bags*?

EI: *Man with Bags* was a political play, so it was very poorly received. It was a political dream, a nightmare. I dreamed that I found myself in my native land and that I could not leave, and that it was a totalitarian country. So it was immediately considered bad by the left, which was very strong in France at that time, because it was a criticism of a totalitarian regime.

JW: What was your experience with the productions of *Journeys among the Dead*?

EI: The play was performed in France, Germany, and England. In France it was well received I think only because the director was a man of the Left. It was poorly received in Germany because it was not a leftist play. There were other reasons too—simply that they didn't understand what it meant.

JW: Have you written other plays since *Journeys among the Dead*?

EI: I started a play about Kolbe, the priest in the concentration camp, but it hasn't worked. I wrote one act; it's a rather conventional play. But I still think about writing other plays.

JW: In Claude Bonnefoy's book of interviews with you, *Entre la vie et le rêve*, you spoke of the *style de lumière* of certain writers. Whom did you have in mind?

EI: I was thinking of Charles Du Bos, of Valery Larbaud, perhaps others. I felt that their writing had a certain luminous spark; the words were luminous. But it was a very subjective impression.

JW: Did the futurists interest you?

EI: The futurists, the dadaists, the surrealists, yes, somewhat. Soupault, Breton, Tzara, Marinetti, I knew all that. But I haven't been influenced by playwrights. I parodied Shakespeare, that is, I parodied him in trying to add something, the problem of politics, in *Macbett*. I've been influenced by writers like Dostoyevsky and especially Kafka.

JW: How did Kafka influence you?

EI: I couldn't say exactly what form that has taken, because it's an influence where the bigger it is, the less explainable it is. But I have felt it in myself, and I have admired him very much. And on another level, I've been influenced by Baudelaire.

JW: Did Picasso's theater work interest you?

EI: A bit, yes, I liked it. Because it was theater that was a bit absurd. Philosophical, more so than mine, and absurd at the same time.

JW: In *Antidotes*, the book of articles and essays, you wrote that Denis de Rougemont and Jean Grenier "could be the authentic thinkers of our time." How so?

EI: On the level of politics and on the level of morality. On the level of religion they were believers, but they weren't believers like Kafka, for example. In that sense Kafka reinvented religion because he lived it in an entirely internal manner, whereas Denis de Rougemont or Jean Grenier lived it in an external way, rather practical. With Kafka it was a living faith, an ardently spiritual life, and I don't even know if he himself knew that he believed.

JW: And where were de Rougemont and Grenier politically?

EI: They were anticommunist and anti-Nazi.

JW: The women characters are usually very crucial in your plays. It's been said that you are one of the best writers for women. Does that correspond to your intentions?

EI: They have a great importance. I've written for women and against women. *The Painting* is antifeminist. But *Hunger and Thirst* is for women. Also a play like *A Stroll in the Air*, where I try to explain the distress of the woman, her solitude. *Amédée* is against women, because they are sometimes crabby and tough, but at the same time it is for them, because the woman there is the one who does all the work, she's the one who puts up with everything—who even puts up with a man, which isn't easy. Like the character, and like myself. But in the end the man-woman question doesn't really enter into my plays.

Carlos Fuentes

History, civilizations, and the complex cultural identity of Mexico have been the stuff from which Carlos Fuentes' twenty books are made. The open adventure of his novelistic structures is indicative of the new language wrought by recent generations of Latin American writers, many of whom he has helped to get their work read beyond their own borders. A keen interpreter of politics, a sincere advocate of culture and thought, Fuentes is above all a man of conscience. Mexican ambassador to France from 1975 to 1977, he resigned his post in protest when former president Gustavo Díaz Ordaz, responsible for the massacre of hundreds of students by police at Tlatelolco in 1968, was appointed ambassador to post-Franco Spain.

For the French publication of his latest novel, Distant Relations, *Fuentes was back in Paris again, where this interview was conducted in the offices of his publisher, Gallimard, in late December 1981. We began by discussing his massive novel of 1976,* Terra Nostra, *which Gabriel García Márquez has said requires a one-year fellowship to read.*

JW: In reading *Terra Nostra* it is surprising how much turns out to be factual. So that discovering more about the history, one discovers more about the book.

CF: Yes, certainly. After all, history is only what we remember of history. What is fact in history? The novel asks this question. We made history. But history doesn't exist if we don't remember it. That is, if we don't imagine it, finally.

JW: Did you have a specific sense of where fact and fiction diverge while writing *Terra Nostra*?

CF: Well, I have another book, it's an anti–*Terra Nostra* in the sense that it's so short: *Aura*, a novella. And the protagonist of *Aura*, who is caught by this sort of witch in this house in Mexico City, says, "Well, I'm here to work and make enough money so that I can write what I've been imagining all my life I could write. A great opus of the Renaissance world, of the discovery of the New World, of the conquest of the Americas, the colonization." I mean, this is a historian who would like to deal with fact. But of course he is caught in a world of pure fiction, a surreal world. So, I guess that from this mold, from this matrix, came *Terra Nostra*. It is written by the protagonist of *Aura*, who is a man caught between life and death, between youth and old age, between reality and surreality, so he writes *Terra Nostra*. But it's not the book he wanted to write, it's not the history book he wanted to write, it's a book in which he has to imagine history, that is, to reinvent history. That is, to write history, really.

JW: How long did you spend researching the book?

CF: All my life. I never consulted a note when I was writing *Terra Nostra*. Because this is something I've carried with me all my life, this is my whole heritage. As a Mexican, as a Latin American, as a man of the Caribbean basin, of the Gulf of Mexico, of the Mediterranean, all the things I am are there. So I never had to consult, I just had to imagine my history and kill a few characters, because of psychological reasons, create or resuscitate others, that's it. But, basically, as a writer and as a man of political preoccupations at the same time, I've always been very impressed by the writings of Vico, in the eighteenth century. Because Vico's probably the first philosopher who says *we* create history. Men and women, we create history, it is *our* creation, it is not the creation of God. But this throws a certain burden on us. Since we made history, we have to imagine history. We have to imagine the past. Nobody lived in the past, nobody present lived in the past. So we have to imagine the past. And I've always had that as a sort of credo. And for *Terra Nostra*, of course, that is essential, to imagine the past.

JW: And then there is the notion of history as of people, rather than history of leaders.

CF: But here of course there is an element, in *Terra Nostra*, which one could call madness in high places. Something Americans know a great deal about in recent times. Because in societies that have always been pyramidal and authoritarian, as the Hispanic societies—Queen Joan of Spain, Philip II—they count a lot in our lives. When Franco died, Juan Goytisolo wrote a very beautiful piece called, "In Memoriam Francisco Franco." Of course he was in opposition to Franco all his life, but he said, "Why have you died on me? What can I do without you? I was born when you came to power, you told me what I could read, what movies I could see, what I should be taught in school, how I should make love, how I should pray to God, you taught me everything. Suddenly I'm an orphan without you. Here I am at forty, an orphan because you have left us."

JW: What brought about your latest novel, *Distant Relations*? What was the seed of that?

CF: So many things. It's difficult to pinpoint one origin. Because, of course, by now I have managed to understand more or less what I am writing and how it all fits in. So this is part, really, of *one* novel I am writing, a novel I have imagined with twenty titles—most of which are written, by the way—and twelve different sections. And one of these sections is three novels that deal with another reality, with a parallel contiguous reality, and they are *Aura, Cumpleaños*, which is a novel that has never been translated, and *Distant Relations*. And it has to do with *Terra Nostra* also.

But it has to do with writing, above all, it has to do with fiction. Although on the surface you would say, "Okay, it's a novel about these contacts that have taken place throughout history between France and Spanish America." There's a lot of stuff about this, about this quantity of poets and politicians and musicians of Latin American origin that have had a prominent role in French life. Lafargue, who was the son-in-law of Karl Marx, and the poets Heredia and Lautréamont and Supervielle and Laforgue, and the musician Reynaldo Hahn, who was so close to Proust, came from Caracas, etcetera. At one level, it is that, but then it is about a family called the Heredias, who have a homonymic counterpart in France, a French Heredia family, and a person who is narrating the story, a French count, Branly, who through the contact of the two Heredias discovers in a way the past he himself had forgotten, as the past of the Heredias is recovered basically through the encounters of two children, whom we are at difficulty to define or to understand the nature of their relationships. Finally, there is a delving into the family tree of the Heredias, but one discovers as one reads that genealogy is very much like fiction. You cannot know all the story. I think the clue to *Distant Relations* is the final phrase, which says, "No one remembers the whole story." No one knows the whole story of the Heredia family and therefore no one can tell the whole story. But this can be said of all fiction. It is a fiction to say that fiction can end, that it has a beginning and an end. Because there is a reader. If you are an active reader, you will not let the author finish the story, you want to finish it yourself.

JW: About halfway through the book, French Heredia says, "The new world was the last opportunity for a European universalism: it was also its tomb. It was never possible to be universal after the century of the discoveries and conquests. The new world turned out to be too wide, on a different scale." What does that mean for you?

CF: It means that America was invented by Europe, that America is an invention of the European mind. As the Mexican historian Edmundo Gorman has said, America was discovered because it was designed, and it was designed because it was needed by Europe. Europe wanted a place to regenerate history, to regenerate man. It wanted to find the golden age and the good savage. It came over and it burned the golden age, razed it to the ground, and it enslaved the noble savage. So that the utopia on which the New World is premised was promptly corrupted by the epic of the colonization and the universality of the utopia broke up into the particular histories, the balkanization of the different epics that took place.

The dream was killed, yet the dream remains alive. Latin America wants to be utopia, wants to be utopia desperately. And so does the United States. Therefore, we cannot have tragedies, which I think is a tragedy. That Latin America cannot give anything to the very great need of restoring tragic values in this terrible world of ours in which instead of tragedy we have crimes. Because we have not been capable of understanding the conflict between good and good. We have only the Manichean vision of good and bad, of good guys and bad guys, white hats and black hats, this sort of very Ronald Reagan vision of the world. But the only tragedian, I think, of the New World is Faulkner. There's no other writer who really understands the nature of the tragic and he extracts it from the South, from the defeat of the South, and tells it in baroque terms. Which is something we should have done in Latin America. But we can only tell our great mock epics, our very funny mock epics, like *A Hundred Years of Solitude*, which resembles *Don Quixote* so much, in that it is not a tragedy, it is a grandiose hyperbolic mock epic of sorts.

JW: What do you think accounts for the urge to want to embrace everything, among many Latin American writers, which doesn't particularly exist in North American writers?

CF: Well, I'm thinking of Thomas Pynchon, who raises it a great deal. And John Barth, in many of his works. You do have that sort of writer also.

JW: But it doesn't seem to be as prevailing. For instance, in your book-length essay on the new Latin American novel, *La nueva novela hispanoamericana*, you talk about how the New World was too wide. But that has many different results between Latin America and North America, which is also a very wide country, if not as wild in a sense.

CF: It was big and vast, but it was empty. There was hardly anything in the North American continent. There were many obstacles in Mexico and Latin America, the first of them were civilizations that had to be destroyed. Of course, the North Americans destroyed civilizations also, they killed Indians. But the colonization of the United States doesn't have an epic like the *Chronicle of the Conquest of New Spain* by Bernal Díaz, which is really the foundation of our literary life, of our novel. It's an epic, as of the world it has discovered. Read the chapters when he enters Tenochtitlán, it's fantastic, it's like entering a story in the Arabian nights. And then he is forced to destroy this, his dream has to become a nightmare, and yet he wants to love what he has destroyed. And then he has to remember what he has destroyed fifty years after the events, when he writes the book, which is like Proust, *A la recherche du temps perdu*. So you have all these very complicated cultural facts which were not present in the colonization of what was to become the United States. It's a very different cultural program and cultural perspective when you have killed a civilization.

JW: How much, when we speak of this, do you think we can talk about Latin America and how much does it apply specifically to Mexico?

CF: I'm talking about Mexico mostly. Of course in Peru, maybe, in the Quechua empire. And the Aztec empire. It certainly doesn't apply to Argentina or Chile, although the Araucanos gave a lot of resistance in Chile, but in Argentina the tribes were decimated and finally really killed by the republican presidents of the nineteenth century, very similar to what happened in the United States. So the sense of a cultural genocide is much stronger in Mexico and in Peru, but it's also very strong in the Caribbean because really there the population disappeared completely, completely. Not a single Caribe Indian was left.

JW: Your books talk a lot about a sense of identity. What do you sense as a kind of identity that comes out of the North American experience, which is very different and in a way is more confused because it has so many more elements?

CF: Well, I see a lot more homogeneity in the United States than I do in any Latin American country.

JW: Yes, but it's not a homogeneity of the peoples in it. It's a homogeneity of the dominant class.

CF: Of the dominant class, what it offers, what it gives as entertainment, what it gives as styles of living, architecture, eating. That is tremendously homogeneous and terrible. It destroys variety a great deal.

JW: And it's only been within the last twenty years that people are paying more attention to the cultural heritage as well as the cultural contribution in present tense.

CF: The great effort is of course to absorb people into the mainstream, to absorb blacks into the mainstream. I think the great challenge is going to come from the Hispanics, because they're much less assimilable than anybody else, for the simple reason that they have their cultures right over the border or in an island fifty miles away or whatever. They do not give up their culture so easily or their language. So it's very different when you have come from Sweden or Poland or Italy, or even from Africa, to assimilate into the mainstream. It's much more difficult for the Hispanics.

JW: How much, in Mexico, has there been a reconciling of the Indian cultures and the Spanish?

CF: Well, Mexico is probably the only country in Latin America that has made heroes of the defeated and not of the conquerors. In Lima you have the statue of Pizarro in the central square. In Mexico you have the statue of Cuauhtémoc, and there is no statue of Cortés, which is a mistake I think. Because we are the descendants of Cortés also and of Spain and of its culture. But, Mexico has always made the decision to sing the eulogy of the defeated, of the Indians. Is this only rhetoric? Well, if it's rhetoric, we're all educated in that rhetoric. Mexicans are educated in the rhetoric of respect for the fallen Indian civilizations and respect for the Revolution. So, this is the only real form of checks and balances we have in our country, that generation after generation of Mexicans are educated in liberal ideas. And they go into society and they are formed by these ideas. So, the problem there is not that we have not recognized the heritage, we have done so. You go to the anthropology museum in Mexico City, and you see that it is mostly children who go there. You see children and students. It means that generation after generation of Mexicans are being educated in the respect and understanding of the old civilizations. Now, the Indians that exist in Mexico today are part of another social and economic structure. There are about four million Indians and they, many of them, like to live in their communities and protect their values and their sense of the sacred and things that have little to do with the modern world. Then there is a double problem, there is a problem of respect to these values and the integrity of these communities, which is sometimes achieved, sometimes it is not. They are exploited, they are corrupted, and that is where a lot of work has to be done.

JW: How much of the snobbish pride for the pure-blood Spanish ancestry is there in Mexico?

CF: Very little, because there are so few pure whites in Mexico. Very, very few pure whites. If it's three, four percent of the population . . . We're all mestizos. I'll tell you, I have forebears that are Spanish, Moorish, Jewish, German, and Yaqui Indian. And I'm a typical Mexican in that sense, I have a total mixture of ancestry. There are very few people who came to be pure Caucasian. You have only to look at us: where are they? I don't think it's a racist country. It's a country that has many social and economic injustices, but racism is not among the injustices of Mexico, I think. Besides, whom would you discriminate against?

JW: And that's part of the central difference between Mexico and the United States, in that in Mexico the Spanish not only conquered the Indians but they bred with them.

CF: The great difference, of course, is that the United States, in spite of the melting pot, has tended to nurture, as we say, a homogeneous culture. The ruling classes in the United States tend to believe that it is in uniformization, and then atomization within the uniformization, that you have power. In Mexico we're very conscious that we coexist with many cultures and many times. It's a country of many historical times, of many different cultures coexisting. This is the nature of the country, and it is a value. I think it is a great value and it has to be protected. And Mexico is a country that has been very isolated. First, because of its geography. It's a country of deserts and mountains, chasms, canyons. Very difficult, the communication in Mexico. When Charles V asked Cortés to describe the country to him, Cortés picked up a very stiff piece of parchment from the table of the emperor and crushed it like this and put it on the table and said, "That's Mexico, that's the country I've conquered."

And I imagine a very moving thing that happened to me, visiting a part of Jalisco, the country of the Huichol Indians, with the president, Echeverría, at that time. And a strip was made in one of the Huichol towns for us to land. The plane landed there, and the Indian chiefs were there in their attire, very beautiful, and said hello to the president. This little village was situated next to a gorge, an enormous canyon, the canyon of the Santiago River which is as deep as the canyon of the Colorado River in the United States. The president said, "What can I do for you?" etcetera, and the Indian chief said, "Something very simple, look over the canyon at those people waving at us from the other side. They are our brothers but we have never been able to touch hands with them. Never, never, never, for thousands of years. So would you take us in your great white bird to the other side of the canyon so we can finally embrace and touch hands?" Well, this is a great image of the isolation of Mexico.

You know, the Mexican Revolution had one great success, its cultural success, especially in the sense that it destroyed that isolation to a great degree. The sense of all these great cavalry charges, of Villa from the north, Zapata from the south, means that Mexicans were moving for the first time and meeting each other and learning to cry together and sing together and what their names were and what they talk about, etcetera. So there is a breakdown of this lack of communication. But not only in an internal sense, also in the international sense. Traditionally, Mexico has been like a cat who was burned with hot water: too many invasions, all contacts with foreigners have been terrible, we lost half our territory to the United States, we were invaded by Napoleon III, we were invaded by Pershing, the Marines took Vera Cruz, don't have anything to do with foreign countries, we got into trouble. In the last decade, during the governments of Echeverría and López Portillo—and oil had to do with this but also a cultural image of ourselves—we have come out much more into the world. In contact with other Third World nations, in contact with countries that offer us an opportunity to diversify support—political, economical, cultural—as is the case today with the Mitterrand government in France, there's a very close relationship between the two governments.

JW: Mexico also serves as a sort of crossroads between the rest of Latin America and the United States.

CF: Well, yes, the United States has the great, great advantage, the great boon, of having friends on its borders, Mexico and Canada, and not satellites. And friends are not yes-men. People who go around saying yes are false friends, they prove to be false; they're good for our ego, for a couple of days probably, but no more. So, Mexico, a country that has a long experience in the Central American–Caribbean area, tells the truth to the United States. Sometimes a harsh truth, a truth the Americans don't like but we do tell it. Because they might avoid making some of the mistakes they have made traditionally, which cost everybody a lot of suffering.

JW: How have you, as a writer and intellectual, managed to reconcile your literary interests and political concerns? How do you find to best express and act upon your political beliefs?

CF: Let me say several things about this. First, my writing is not political in the sense that it's pamphletary writing or anything of the sort. It's not even popular writing. It's rather elite writing, it takes a lot to get into my books and to win readers for my books. I like to win readers, not to have ready-made readers, I don't care for that. I prefer to have more readers by the year 2000 than to have fewer readers by the year 2000 than I have today. And that is in a sense of the integrity of the work, I think, it has something to do with that. But I do think that there is a political element in literature always, because we are political beings, because we live in a society. Now, the thing is not to write pamphlets certainly, because that is paving the sidewalks of hell with good intentions. We've had too many novels and poems in Latin America that pretend to be political but do not serve either literature or the revolution. They're just bad writing, they don't serve anybody, it's useless. So, what I aim at, I hope to, because these are great models—my God, I'm not comparing myself to them—is what you find in Balzac or Dostoyevsky. And that is that the political reality you find in *La comédie humaine* or in *The Possessed* is in constant tension with what Balzac would call the search for the absolute or the metaphysical urge in Dostoyevsky. And this extraordinary tension between what is most passing and brittle, which is the political reality, and something that should be lasting and permanent creates the marvelous tension of these novels. In that sense I would like to write political novels, like *The Possessed* or like *Lost Illusions*. But who knows?

Anyway, writing's a rather solitary activity, an extremely solitary activity, and I am a gregarious man. I am not a solitary man and I suffer greatly from spending eight or nine or ten hours a day sitting alone, hunched, drawing a hump, and scribbling little fly's feet on white paper. This can drive you nuts, absolutely. It's a form of torture and it is against nature. If there's anything against nature, it is writing. So, my political preoccupation—which is authentic—is also a way of getting together with people, of establishing contact with people. But I try to do it mostly as a citizen than as a writer. Or as a writer who writes journalism. Because I love journalism, I love writing in papers, and I love friendship and contact and conversations with journalists. So it is at that level of journalism and teaching and lecturing that I try to have a certain political bearing on things.

JW: But as far as your political concerns, does that seem to be a main thread in the Latin American cultural identity?

CF: Yes, yes, yes. Because I'm very conscious . . . you know, a lot has been said about the ideological nature of Latin American writers, and I disagree with this, on the level of the greatest writers. I mean, of Pablo Neruda, or Vallejo, or Octavio Paz, Cortázar, García Márquez, Carpentier. We're not dealing with ideology. We are dealing with writers who are restoring our civilization, the facts of our civilization, who are creating our cultural identity. This is not the same as offering ideological ghosts for political consumption, it is *not* the same, it is very different. And I think, yes, we are all in the same boat of trying to reconstruct, in order to construct for the future, the house of our civilization.

JW: It's interesting to hear you say "reconstruct" with a writer like Cortázar. In his work most often it's less a sense of history than a sense of what is behind the door that you didn't bother to open.

CF: Yes, exactly. But that can be history too, what is behind the door. When you recognize yourself in the little axolotl, when the house is being taken over, you are understanding that behind the appearances of reality, of everyday reality, in the world but also in Latin America, there is another reality. Which is basically what García Márquez and Carpentier and the poets are saying also. Because that is our problem, discovering the true reality. And in trying to discover it, adding to that reality, adding something new. Not reproducing reality, but adding something to it.

JW: Which seems, again, a certain divergence between the realism of the North American writers and the heightened realism and the fantastic of the Latin American writers.

CF: Well, there is a great tradition of the supernatural in American fiction. And I, for one, have learned a great lesson from the literature of the United States. There's a very famous page where Nathaniel Hawthorne asks himself if North Americans can write books of romance and gothic fiction, since they do not have the romantic décor, they don't have the castles, the moats, the dungeons, all that goes with it. He says, "Well, but I prefer the blessed, sunlit, prosperous tranquility of my native land to all the gloomy gothic backgrounds of Europe." Well, of course, he wrote supernatural stories. And so did Edgar Allan Poe. That's a fictional gothic world, the House of Usher doesn't exist really. But Poe discovers something marvelous for all of us in the New World. He discovers that the heart of fiction, of the supernatural, is really the telltale heart. That it's not in the décor, it is in your heart and your mind. Then James brings the ghosts out at noon, they don't know they're ghosts. Their life goes by waiting for an event and the event doesn't happen, and it proves they are spectral.

So I think with these three illustrious North American antecedents, one cannot talk about a lack of the supernatural dimension in North American fiction. And then I think Faulkner has decidedly a flavor of the spectral in him. There are lots of ghosts and the fact that all his novels are novels in which you remember the past, but you remember it in the present, and the past only takes place in the present or as he said, "The present began ten thousand years ago," he says in *Intruder in the Dust.* Well, this has a lot to do with us. We're facing a lot of common problems in the New World, be it Anglo-Saxon or Iberian. But, of course, there are a lot of differences also because the social and economic conditions of the two worlds are very different.

JW: Though there seems to be more of a sense of the autobiographical in North American writers.

CF: Yes, perhaps the autobiography is more collective in Latin America in a way. But, in another way, we need very much books of memoirs, we don't have this. We don't have the personal recollection. The Donoso book (*The Boom in Spanish American Literature, a Personal History*) is very interesting in this sense, it's a wonderful book which I hope will start a trend. Or Guillermo Cabrera Infante, the Cuban writer, with his *La Habana para un infante difunto*, which is a marvelous book of his memoirs as a child in Havana. But when I think of books like *Sophie's Choice*, or *The Ghost Writer*, or even *The Executioner's Song*, I find that we are facing a mutation in North American letters, in which we are coming together a lot more than is perceptible to the naked eye. Styron is re-creating the forces of a civilization as it destroys itself, as it meets its opposites, its parallels, Poland and the South in the United States, Stingo in Brooklyn and a Catholic Polish woman at Auschwitz. The extraordinary play on history that Philip Roth offers us in *The Ghost Writer.* Or the transformation of reality and naturalism through the sheer exercise of language in Norman Mailer, in *The Executioner's Song*, where you are creating a world with language even if you know the story of Gary Gilmore. It is a different world because Mailer has written it. And besides, the language of the West appears and appears and appears in that novel and suddenly takes over the novel, and it is not the same language of the East. It is finally the language of a different civilization, of a cultural component that is different. So here we are dealing with civilizations, with cultures, with societies, which were not the great preoccupations of most psychological or realistic writers in the past, in the United States. You have a much broader canvas in the works of any of these three writers I have mentioned.

JW: Do you have a sense of North American writers being influenced by Latin American writers?

CF: Well, I hate the word "influences" but I think that we all form part of a tradition, and if you mean that we recognize more and more, north and south in the Americas, that we belong to a tradition and that there are many common points in that tradition, that is right. Allen Tate once called William Faulkner, I guess with a pejorative intention, a Dixie Góngorist. Well, I don't find anything pejorative about being compared with the greatest European poet of the seventeenth century. But the fact is that without the previous poetic experience of Góngora, probably the North American and the southern writer Faulkner could not have written his novels. And without the novels of Faulkner, many of us would not have written our novels. It is in this sense that the health of literature is the openness of its tradition, the openness of its several streams. Who is not influenced, of course! Books are the products of other books, certainly.

JW: What are you working on now?

CF: I'm in the middle of a novel. I think at this stage of my life and my career, I know more or less how many novels I carry in myself. Basically, three big novels I want to write. And I hope I have time to write them. I couldn't write them before because I didn't know how to write them. I've carried them with me since I was twenty. Now I know how.

JW: There's something in *The Death of Artemio Cruz*, where he talks about how he could never see things in black and white like the North Americans. First, is that a statement representative more or less of your own attitude, and also do you think that North Americans can ever learn to see those colors and shades of gray?

CF: Yes, I think you do not understand the world in its shadings.

We were talking about the Manichean perspective, the black and white thing, a while ago. And this has a lot to do with success. Rome tended to see the world in black and white, so does the United States. And I think it's only through the experience of failure that you understand the shadings of the world. And the experience of failure is a rather universal experience, it's much more universal than success. So I think that in the measure that the United States meets failure—and it has met it in the last fifteen or twenty years, God knows it's met it—it will become really a more civilized nation. A nation more capable of these shadings, of which its intelligentsia is capable. Because this way you understand you are part of the human race. You have a better chance of saving yourself if you know you are human than if you think you are superior to the rest.

JW: In some of your books, the accumulative awareness of one's past and of a nation's past becomes an identity. Then, what about the history that isn't written or isn't remembered, but is there just the same? Does that then become part of the identity that is always discovered?

CF: This has for me a very important literary dimension. To take it by parts: when I hear your question, I think of Kafka. Imagine, of all things. I think of several things in Kafka. One of the impulses of the modern novel as conceived basically by the English writers of the eighteenth century, by Defoe and Richardson and Fielding, and certainly by Madame de LaFayette in France, is the characterization process. The process of differentiation of characters. So that they not be allegorical characters, as they were in some of the medieval writing. And this I think is taken to its very culmination by writers such as Balzac and Dickens. In Dickens it is by differentiation that you know the characters. They're so peculiarly characterized in the way they speak, they dress, they move, their names, everything, Micawber, Uriah Heep, etcetera. Flaubert makes us understand that the characters are the product of the writing, of their names, and that their actions are verbs. I was talking to Susan Sontag the other day and she says, "How difficult it became to write after Flaubert." Because you are self-conscious, because you're conscious of every adjective, of every verb, of every noun, every single thing you write. It is no longer innocent after Flaubert, and it's certainly not innocent after Proust, who I think takes psychological writing to its very culmination. There's very little you can do after that in the investigation of the self, of the individual, of his internal characterization.

And then we have a man without a face, who is the man of Kafka. I ask myself, when I read Kafka, this man has no face, K. has no face. But then, because he has no face, should I guillotine him, should I chop his head off? Or can I give another kind of face to him? And I realize that Kafka is writing stories at the same time which are about forgotten myths, myths he finds in the basements of history and of the mind, things that had been forgotten, precisely as you say, and then recreates them. And he says so, he declares, "I only want to rewrite the old German and Jewish myths and fairy tales, that's all I want to do in this life." But of course in rewriting them, he writes a new myth, a new fairy tale, through the appropriation of the forgotten, of the old memory, the forgotten memory. And in this double creation of the new character, this devastatingly solitary and faceless man who becomes a bug, Samsa, in the writing of his fable, we suddenly come upon the meaning of all the opportunities of modern fiction, I think. Kafka said a wonderful thing, "There shall be much hope, but not for us." And he's offering a sacrifice of literature and himself for the future, which I find very very moving.

And through this understanding of Kafka, I understand a lot of what we're trying to do in Latin America, which is not to create psychological characters in the Flaubert sense or differentiate characters in the Dickens sense, but to discover something new which I couldn't name for you. Which perhaps we could call figures. I support myself a great deal on archetypes, especially the great archetypes of Spain: Don Juan, and La Celestina, and Don Quixote. But these are archetypes and I'm interested in figures. I'm interested in three young men thrown on a beach with no identification and no memory. So as to surprise them in the moment in which their character is totally unconstituted and see where we can go from there and how we can construct a new character, a new personality, a new identity, through a more intimate relationship with the facts of our civilization, of our culture.

JW: But is there, in the end, with Kafka or elsewhere, anything that can differentiate the resonances of a story that is fable-like or myth-like as opposed to one that is a new version?

CF: Of course. The old myth disappears in a way. What you get is a story called "The Judgment," or "The Metamorphosis," or "In the Penal Colony." And the original myth is lost. Sometimes in his little, little fables and versions of Prometheus and of Ulysses, he lets you take a look at the way he goes about it. "Did Ulysses hear the sirens or not? Did he plug his ears or did they know that he would have his ears plugged, because he is wily, and therefore that time they didn't sing?" And what happened to Prometheus? And finally how bored and how tired we are of Prometheus, and the eagle, and the liver, everybody's tired of the tragedy. These things he lets you perceive, but when he goes into his major works you don't perceive them, you are right.

JW: Are there particular writers you like to read?

CF: Well, I've already mentioned the novelists of the present, I think that fills in the picture quite well. But, in the past, I'm a great reader of Cervantes. That is one book I read every year, I can't live without that book. There's a Guatemalan author who lives in Mexico, Tito Monterroso, who has a volume of *Don Quixote* open in every room in his house, at a different page. And he goes from room to room reading this, he always has *Don Quixote* open. I would like to imitate him. That's one book I can't live without.

Jean-Claude Carrière

*Jean-Claude Carrière is probably best known as the screenwriter for
nearly all of Luis Buñuel's films since* Diary of a Chambermaid
(1964), including Belle de Jour *(1967),* The Milky Way *(1968),*
The Discreet Charm of the Bourgeoisie *(1972),* The Phantom of
Liberty *(1974), and* That Obscure Object of Desire *(1977). That
work alone would make him unique, but Carrière has also written for
a host of other internationally prominent directors: Louis Malle (*Viva
María, Le Voleur*), Jacques Deray (*Borsalino*), Milos Forman (*Taking Off, Valmont*), Volker Schlöndorff (*The Tin Drum, Swann in
Love*), Andrzej Wajda (*Danton, The Possessed*), Carlos Saura
(*Antonieta*), and Philip Kaufman (*The Unbearable Lightness of
Being*). He has had occasional small acting roles as well, especially in
the Buñuel films. In addition, since the early 1970s he has worked
regularly with theater director Peter Brook, a collaboration as important for him as that with Buñuel. Working on every major Brook production, he has contributed new French adaptations of Shakespeare,
Chekhov, a version of Attar's epic,* Conference of the Birds, *and also
of the monumental Indian epic,* The Mahabharata.

*In effect, Carrière is a translator of sorts. With a daring unmatched
by others in his field, he has taken up complex visions and difficult works*

of literature, rendering them in theatrical terms that are notable for their resourcefulness. Above all, he is an ardent practitioner of the imagination. "The imagination must undergo an incessant training," he insists. "You can't let it sleep. In no case should it fall into intellectual comforts." The following interview took place at his Paris home, in early May 1983, before the English language publication of Buñuel's memoirs, My Last Sigh, *in which Carrière's role was essential (Buñuel died in late July of that year).*

JW: What was your part in Luis Buñuel's book of memoirs, *My Last Sigh*?

JCC: Through eighteen years of collaboration I'd been taking notes on his life, classing them by chapter. There's a bit of everything. After *That Obscure Object of Desire* we worked on another screenplay, *Une cérémonie somptueuse*, which is part of a phrase by André Breton about eroticism. We didn't finish this script, Luis fell ill and he stopped making films. That was in '79, and he began to get very bored. He was declaring that he was going to die, but that was four years ago, and he's still alive. So, I took out these notes and said, "Let's write a book, on you—your life, your ideas, your sensations." Well, his first response was one of strong refusal. He said, "No! Oh horrors! An autobiography, every chambermaid writes her memoirs, everyone writes now. Horrors, no, no, no!"

So, I wrote by myself—in the first person, and for me it was a very interesting exercise, to write while playing Buñuel—one of the chapters, the one about bars, alcohol, and tobacco. The idea was to do a book like a screenplay, taking his life as the subject. Because I told myself that could be really new, as a book of memoirs that would be rather unconventional about one's life, with interpolations like those we did in the films we made together. That is, we stop the life story and we tell a tale about something. About what's important: God, death, women, wine, dreams, what's really important for him.

He read this chapter and he was very surprised, he said to me, "But I feel like I wrote it!" Because I'd done some research. Of course I know his vocabulary, his way of speaking. I tried to identify him as if he really had written it.

JW: Yes, I wondered if you had actually done the writing.

JCC: That's one thing. Second, a few years ago a big Spanish paper from his part of the country, Aragon, had asked him to write something about his childhood, about his oldest memories. We were in the process of writing a script, *That Obscure Object of Desire*, and he said, "That annoys me, I don't write, I don't know how to write." So I said, "Luis, if you like, we'll stop the screenplay for a day or two, you tell me about your childhood," which I already knew about because he'd spoken a lot about his life to me, "and I'll try to write it and you translate it into Spanish." So, we did that, and the result was published, with the title, "Medieval Memories of Lower Aragon" no less!

Well, we had these two documents, this thing which already existed and the chapter that I'd written. And these two things gave the book's tone, one which was autobiographical and the other which was like an essay on something. So then we set to work. I went to Mexico three times, for weeks at a stretch. In the morning we worked at his house, I asked him questions, I took notes, he responded, we went deeper with one question or another, in the afternoon and the evening I wrote. I'd made photocopies in a little bookstore there, the next day I brought them to him, he read them over again. It was a lot of work, he edited, corrected, and so on. And it was a very uneven task, in certain cases there were chapters that were written all by me, I almost didn't need him because I had everything in my memory.

Other chapters, like the one about the Spanish Civil War, for example, that was weeks' worth of work. Because I told myself that for the first time in my life I would try to understand something about the Spanish Civil War. No one's ever really understood anything, because all the accounts have always been from one side or another. They've always been very partial. So, with his indisputable authority in the Spanish world, where he is an immense figure, he could say what no Republican would have said, that Franco had helped to save the Jews, and that famous sentence about Franco: "I'm even ready to believe that he kept Spain out of World War II." That sentence was like a bomb in Spain: that Buñuel who was of course anti-Franco during the war could say that today, that contributed to the national reconciliation in Spain and to the success of the Socialists in the election, really. Considerably. That is, he was like the father long in exile who remains nevertheless a force in Spain. You know, Buñuel is clearly a greater man than Picasso. You have to go all the way back to Goya to find a figure of that importance. That is, Picasso is a great painter, but he's only a painter. You can write books, make films, without ever thinking of Picasso. But whatever you do in the Spanish world, whether you're a novelist, painter, filmmaker of course, man of theater, at a given moment you're going to meet up with Buñuel. He's touched everything. He's found some of the key images of the century in the Spanish world. In the United States, in France, in Italy, he's considered a great filmmaker and, since his book, a great man. But with something marginal about it. They always say he's a surrealist, he's not really a classic, he's not really a master of thought. In Spain, he's not a surrealist at all, not at all. He *is* Spanish, period. What we find in him as bizarre, cruel, peculiar, in Spain is only natural.

JW: When did you meet Buñuel?

JCC: Exactly twenty years ago. At the time he was looking for a young French screenwriter who knew the French countryside well. He'd worked a lot with the older French screenwriters. People were talking about the Nouvelle Vague then, he really wanted a young person. I'd done two films, that's all, I was a beginner. I had gone to Cannes, and he was seeing various screenwriters there, I had lunch with him, we got along well, and three weeks later he chose me and I left for Madrid. Since then I haven't stopped.

JW: How did you two know you could work together?

JCC: It's hard to say. Purely by instinct, I think. We discovered a lot of affinities. We're both Mediterranean, that's important, both Latin. I was born not far from the Spanish border. I had a Catholic education. I'm a wine producer. The first question he asked me when we sat down together at the table—and it's not a light or frivolous question, the way he looked at me I sensed that it was a deep and important question—was, "Do you drink wine?" Just like that. That is, a negative response would have definitely disqualified me. So I said, "Not only do I drink wine, but I produce it. I'm from a family of wine growers." It's true. Well, right away something quite rare had happened, to come upon a screenwriter who was a wine producer. And wine has been with us throughout these twenty years. We've tasted wine, talked about it, sung it. We've made some excellent meals. We've had more than two thousand meals together, through all that time. I figured that out the other day and I was very surprised. Many of them were here with friends who brought exceptional wines. I went to Mexico last week, I brought him wine and cheese. So that first question was followed by a thousand attempts at a response.

Then there was the fact that I'd written books, of course. But it was an ideal affinity. I'd liked him a lot for a long time, because at the age of eighteen I was already in charge of a film club at the university, and the films we knew then were his surrealist ones, the first three. After that, I was very stirred up at the age of twenty by *Los Olvidados* and *El.* And when I met him I'd just seen *Viridiana* and *The Exterminating Angel.* It was very important for us. *Los Olvidados* was a real shock. Imagine today, for a young man of twenty in 1951, in the French cinema which was a bourgeois, artificial cinema, made in the studios—Jean Marais, Michèle Morgan—to receive *Los Olvidados.* It was an enormous shock, worth changing one's life about. Certainly it's one of the films that made me decide to write. The dream of the meat, in *Los Olvidados*, it's an image from the Third World, the twentieth century. It's a key image, a key to open that universe.

JW: When did you start to write?

JCC: I was writing novels from the age of twenty-three or twenty-four. I'd even met Jacques Tati in 1956, I was twenty-five.

JW: It was through Tati that you started in film?

JCC: I began by writing novels from two of his films, *Mr. Hulot's*

Holiday and *My Uncle*. So, I was doing the opposite of what I was going to do so often later. I'd already written a novel, and then Tati had a contract with Robert Laffont, his publisher, who had a sort of little contest among his young writers and my chapter based on the film was chosen. Through that I met Pierre Etaix, with whom I wrote several projects. Then the Algerian War came along and I was called up, which lasted nearly three years, so it completely interrupted any sort of work. And on my return, I was thirty, I started right away to work on some film shorts with Etaix, in '61, and one of those won the Academy Award for Best Short Film. It was called *Happy Anniversary*, about a man who is bringing some flowers to his wife for their anniversary but gets caught in traffic jams. We made a feature film after that. And then I met Buñuel.

JW: What was the most difficult for you to learn about writing film scripts?

JCC: Well, it's always very difficult. If you want the work to have a chance of being interesting, escaping routine is an absolute necessity, to never say I know how to write a script. Each script must be the first one. Of course, experience does count for something, but no film that I've written resembles any other, I think. Each time I've tried, I still try, to find new ways, and I've worked with rather different people. *Danton*, with Wajda, for example, was quite serious, I'd never done a script with so much dialogue. Nor with a young actor (Gérard Depardieu) so lyrical, so determined, so tense. So, although previous experience does not count, secretly it does count all the same. I mean, if you rely consciously on your experience, to say, "I did it like that, so I know how to do it," you run the biggest chance of going wrong. I've experienced that often enough. This sort of uncertainty is only acquired after a long series of setbacks, of choices made. It takes a lot of time, a lot of patience, and a lot of humility to arrive at this uncertainty.

JW: Even so, you've had a lot of success with your scripts.

JCC: Yes, about one out of two. And in theater, about the same. That is, meeting Peter Brook was as decisive for me as meeting Luis. What's more, our work has helped me a lot in screenwriting.

JW: You're also a designer as well.

JCC: Amateur. I supported myself as a designer when I was a student and I continue to draw now and then. But I don't really have the time for it. Drawing is like the piano, you have to do it three hours a day. If not, you don't develop. Writing too is like that.

JW: Has drawing helped you with writing, in seeing how things might go?

JCC: Enormously. Almost every scenario I've worked on, I illustrated as well. For some it avoids long explanations with the producers. For *Belle de Jour*, for example, I did at least twenty-five or thirty drawings, and the producers sold the film with that. And with Buñuel, he's always asked me to illustrate the screenplays. There are some that have been very elaborately illustrated. *The Tin Drum*, for example, with Schlöndorff, was very thoroughly illustrated, and the film is entirely faithful to that. In the design, the décor, the characters, the costumes. And besides, something very curious is proved. For example, we're working on a scene, without saying anything about the décor. And then I decide we should talk about the image we have of the scene. I cover up the page and I ask Luis, say, "Which side is the door on?" He'll say, "The left." "Which side is the lamp?" "The right." Everything always coincides. It's all so extraordinary, we find that we've been working with the same mental image of the scene.

JW: In the way you write the script, has there been a big difference for you between adaptations from books and original stories?

JCC: Yes, it takes longer when it's an adaptation. Because it always takes a good while, several weeks, before you're completely free of a book. You're always somewhat of a prisoner to the book, from the point of view of the screenplay. Since if an author put something in that we want to omit, still he did have his reasons. So perhaps we should think about it, examine it, as much as we can, and that takes a lot of time.

Out of the six films I did with Luis, three were from books, though *That Obscure Object of Desire* was very far from the book.

JW: What do the new images come out of?

JCC: That's a mystery. It's an instinctive springing forth of images. That is, it's not thought out. And each of us has the right of veto with the other. So, on the one hand these images arise from the free play of the material, and on the other hand they don't really come from us. And if you ask me to explain, I can't. I don't know why these images, which apparently spring from the disorder of the spirit, become ordered when they enter into play, by which I mean the drama. You have to play a scene, and then you can write it. The simple fact of playing introduces an order, the dramatic action will inevitably follow from that moment. It begins with saying, "Here's a place with this or that image," I am introducing an order among the images that will arise. And the whole work of the scenario is born from this dialectic between the liberty, the phantom of liberty as Luis says in his film, and the order that proceeds from it, the dramatic order, which is implacable and won't put up with just anything. Or it wouldn't make any sense. That is the great mystery we've been confronted with daily for some time now, without ever theorizing about the scenario. I'm not a theoretician. What I'm telling you now I never talk about.

JW: You've said that psychology doesn't interest you when you do characterization.

JCC: I'll tell you why. Because the psychology on which traditional bourgeois theater relies supposes that we know the character before the story has ever begun. So, farewell to the free play of the imagination. If you're a character that I have defined psychologically, in a completely arbitrary way, at that moment my imagination is paralyzed. I wouldn't be able to make you do anything that's going to go against that image. So, for the initial stage of work especially, psychology is enemy number one. Because it paralyzes and limits. And as Luis is fundamentally surrealist, it's the irrational and not the rational that leads the way.

JW: Though in other work you've had to approach a bit closer to the psychological, as in Carlos Saura's *Antonieta*.

JCC: When I speak about psychology like that, I'm talking about with Buñuel. For other subjects without doubt it's indispensable to follow a certain line of a character. The problem with *Antonieta* is entirely different, because she's a true character who really lived, so I can't invent.

JW: How did you choose the subjects in the Buñuel films that were not adaptations? What determined the action?

JCC: Well, we never really chose a subject; in reality everything is the subject. Though *The Milky Way*, no, we did have a subject, we had a word: heresy. So, I had to find out all I could about the heresies, and then we created a subject, but the subject remains indefinite.

As for *The Discreet Charm of the Bourgeoisie*, we never really chose a subject. That is, we speak about everything and nothing. About the same things as in *The Milky Way* really, but in another way. There the process of writing was completely different. I'd said to him, "There are things in your films that you repeat." He said, "Yes, I like that. I'd like to do a story that repeats." So, we chose that as a theme of discussion, you know that's very vague. We started with a story about a crime where the criminal escapes, the crime is reconstructed. We worked two weeks and didn't like it. And then completely by chance, we came upon this idea one day of a meal, about these friends who want to get together for dinner. We worked on it for two years on and off. Because it was very difficult to work without a subject, the danger was either we were making a completely gratuitous, surrealistic film, that would be "unlikely," or else on the other hand a film that would be just flatly realistic. So, between the two, we chose the path of what is probable, but just at the limit of the probable, at the borderline. That's what interested me, but that is very difficult to maintain.

JW: How did *The Phantom of Liberty* come about? How did you proceed?

JCC: When we got together after *The Discreet Charm of the Bourgeoisie*, which was a big success at Cannes, we wondered,

"Now what are we going to do?" We couldn't just make another popular film. We started talking about liberty, and the title came from the end of *The Discreet Charm*, about the phantom of liberty. There was a principle to the tale. We asked ourselves why, when one tells a story, one tells this and not that? By what arbitrariness does one decide to tell what story? And we decided we really don't know. Because it's that, the phantom of liberty, deciding what a film passes through. So we imagine a couple who's waiting for a very important telegram that's going to decide the course of their lives. Their thoughts are only on the telegram. The telegram carrier rings, they take the telegram and close the door, and we stay on the carrier and follow him, leaving the couple behind. Naturally, that's the opposite of what one expects.

JW: And each time the film follows the person who's arrived.

JCC: That's right. Whoever interrupts the action, and we follow him because *perhaps* he has a story to tell, we're going to see. That's a principle which I think has never been used elsewhere. We were just speaking about an order that you have to find in the disorder, but there it had to do with a great disorder that we were forced to follow through to the end. In my opinion it's one of Buñuel's favorites of his films. At any rate, there are three or four scenes that are among his best, such as the little girl who is lost but who is there. But it's a film that for certain people remained unpardonable, because it goes against all story conventions. He'd truly opened a surprising door. Like in his last film, in entrusting two actresses with a single role, that's yet another door. So, up to the age of seventy-seven, Luis continued to open doors. Perhaps one day someone will come along and enter them.

JW: What about the last script you were working on for him, *Une cérémonie somptueuse*?

JCC: There was a key word, terror. It told about a young woman terrorist who's sentenced to years in prison. But this prison was also the place where her dreams, her images, gathered. That is, the doors of her prison could never close on the world. But I never finished it.

JW: How did you get involved with the Proust film, *Swann In Love*, that's being made now?

JCC: Peter Brook and Nicole Stéphane, who holds the rights, asked if I'd be interested in working on a film of Proust. I said yes, on the condition that we limit ourselves to the part without Proust. That is, where the narrator isn't there, *Un amour de Swann (Swann in Love)*, because we felt it would be extremely difficult to represent Marcel, and the whole work, adequately in a film. So, starting from there, we worked long and hard, deciding that to do *Un amour de Swann* we should extend the story of Swann until his death, and we've included many things from the ensemble of the work. We did a very careful study of the whole work and certain traits from it are found in the script. Because Proust, contrary to what people think, is a great realist, he tells you what everything looks like. But the film remains first of all a résumé of twenty-four hours in Swann's life. So, it's about a man, Swann, who is very worldly and cultivated, and who is struck by love—by chance, like a cancer—and eventually dies from it.

JW: Did you write the script alone?

JCC: With Peter Brook. And he was going to direct it originally, but then he didn't have the time and Volker jumped in at that point.

JW: Did the scripts from previous attempts at the project help at all, such as Pinter's script?

JCC: I read three or four adaptations. Visconti's is the one I prefer, but it was totally different. Like Pinter's, it dealt with the whole work. But the part we're doing neither Pinter nor Visconti dealt with, because the narrator isn't there, it's before the narrator's time. Visconti's script was very exciting, it focused on the Charlus story. As for Pinter, he tried to do an impressionistic summary of Proust's work, *without* Swann. It's a rather brilliant exercise.

JW: Would you speak about your collaboration with Peter Brook and his theater at the Bouffes du Nord? What, for instance, was the nature of your adaptation of Chekhov's *The Cherry Orchard*?

JCC: With Chekhov it was a problem of language. Chekhov's language is really much like Beckett's, with very strong, dense words, very alive. It's not at all a bourgeois language of fashionable society, as in all the French and English translations. For example, a woman calls a man a "kolossus," with a "k," and in all the translations you will find, "Oh, he is a very *intelligent* man." So, I worked with a Russian translator to do a new version.

I've been working with Peter for twelve years, though we've known each other for twenty. It's very profound work, of course, very exciting, that serves as a base for us. We meet every day, it's work that deals directly with the most essential. Peter is the opposite of someone who imposes his way, he searches with me. And what's more, he only finds what he's after in the last few days. Things are really not set in place until the last minute.

JW: But what motivates the work of that searching?

JCC: There is no motive. Peter comes in with no plans. There's just him, me, and the actors. He searches. It's hard to admit—people always figure that we're starting with some objective.

JW: And so at what point do you write the texts then?

JCC: That depends. There's no clean separation between the writing and the staging. That is, he participates in the writing and I in the staging, it's like a "fade-out fade-in."

There is a very ancient text from India that gives three rules for theater: 1) It must be encouraging and amusing to the drunk; 2) It must respond to the one who asks, "How should I live?"; 3) It must respond to the one who asks, "How does the universe work?" All three at the same time. That's ambitious!

Milan Kundera

At fifty-five, Milan Kundera has matured handsomely. Yet the boyish quickness still lingers, in the penetrating light of his smile and in the way he bounds across the bright living room of his Montparnasse apartment in Paris to answer the phone. Tall, slim, gracious, he seems hardly fazed by his growing celebrity.

After the 1968 Soviet invasion of Prague, Kundera's books were banned in his native Czechoslovakia. In 1975 he and his wife came to France and since then his books have had their first publication in French translation, with a small Czech edition published in Canada. His novels have won major awards in France, Italy, and the United States, and his latest work, The Unbearable Lightness of Being, *was made into a major American film in 1988.*

Kundera thinks of the novel as a form of meditation. In his work, the story is like an object turning in the writer's hands, gathering reflections as it goes. His lucidity stokes the narratives along, at each bend revealing the human paradox. At the same time, Kundera tells a good story, and his formal innovations have enabled him to employ a wide range of modes in his novels.

The following interview took place in late November 1984.

JW: How did you begin writing your latest novel, *The Unbearable Lightness of Being*? What was the seed? How did you develop it?

MK: That's rather a long story. For example, I'd wanted to write the meeting of Tomas and Tereza around twenty-five years ago. It was even a first novel that I wrote, but completely unsuccessfully, which I set aside. But I held onto it anyway, this story that I didn't know how to write. It was a very very long gestation. I wrote other novels, but always with an idea that one day I'm going to return to this story. When I came to France, I told myself, "Now I'm going to write this novel about Tomas and Tereza," though at the time they had other names. All of a sudden I had the feeling that I wasn't strong enough or ready enough to do it. So, I put it off once more, and I began *The Book of Laughter and Forgetting*. After finishing that book I set about once again to write this novel. From the point of view of the motifs, it was already prepared.

For me, it's always a question of counterpoint. You have a story, for example that story of Tamina in *The Book of Laughter and Forgetting*, it fascinated me a lot but it was never right. Suddenly, I was searching for another motif that could create a harmony with this story. I found this harmony in the idea of joining it with a memory that was completely real, the death of my father. And at that moment, I knew that was it. Here perhaps it's the same thing, the counterpoint of this story was the one about Sabina and Franz. That was the long search, it was a wandering, really. The moment I understood that it really does form a whole novelistically, then I saw that it worked.

JW: With this notion of counterpoint, how do you manage to find a balance among the elements? How do you search for it?

MK: It's a question of sensibilities. You know, all the theories that I'm telling you, they are *a posteriori*. I never realized that that's what polyphony is, it was only after the fact when I began to reflect on what I'd done. So I said that it's a certain method, but a spontaneous one. It's not cerebral.

JW: Discussions, the play of ideas, are always present amid your stories. Even the title of your last novel could be that of a philosophy book. Does it ever worry you that you might be getting too close to the realm of ideas and lose the story?

MK: Not at all. Of course, from the point of view, I don't know, of Flaubert, to intervene in the story in this way would be impossible, in bad taste. Because it's another aesthetic, one that wanted the author to disappear completely from the objectivity of his observations. But my aesthetic is different; it's the opposite. I would like everything to be reflected upon. Even if I relate how you're drinking whiskey right now, that must be part of a reflection, but not one which is philosophical; rather, a novelistic reflection. That's different. You know, it's a mistake for us to consider thought as boring. That's not true. Novelistic thought must be the opposite, it engages the attention. We have to make thought captivating, we have to give it suspense. We mistrust thought, which is perhaps the question of the revolution of modern society, because we cease to think. That is, when someone starts to think, to reflect, then we're a bit shocked: is it possible? How? I think of the novel as a form of meditation. But I know that I'm going against the current of the times.

JW: Reading the passages where there are discussions of ideas, one might expect that it'll soon get boring, but it doesn't.

MK: No, because it's always connected to the story, to the situation; it's always connected to the characters. I start with Nietzsche in *The Unbearable Lightness of Being*, but one doesn't realize that this beginning with Nietzsche is an introduction to Tomas, to the problematic existence of Tomas. So, it's a novelistic meditation, connected to a character. Second, it's a provocation. What I say about the eternal return, it's an intellectual provocation.

JW: If you see yourself as going against the current, what is the current then?

MK: Journalistic thought. I'm not thinking only of being counter-current to the evolution of the novel. On the contrary, it's to the spirit of the times. We leave less and less room for thought, for really thinking. And we replace thought with the nonthinking of the mass media. We're encumbered by information, but we no longer try to ask questions. To stop, to reflect, is something which modern society gives no place to anymore.

JW: Considering your concern with the rational, were you ever interested in surrealism, say, where the irrational is so important?

MK: I'm not going to contrast the irrational with the rational. That opposition doesn't even mean much to me. Because we are rational in order to get hold of the irrational, right? We are irrational in order to awaken the imagination, and it's the imagination which is there to understand the world better. I want to cultivate both my irrational and my rational sides, so, both the lucidity of reflection and the imagination completely unbound. I would even say that it's my greatest aesthetic challenge, to create in the novel a space where the coldest rationality could cohabit with the freest imagination. Which isn't easy. But I believe the novel gives you the opportunity to connect such things.

JW: One of the themes that runs through all your books is the separation of the body and the soul, which is a rather fundamental concern for religion too. Has the religious or even the mystical aspect of that question been of much interest to you?

MK: No. For me the question of the body and the soul is the fundamental question in the metaphysics of love.

JW: I'm fascinated by the sinuous play of the plots in your novels. You seem to delight in their possible twists, pushing them to the limit.

MK: The modern novel has had a sort of complex, as if the novel were ashamed of being a novel. A novelist often says, "But what I've written, it's not really a novel." The *nouveau roman* novelists in France said, "We're writing an antinovel." This shame about the novel is something I do not share. On the contrary, I think that the importance of the novel in European culture has been enormous; European man is unthinkable without the novel, he was created by it. For centuries it was the first thing one read. The love of adventure, which is so European, adventure understood as a value. If you say, "I lived my life without adventure," then it's a failure, right?

Well, it's the novel that impressed upon us this love of adventure.

And the understanding of others, the element of characters, which is another source of shame for the novel. The French no longer say "the novel," they say *l'écriture* (writing): "In my writing, the character is already a thing of the past." Trying to construct someone who isn't you is an extraordinary way out of your egocentricity, to understand someone who thinks differently from you. And not only to understand him, but in a certain sense to defend him against yourself even. And that's very European.

The novel has not exploited all its potential. There are lots of things the novel could have done and didn't, because after all every story is in a certain sense a failure. Every life is a failure: at the end of your life you might say, "I should have screwed more women, I should have written better things," etcetera. And at the end of the life in the novel you can have the same regrets. That is, I do not have that sense of shame either about characters or about adventure. Why be afraid to relate an adventure? That all depends on how you tell it. You can tell it in a way that's so conventional that it doesn't mean anything. But being against the conventional novel, I would never speak against the *traditional* novel. For example, here in France this break in the discourse among people who speak on one side for the modern novel and on the other side for the traditional novel: I find that to be extremely stupid. Because, first, what *is* the traditional novel, where does it end? It's an amalgam; there are various phases of the novel. And then, each phase of the so-called traditional novel was always the anticonventional novel of its time. Flaubert is a traditional writer? How can that be? His work was the biggest revolution in the history of the novel. But one is against the conventional novel, the novel that discovers nothing new.

JW: You first read Kafka when you were fourteen. What did his work mean for you in your development as a writer?

MK: The great experience of reading Kafka changed my way of seeing literature. Above all, it was a lesson in liberty, suddenly you've understood that the novel isn't obligated to imitate reality. It's something else, a world that's autonomous. How you construct this autonomous world, that's already your business. But Kafka says you mustn't naïvely imitate reality, you are completely free, you can invent whatever you want, now it depends on you. That is, there are thousands of possibilities; Kafka's lesson is an aesthetic one rather than philosophical. And then, he also tells us that the novel is a question of the imagination. Because in the nineteenth century the aspect of observation in the novel had evolved greatly, with Flaubert. It was brilliant, the novel knew how to see, to observe. And Kafka held on to that faculty of observation, but he says at the same time that you also have to engage an imagination, you have to know how to free it. I'd say that the density of imagination—if we could measure the quantity of imagination within a certain space—well, the density of imagination for Kafka is a hundred times greater than for any other writer. And that is Kafka's invitation: free yourself.

JW: In *The Joke*, Ludvik says at one point, "Youth is a terrible thing." Was your youth so terrible?

MK: Certain experiences are personal ones. When I was twenty, it was the arrival of Stalinism, of the terror of Stalinism. And that terror was supported above all by the young people. Because the young saw in it a revolt, against the old world and so on. Little by little, that led me to ask myself not only the question of terror but also the question of youth. So, I never had that adoring attitude that people have toward the young. Even when I was young myself.

JW: The character Ludvik goes on to reflect on "the terrible restlessness of waiting to grow up." You started your first novel when you were in your early thirties. Why did you not start writing earlier?

MK: I can't even imagine writing a novel before the age of thirty. I don't think it works. Because not only is there not enough experience, but especially there isn't the experience of time. I felt myself to be very young then, and I was, thirty-three, that's young. So, the critique of youth has always interested me a lot. And it's not bitterness either, rather it's a self-critique. Because if I recall myself as a young man, I am not at all filled with enthusiasm or lyrical nostalgia. I more likely tell myself, "This jerk that I was, I wouldn't like to see him." I am not comfortable with myself at twenty. I think I was an absolute jerk from every point of view, and it likely comes from there, this suspicious attitude toward that age, especially with regard to a certain lyricizing.

JW: You came from a musical family. Did you never think of a career in music?

MK: Yes, I even had a certain musical education, which I abandoned completely at the age of eighteen. But it left me with quite a large knowledge of music and a love of music too.

JW: You've often spoken of the importance of counterpoint in your writing. Has music brought other contributions to your work?

MK: Certainly. Especially the sense of form, the sense of rhythm, tempo. Repetition, variation.

JW: You also played jazz when you were young.

MK: Jazz perhaps isn't the right word. At a certain point without work, when I was very young, twenty-two or twenty-three, I earned my living playing piano with a few friends in the bistros.

JW: Did you like listening to jazz much?

MK: Yes, quite a bit. You know, it was at the time when the Iron Curtain had really fallen, after '48. That is, we didn't know contemporary jazz; what we did was our own memory of jazz, our own imitation of what we considered to be jazz. I played something like jazz, but with terrific musicians, because they were chased out of the conservatories for political reasons and so on. Perhaps we even played well. It was unclassifiable, because we played before a public that was absolutely naïve, in popular bars for people to dance. So, it wasn't a demanding public. But there was behind all that the love of jazz. Whereas popular music interested me more from the point of view of theory rather than practice, in the harmonies, the rhythm.

JW: You've written certain essays, such as your piece on Kafka, in French rather than Czech. Has that changed the way you write, working in another language?

MK: What changes is your contact with translators. Because you look at your text in the mirror of the translation. That changes something, because it is the perpetual control of their attitude toward what you're saying. So, the fact of being translated forces you toward the greatest clarity possible.

JW: Yet one of the more difficult things to translate is the rhythm itself of the prose.

MK: You know, in translation the first thing is the willingness to be faithful, and that's what's missing with the majority of translators. Because the rhythm, what is that? The rhythm is, for example, your punctuation or the repetition of a word. You start three sentences one after the next using the same word, like that you create a certain litanic melody. It suffices to be faithful and the melody is completely retained.

Nathalie Sarraute

Nathalie Sarraute was eighty-three when she first published a best-seller, Childhood *(1983). Unlike her previous books it treated auto-biographical events. In the book, memories from her Russian and French childhood emerge from a word or a gesture recalled, burn brightly for a moment, and fade. Quietly the mosaic takes shape, in her compassionate regard for the parents whose early divorce divided her love.*

Born in 1900 in Ivanovo, near Moscow, Sarraute has made a life-time of seeing inside being human. Her first book, Tropisms, *a collection of brief texts that appeared in 1939, marked a fresh direction in French literature and established her as the first of what came to be known as the* nouveau roman *group of writers. She describes tropisms as the "interior movements that precede and prepare our words and actions, at the limits of our consciousness." They happen in an instant, and apprehending them in the rush of human interactions demands painstaking attention.* Tropisms *became the key to all her subsequent work.*

Highly respected in France, Sarraute has been translated into twenty-four languages; her eight novels and other books are all avail-able in English. Since the 1960s she has been a regular traveler, in-

vited to universities around the world. Her husband, whom she met in law school, always accompanied her. She has been all over the United States, visiting every few years, and was last in New York in September 1986 for the American premiere of her play, Over Nothing at All. *In the fall of 1990 she was invited to visit the house where she was born in Ivanovo.*

For the past twenty years Sarraute has gone every morning to write at the same neighborhood café in Paris. The following interview took place on two cold January afternoons in 1987, at her home in the sixteenth arrondissement, near the Musée d'Art Moderne.

JW: In your books you have a very fine ear, for the interior voices as well as for the development of the text. Another domain of listening, of course, is music. Do you listen much to music?

NS: I like music a lot, almost too much. Sometimes so much that it gives me a sort of feeling of anguish. But I haven't listened a lot, partly because of that. It's quite curious, the effect it has on me. And precisely in the works I prefer, it's a sort of anguish that I never have from painting, which always gives me a feeling of eternity, security, peace—of immobility. I love painting a great deal. Music at times reaches something that is almost superhuman, divine. One listens to Mozart and says, "It's not possible that a human being did that."

JW: Were you ever tempted to write another sort of literature, such as the fantastic?

NS: Not at all. Because each instant of the real world is so fantastic in itself, with all that's happening inside it, that it's all I want.

JW: At the time of your first book, *Tropisms*, what was your relationship with the literary world?

NS: I didn't know anyone, not a single writer. I didn't meet Sartre till the war. After the Liberation, he wrote the preface for my first novel, *Portrait of a Man Unknown* (1947).

JW: How did you arrive at the form of those first short texts?

NS: The first one came out just as it is in the book. I felt it like that. Some of the others I worked on a lot.

JW: And why did you choose the name *Tropisms*?

NS: It was a term that was in the air, it came from the sciences, from biology, botany. I thought it fit the interior movement that I wanted to show. So when I had to come up with a title in order to show it to publishers, I took that.

JW: How did you know what they were at the time, these tropisms? How did you know when you'd found one?

NS: I didn't always know, I might discover it in my writing. I didn't try to define them, they just came out like that.

JW: The tropisms often seem to work through a poetic sensibility.

NS: I've always thought that there is no border, no separation, between poetry and prose. Michaux, is he prose or poetry? Or Francis Ponge? It's written in prose, and yet it's poetry, because it's the sensation that is carried across by means of the language.

JW: With the tropisms, did you feel that it was fiction? Did you wonder what to call it?

NS: I didn't ask myself such questions, really. I knew it seemed impossible for me to write in the traditional forms. They seemed to have no access to what we experienced. If we enclosed that in characters, personalities, a plot, we were overlooking everything that our senses were perceiving, which is what interested me. One had to take hold of the instant, by enlarging it, developing it. That's what I tried to do in *Tropisms*.

JW: Did you sense at the time that this was the direction your work would take?

NS: I felt that a path was opening before me, which excited me. As if I'd found my own terrain, upon which I could move forward, where no one had gone before me. Where I was in charge.

JW: Were you already wondering how to use that in other contexts such as a novel?

NS: Not at all. I thought only of writing short texts like that. I couldn't imagine it possible to write a long novel. And later, it was so difficult to find these texts—each time it was like starting a new book all over again—that I told myself perhaps it would be interesting to take two semblances of characters who were entirely commonplace as in Balzac, a miser and his daughter, and to show all these tropisms that develop inside of them. That's how I wrote *Portrait of a Man Unknown*.

JW: In effect, one could say that all or most tropisms we might find in people could also be found in a single person.

NS: Absolutely. I'm convinced that everyone has it all in himself, at that level. On the exterior level of action, I don't for a minute think that Hitler is like Joan of Arc. But I think that at that deep level of tropisms, Hitler or Stalin must have experienced the same tropisms as anyone else.

JW: The tropisms would seem to enter the domain of the social sciences as well.

NS: Yes. I've become more accessible, besides. It used to be entirely closed to people. For a long time people didn't get inside there, they couldn't manage to really penetrate these books.

JW: Why do you think that is?

NS: Because it's difficult. Because I plunge in directly, without giving any reference points. One doesn't know where one is, or who is who. I speak right away of the essential things, and that's very difficult. In addition, people have the habit of looking for the framework of the traditional novel—characters, plots—and they don't find any, they're lost.

JW: That brings up the question of how to read these books. You do without a plot, for example.

NS: There is a plot, if you like, but it's not the usual plot. It is the plot made up of these movements between human beings. If one takes an interest in what I do, one follows a sort of movement of dramatic actions which takes place at the level of the tropisms and of the dialogue. It's a different dramatic action from that of the traditional novel.

JW: You've said that you prefer a relatively continuous reading of your books. But all reading is a somewhat fragmentary experience. With a traditional novel, when one picks it up again to continue reading, there are the characters and the plot to situate oneself, where one left off. In your books, do you see other ways of keeping track of where one was?

NS: I don't know. I don't know how one reads it. I can't put myself in the readers' place, to know what they're looking for, what they see. I have no idea. I never think of them when I'm writing. Otherwise, I'd be writing things that suit them and please them. And for years they didn't like it, they weren't interested.

JW: Even after several books you weren't discouraged?

NS: No, not at all. I was always supported, all the same, from the start. With *Portrait of a Man Unknown*, I was supported by Sartre. At the time Sartre was the only person who was doing something about literature, he had a review. My husband as well was tremendously supportive, from the very start. He was a marvelous reader for me, he always encouraged me a great deal. That was a lot. It suffices to have one reader who realizes what you want to do. So, it was a great solitude, if you like, but deep down inside it wasn't solitude. Sartre was impassioned by *Portrait of a Man Unknown*. So, that was very encouraging. Then when *Martereau* (1953) was done, Marcel Arland was very excited and had it published with Gallimard. He was editing the *Nouvelle revue française* at the time. I always had a few enthusiastic readers. When *Tropisms* came out, I received an enthusiastic letter from Max Jacob, who at the time was very much admired as a poet. I can't say it was total solitude.

JW: Did Sartre or others try to claim you as an existentialist?

NS: No, not at all. He had published the beginning of *Portrait of a Man Unknown* in his review, *Les temps modernes*, and then he wrote the preface because he wanted to. And he told me, "Above all, they shouldn't think it's a novel that was influenced by existentialism." Which couldn't be the case, because *Tropisms* came out almost at the same time as *Nausea*.

JW: It was rather another existentialism.

NS: He was entirely conscious of that. And very honestly he said, "It is existence itself."

JW: You've said that it was during your law studies that you became attracted to the spoken language, which became your written language in effect. How did that opening come about?

NS: When I was working in law I didn't practice much, but I prepared probate conferences, which were literary; one said them, it's a spoken style. I'd worked those conferences a lot, they went well. And so, I think that tore me away from the written language, which I'd always been subjected to since childhood by the very strict French homework. It gave me a kind of impetus toward the freer language, which is spoken French. It did play some role.

JW: The language seems lighter, there's a greater facility in the flow of your writing.

NS: That facility demands an enormous amount of work. What a job!

JW: Did you look for models elsewhere?

NS: No, I never thought of comparisons. They were things that I felt spontaneously really. It wasn't taken from literature but from life.

JW: Do you imagine other ways of writing about tropisms?

NS: No, because for me form and content are inseparable. So that would be something else. If the form is different, it will be another sensation. And for this genre of sensation it's the only form.

JW: Do you feel there are other writers who have found certain lessons in the domain of tropisms?

NS: I don't feel I have any imitators. I think it's a domain that is too much my own.

JW: Would it be possible to use the tropisms in a more traditional novel?

NS: I don't see how. What interest would there be? Because in a more traditional novel, one shows characters with personality traits, while tropisms are entirely minute things that take place in a few instants inside of anybody at all. What could that bring to the description of a character? On the contrary.

JW: As if at the moment of tropisms, the character vanishes.

NS: He disintegrates before the extraordinary complexity of the tropisms inside of him.

JW: Which is what happens in *Martereau*.

NS: Martereau disintegrates. And in *Portrait of a Man Unknown*, the old man, the father, becomes so complex that the one who's looking to see inside of him abandons his quest, and at that moment we end up with a character out of the traditional novel, who ruins everything. In *Martereau* it's the character out of the traditional novel who disintegrates at the end.

J W : Yet in *The Planetarium* (1959), it seems that more than ever you're using traditional characters.

N S : On purpose. Since they are semblances, it's called *The Planetarium* and is made up of false stars, in imitation of the real sky. We are always a star for each other, like those we see in a planetarium, diminished, reduced. So, they see each other as characters, but behind these characters that they see, that they name, there is the whole infinite world of tropisms, which I tried to show in there.

J W : Considering the interiority of your writing, has it sometimes been difficult to remain at such depths?

N S : No, what is difficult is being on the surface. One gets bored there. There are a lot of great and admirable models who block your way. And once I rise to the surface, to do something on the surface, it's easy, but it's very tedious and disappointing.

J W : In *Portrait of a Man Unknown* the specialist consulted by the narrator tells him: "Beware of this taste for introversion, for daydreaming in the void, which is nothing but an escape from effort."

N S : Yes, because he feels that he is marginal, he feels that he's not normal. It's entirely ironic. He goes to see a psychiatrist who tries to put him on the right path. In my books there are always these normal people who don't understand these tropisms, who don't feel them.

J W : With *Portrait of a Man Unknown* had you decided to avoid using characters?

N S : No, on the contrary, I wanted to take semblances of characters, types, the miser for example, like Père Grandet, and then try to see what really happens in him, which is enormously complex. It is so complex that the character who is searching him out abandons the search, he can't go on anymore. And at that moment the character from the traditional novel is introduced, who has a name, a profession, who marries the daughter, etcetera. We fall back into the traditional novel and dialogue.

J W : While you were writing this book, did you know how it was going to end?

NS: No, I found the ending when I got to the end. Usually, it develops like that, like an organism that develops. Often I don't see the ending at all, it comes out of the book on its own.

JW: You've said that with your novels you wrote the first draft directly from beginning to end.

NS: At first. I always have to make a beginning that's entirely finished, the first few pages must be fixed in place. Like a springboard that I take off from, I don't rework it any further. I work on it a lot, and then it's finished. But after that, I wrote from one end to the other. I used to work like that, not now. I wrote from one end to the other, in a form that was sometimes a bit rough, I found the general movements, and then I rewrote the whole thing. For a while now, though, I'm afraid of waiting two or three years like that before starting over. So, I write gradually, I finish each passage as I go along. I changed my system about six years ago, since *The Use of Speech* and *Childhood*.

JW: In *Martereau* the narrator speaks of the importance of words, of what they hide. For Martereau, who is rather a traditional novelistic character, words are "hard and solid objects, of a single flow." One would say that in your books you feel a certain seduction of words.

NS: Yes, it's words that interest me. Inevitably. It's the very substance of my work. As a painter is interested in color and form.

JW: Some say the most important problem in the novel is time. In your book of essays, *The Age of Suspicion* (1956), you said that "the time of tropisms was no longer that of real life but of an immeasurably expanded present." In the novels time is surely complicated then.

NS: There are always instants. It takes place in the present finally. I'm concerned with these interior movements, I'm not concerned with time.

JW: Is that because you often do without plot?

NS: Completely. It has to do with a dramatic development of these interior movements, that's the time. There is no exterior reference.

JW: So then it's a sort of freedom from time.

NS: Time is absent, if you like.

JW: How was it you realized you could do without a plot in the first place?

NS: The question never presented itself for me. Given what I was interested in, plot didn't enter into it. I was involved as with a poem, one writes a poem and isn't concerned with such matters as plot. It was a free territory, there were no pre-established categories that I was obliged to enter into.

JW: In effect there are quite a few correspondences with poetry in your work.

NS: I hope so. There was a book by an Australian, on my novel *Between Life and Death*, who called it a "poetry of discourse." He called it a novelistic poetry. Not a poetic novel, because that's been done.

JW: Have you read a lot of poetry?

NS: Not especially. I've read some. You know, outside reading has not played a big role in my work.

JW: Well, what sort of reading was important for you?

NS: What really turned me around was reading Proust, it was a revelation of a whole world, and reading Joyce too. The interior monologue of Joyce. They're things without which I wouldn't have written as I do. We always start from our predecessors. If I'd written in the eighteenth century, I wouldn't have written like that. There had to be writers like that before me, who opened up such realms.

JW: Were you fairly young when you read them?

NS: Yes. I read Proust when I was twenty-four and Joyce at twenty-six.

JW: In your essay, "From Dostoyevsky to Kafka," you say that Kafka "traced a long straight path, a single direction and he went all the way." Don't you think there is any continuation beyond him?

NS: I don't think so. They've sought to imitate him a lot, at a certain moment it was fashionable to write like Kafka, but in my opinion that didn't lead anywhere.

JW: It seems, however, that there is more than a single direction in Kafka. There are various levels, that of the story, of the way he tells it, but there is also the poetic dimension, the parables.

NS: I wasn't concerned with all that. It was a period when there was a hatred, a mistrust, of "psychology." People were divided between those who were for Dostoyevsky and those for Kafka, that is against psychology. At the time I didn't know Kafka's work at all. I read Kafka very late, after the Liberation. I didn't like "The Metamorphosis," I only liked *The Trial* and *The Castle*. So, they were contrasting Kafka with Dostoyevsky; in Kafka they said there was emptiness, no psychology. I wanted to show that even in Kafka there was psychology, we can't do without it. It was a psychology pushed to the ultimate despair, the total absence of human contact. I was never concerned with a full analysis of Kafka, I'm not a critic. And then Kafka is not an author who influenced me. I must have been about forty-five by the time I read him.

JW: The central concern of the essay was with the psychological.

NS: That's right. I wanted to defend this conscience that was so despised, which Kafka supposedly didn't have. I found that he had a lot of it, and that every writer worthy of that name cannot do without the internal life.

JW: Elsewhere in that essay you made a distinction between the characters in the work of those two writers, saying that "while the quest of Dostoyevsky's characters leads them to seek a sort of interpenetration, a total and always possible fusion of souls, with Kafka's heroes it has to do with simply becoming, 'in the eyes of those people who regard them with such scorn,' not perhaps their friend but finally their co-citizen." Isn't this distinction a condition of the Christian and Jewish contexts of the two writers?

NS: I never got involved with that question, because I think that what's interesting there is to step outside of those contexts and to see the human being in depth. Kafka's universe has become a part of our own universe, and the Jewish question doesn't intervene at all. What's more, he doesn't talk about it in either *The Castle* or *The Trial*. We have the right to deal with that if the author himself puts it in his work. But if it remains outside, I don't see why a Christian couldn't read

Kafka's *The Trial* or *The Castle* in the same way as a Jew. It is addressed to everyone, that's why it's a great work.

JW: I was thinking more of their cultural formations.

NS: I'm not concerned with that. I'm not a critic. I'm concerned with what touches me directly as a writer.

JW: In one of the essays you also quote Katherine Mansfield's phrase, "this terrible desire to establish contact." But once a person takes off on a more experimental path, like yours for example, what becomes of that need? Were you yourself thinking along such lines?

NS: No, when I work I never ever define from the outside, I don't qualify what I'm doing. I'm looking to see what is felt, what we feel. I don't know what it is, and that's why it interests me, precisely because I don't know exactly what it is. Those were theoretical essays, they have nothing to do with my work when I write. I don't put myself at that distance, I'm entirely inside.

JW: In the essay "The Age of Suspicion," you said that the novel "has become the place of the reciprocal mistrust" of the reader and the writer. Do you think that with the contemporary novel that mistrust has gotten deeper, more serious?

NS: That's an entirely personal question. I'm not terribly interested, except when I'm reading Agatha Christie or novels that carry me away, in the personalities of the characters or in the plot. When I see a novel written in that form, it might amuse me, it can be slices of life or descriptions of manners, but I can't say that it interests me as a writer. There are those who like that, obviously, people do continue to write in that way.

JW: Do you feel, for example, that the contemporary novel has become more conservative?

NS: There was a period when we fell back joyfully into the tradition. There was a strong academic tendency, in the theater as well, everywhere. And I think all the same we're getting out of that once again. The admiration for academicism is declining.

JW: If there is such a thing as an evolution of the novel, do you see it as a one-way street?

NS: I'm not a critic, you know. I only read what interests me, what passes my way. I don't have any opinion on the current evolution of literature. I think that the writers who were grouped under the term *nouveau roman* have all continued to write in their own ways, works which have remained alive for the most part.

JW: On various occasions, especially in your essay on Flaubert, you've spoken about dispensing with the old accessories such as plot and characters. But are those old accessories so useless as that? Are there no truths to be reached with them?

NS: One reaches certain truths, but truths that are already known. At a level that's already known. One can describe the Soviet reality in Tolstoy's manner, but one will never manage to penetrate it further than Tolstoy did with the aristocratic society that he described. It will remain at the same level of the psyche as Anna Karenina or Prince Bolkonsky, if you use the form that Tolstoy used. If you employ the form of Dostoyevsky, you will arrive at another level, which will always be Dostoyevsky's level, whatever the society you describe. That's my idea. If you want to penetrate further, you must abandon both of them and go look for something else. Form and content are the same thing. If you take a certain form, you attain a certain content with that form, not any other.

JW: But even so the form is something you've discovered each time.

NS: Each time it has to find its form. It's the sensation that impels the form.

JW: In your essay "Conversation and Sub-conversation" you speak of certain ideas that Virginia Woolf and others had about the psychological novel, saying that perhaps it hasn't yielded as much as they had hoped at the time.

NS: That was meant ironically. I agreed with her. I don't really like the word "psychological," which has been used a lot, because that makes one think of traditional psychology, the analysis of feelings. But I would say that the universe of the psyche is limitless, it's infinite. So, each writer can find there what he would like. It's a universe as immense as we all are, and there are writers yet who are going to discover huge areas of the life of the psyche, which exist but which we haven't brought to light.

JW: In the same essay you also speak of the American example as a reason to look beyond the psychological. Who were you thinking of, besides Faulkner?

NS: The behaviorists, they were completely against that. Steinbeck, Caldwell, that wasn't psychological at all. It was because of them that psychology was despised. It had a big influence, besides, on people like Camus, with *The Stranger*. It was fashionable at the time to say that there was no conscience, that it held no interest.

JW: In "Conversation and Sub-conversation," you particularly discuss the problem of how to write dialogues now, so that the sub-conversation may be heard. How did you arrive at your way of reaching all those levels at once, in the way you write dialogue? Was it by a lot of experimenting?

NS: No. That comes uniquely from intuition, it represents a big job of searching, in order to reconstitute all these interior movements. To relive it. To expand it, to show it in slow motion. Because it is very fleeting. It gets erased very quickly. And it's very difficult to get ahold of.

JW: You've written that the traditional methods of writing dialogue couldn't work anymore.

NS: Not for me. Because I would have to put myself at too much of a distance from the consciousness in which I dwell. I'm immersed right inside, and I try to execute the interior movements that are produced in that consciousness. And if I say, "said Henri" or "replied Jean," I become someone who is showing the character from outside.

JW: One of the things that marks your writing is the punctuation, which you work very carefully.

NS: In the last few books there are a lot of ellipses; there were fewer of them before. Because I find that it prevents one from reading these movements, which are very quick and suspended, without breathing. There is a need for a certain breathing when one reads it, and the ellipses create this breathing. They help in the rhythm of the sentence. It gives the sentence more flexibility.

JW: Let's talk about your theater work. Why did you start writing plays?

NS: It was simply a request by the radio in Stuttgart. A young German, Werner Spiess, came to see me for the radio in Stuttgart, he asked me to write a radio play. That was in '64. He wanted something new, in a style that wouldn't be like the usual style; it didn't matter if it were difficult even. I started by refusing. He returned a second time, and I refused again. And then I thought about it one day. I told myself that perhaps I could write a radio play after all, that it would be entirely a matter of dialogue. I hadn't thought I would be able to do it because for me the dialogues are prepared by sub-conversation, the pre-dialogue. The dialogue only skims the surface of the sub-conversation. So, I decided everything will be in the dialogue, what is in the pre-dialogue will be in the dialogue. They later said my plays, in relation to my novels, were like a glove turned inside out. Everything that is inside is now on the outside.

JW: Which play was that?

NS: First it was *Silence*, then *The Lie*, then the four other plays. They were always performed first for foreign radio.

JW: That's why you put hardly any directions in the text, because they were written for the radio.

NS: That's right, because they're not written for the stage. There's only one where I was thinking of the stage, that was *It Is There*. And still, not a lot. Above all, I hear the conversations and the voices, and I don't see at all the theatrical space, the actors. All that is the job of the director. Which is a very interesting job, because everything remains to be done.

JW: Have you attended rehearsals much?

NS: Yes, I've attended rehearsals. First, with Jean-Louis Barrault, then with Claude Régy, then with Simone Benmussa. I don't have a lot to say, except for the intonations, but not for the actors' movements. That's the director's job.

JW: Were all the plays requests like the first one?

NS: It was always for the radio, always the same person who asked me. Then, after the radio in Stuttgart didn't do difficult plays anymore, it was the radio in Cologne. And French radio too. Each time after finishing a novel, I rather liked writing a radio play. It distracted me, it gave me a bit of a change.

JW: Did you have much experience of the theater apart from your plays?

NS: I liked going to the theater, of course. I was quite impressed by *Six Characters in Search of an Author* by Pirandello and *The Dance of Death* by Strindberg. Those two plays impressed me deeply.

JW: You've said that your plays are like a continuation of your novels. What has the theater brought you for the writing of your novels?

NS: Absolutely nothing. It has no relation whatsoever.

JW: Are there voices in the modern theater that have particularly interested you?

NS: No, not so much. Some of Pinter's plays I've quite liked. Where he touches on things that interest me.

JW: Has the experience of writing changed much for you since you were young? Do you have different habits?

NS: I don't feel that it's changed. I think we always have the same difficulties with each new book; there is no acquiring of experience. Each new book is entirely another realm, in which one must try to find its form and its sensations, and the difficulties are the same as at the start. I see no progression. There is no technical experience gathered for me.

JW: Was writing much different for you when your children were young?

NS: No. I started to write when my third daughter wasn't yet born, the two others were little; that played no role. I always had enough time for myself. You know, I don't believe that women of the bourgeoisie can pretend they can't write because they have children. That's absurd. Claudel was the French ambassador in Washington and wrote an immense body of work; he never ceased to be ambassador and all that that represents. So when you've got someone to take care of the children, and later when they go to school, it's impossible not to find two or three hours in the day to work. It's *very* different for a working-class woman, or for a working-class man, it's the same problem. Not entirely the same, because the woman has even more work to do than the man. But there I understand completely that it's impossible. One can't speak like that of women from the intellectual milieu, which is always a bourgeois milieu. Especially before, since now it's become more difficult, but before one found whatever one wanted for taking care of children. There was no problem as far as that was concerned.

JW: Considering the interior quality of your writing, do you see the fact of being a woman as giving you any special access to such a state? As if that predisposed you toward the interior rather than out toward action in the world.

NS: No, I don't think so at all. I don't think that Proust or Henry James or even Joyce was turned elsewhere than toward the inside. It's a question of the writer's temperament.

JW: Do you see any sort of difference between women's writing and that of men?

NS: No, I don't see any. I don't feel that Emily Brontë is a woman's writing, among women who truly wrote well. I don't see the difference. One says first of all, "That's what it is to be a woman," and then afterward one decides that is feminine. Henry James was always working in minute details, in his lacework, or Proust, much more still than most women. I think that if women like Emily Brontë wanted to keep a pseudonym, they were entirely right. One cannot find a manner of writing upon which it would be possible to stick the label of feminine or masculine; it's writing pure and simple, an admirable writing, that's all. There are subjects in writing that are very feminine, which are lived, the women who write on feminine subjects like maternity, that's completely different.

JW: Let's talk about cigarettes. Have you always been a smoker?

NS: Alas! I shouldn't smoke, but I don't smoke a lot. Six or seven cigarettes a day. That's still too much. I have a very bad habit. So, in order not to smoke, I've taken to holding the cigarette in my mouth while I work. I don't light it. That gives me the same effect. Because I forget. I feel something and I forget if it's lit. Since I smoke very weak cigarettes, and I don't inhale the smoke, I feel just as much like I'm smoking even if it's not for real.

JW: As if it enters into the game, in effect.

NS: That's right. It's a gesture, something one feels.

JW: Could we speak about the conception of some of your books? *The Golden Fruits* (1963), for example, did that come out of an experience with the literary world?

NS: Not at all. I take no part in the literary world, I've never gone to the literary cocktail parties. It has to do with an inner experience. It has to do with a kind of terrorism around a work of art that is lauded to the skies and that we cannot approach. Where there is a sort of curtain of stipulated opinions that separates you from that work. Either we adore it or else we detest it, it's impossible to approach it. Above all in Parisian circles, even without going to the cocktail parties, even in the press, there reigns a kind of terrorism of general adulation, and you don't have the right to approach it and have a contrary opinion. And then it falls; at that moment you no longer have the right to say that it's good. That's what I wanted to show, this life of a work of art. And this work of art, what is it? I'd have to approach it, but that's impossible. And then all that we find there, all that we look for in a book, and which has nothing to do with its literary value.

JW: There is often a multitude of voices in that book.

NS: It's like that in most of my books that come later. There are all these voices, without our needing to take an interest in the characters that speak them. It doesn't much matter.

JW: Have there been processes that repeat themselves, either in the conception or in the elaboration of your novels?

NS: Each time it didn't interest me to continue doing the same thing. So I would try to extend my domain to areas that were always at the same level of these interior movements, to go into regions where I hadn't yet gone.

JW: Have you ever been surprised by the fate of one of your books?

NS: No. I was more pessimistic at the start. I really thought that it would not be understood at all.

JW: You've said that the *nouveau roman* movement helped you as a means to get read. But did the idea of belonging to a movement, so-called, constrain you as well?

NS: No. And none of those who belonged, who were classed in this movement, has written things that resemble each other, whatever it may be. They've remained completely different from each other and have continued each one on his own path.

JW: Your essays were among the first to speak of concerns common to the group. Have you ever felt any sort of responsibility to this movement?

NS: Not at all. I had reflected upon these questions about the novel before the others, because the others were twenty years younger than me. I haven't changed my way of thinking since my first books, I haven't budged. I could repeat exactly the same things I said when I wrote *The Age of Suspicion*. I have a deep conviction that the forms of the novel must change, that there must be a continual transformation of the forms, in all the arts—in painting, in music, in poetry, and in the novel. That we cannot return to the forms of the nineteenth century and set another society in them, it doesn't matter which. So, that interested Alain Robbe-Grillet; he's the one who did a lot to launch the *nouveau roman*. He was working at Les Editions de Minuit, he wanted to republish *Tropisms*, which had been out of print. It came out at the same time as *Jealousy*, and at that moment in *Le Monde* a critic had written, "That is what we can call the *nouveau roman*," though he detested it. It was a name that suited Robbe-Grillet quite well. He said, "That's magnificent, it's what we needed." He wanted to launch a movement. Me, I'm incapable of launching a movement; I've always been very solitary.

JW: Were there ever any meetings of the group?

NS: Never. Nor discussions. It had nothing in common with the surrealists, where there was a group, a leader, André Breton, nothing of the kind. We never saw each other.

JW: How did he find all the writers to bring them together as a movement?

NS: It was Les Editions de Minuit. Robbe-Grillet found Michel Butor, who had written *Passage de Milan*, which they published. He found Claude Simon. Robert Pinget as well. Robbe-Grillet and Jérôme Lindon, who is the director of Les Editions de Minuit, they worked together. Like that they formed a sort of group.

JW: Have there been other experimental literary movements that have interested you?

NS: No, I passed them by entirely. The surrealist movement, for example, that might have interested me, but it didn't at all.

JW: What about the Oulipo movement in the 1960s, which included Georges Perec, Raymond Queneau, Italo Calvino?

NS: I liked what Queneau was doing a lot. My first book, *Tropisms*, appeared in the same collection as his book, *The Bark Tree*, with the publisher Robert Denoël. I quite liked *The Bark Tree*.

JW: In *Between Life and Death* (1968), your novel on literary creation, you say that no work is useless, that sooner or later it must give fruit, that it suffices to pick it up again later at the right moment. Have you had that experience, of reworking a text you'd written?

NS: No. I meant that every effort we make always serves for something, all the same. There are certain texts that were projected for *Tropisms* that I brought out later in *Portrait of a Man Unknown*.

JW: Which of your books do you prefer?

NS: That's very difficult to say. I don't reread them. And sometimes I tell myself, "It seems to me I've already done something like that," and I can't recall where.

JW: Has one of the books satisfied you more than the others?

NS: It's all very difficult. There are always doubts about what I wanted to do.

JW: Even the doubts, have they played a constructive role sometimes?

NS: I don't know. I think it's very painful, and it's better not to have any. I envy those who don't have any, I envy them a lot. They are happy people.

JW: In *Do You Hear Them?* (1972), it seems that every movement starts from a central balance: on one side, the two friends and their pre-Columbian stone that they're admiring; on the other side, the children upstairs and their laughter. What impelled you to explore this dynamism?

NS: I've always been interested by the relation between a work of art, the desire to communicate, and what the work of art brings you. Also, the relation between people who love each other a great deal. I thought it was an amusing construction, I don't know. Each time there is a point of departure, but you know it's hardly conscious. It comes and one doesn't know how or why.

JW: We are far from autobiography in your work, so readers and critics end up by being curious about your life. You give little importance to all that. Why, do you think, do so many serious writers insist on not writing autobiography in their books?

NS: I think that in every book we put a lot of experience that we have ourselves lived more or less or imagined ourselves. There is not a single book that doesn't contain such experience. Even with Kafka, he didn't live *The Trial*, but there is a whole universe in which he lived, which was close to him and which he translated by *The Trial* or *The Castle*. It's a transposition, it's a metaphor for something that he felt very strongly. And that we all feel as well.

JW: But it seems sometimes there is a sort of mistrust of autobiography.

NS: When it's a real autobiography. That is, one wants to display everything one has felt, how one has been. There is always a mise-en-scène, a desire to show oneself in a certain light. We are so complex and we have so many facets that what interests me in an autobiography is what the author wants me to see. He wants me to see him like that. That's what amuses me. And it's always false. I don't like Freud at all and I detest psychoanalysis, but one of Freud's statements I have always found very interesting, and true, is when he said that all autobiographies are false. Obviously, because I can do an autobiography that will show a saint, a being who is absolutely idyllic, and I could do another that will be a demon, and it will all be true. Because it's all mixed together. And in addition, one can't even attain all that. When I wrote *Childhood*, I stopped at the age of twelve, precisely because it's still an innocent period in which things are not clear and in which I tried to recover certain moments, certain impressions and sensations.

JW: *Fools Say* was the last novel you wrote. It seems the most abstract of your books.

NS: It's more difficult, the construction is difficult. It works on two planes: there is on the one hand the character, the one who acts like a character, and then the idea, which is attributed to a so-called intelligent character or to a fool. And this idea only has value in the fact that it is attributed to someone of repute. It can be stupid but we can't say so, because it was that person who thought that. On the contrary, the one who has been defined as a fool, whatever he may say, he might be very intelligent sometimes, we say that it's stupid. The idea has no freedom, it's not taken on its own, because it is always attributed to someone. Later, when I had written my book, someone wrote me that Lenin had said, "We must destroy the fools." Who were the fools? Those who didn't think like him. That's what I wanted to show in my book. So, for that I had to create characters. The character of the genius, the character of the fool. But what is a fool? He may be a fool when it's a question of mathematics or political science, and he might be remarkably intelligent when it's a question of something else. Each one of us is at the same time very intelligent and a fool. It depends what is asked of us. It reflects a lack of freedom to declare, "That's what fools say." To class people as fools is already a fascist attitude. It's entirely totalitarian, entirely arbitrary, and absolutely unspeakable. One should say, "That idea there is a stupid idea." But we cannot say of someone, "He's a fool." Because that fool may be much more intelligent than Einstein or someone on another matter.

JW: Did you decide not to write any more novels after that?

NS: No, I never made any decisions. And then, I've never considered them as real novels in the traditional sense.

JW: What are you working on now?

NS: Now too it's something in a form that I've never used, and I don't know what it will be. I've got about two-thirds of the book done now, but I'm not in so much of a hurry to finish it. I don't know what I'll do afterward.

JW: Your book *The Use of Speech* (1980) recalls your first book *Tropisms*. Again there are brief texts completely separate from each other, though here you look at certain things around a specific word, how it works.

NS: As it's called *The Use of Speech*, it always starts off from the spoken word. The word falls into it like a stone and makes ripples.

JW: Was it conceived as a book from the start?

NS: It was conceived in advance that each of its texts was based on a word, whereas *Tropisms* was not conceived in advance. There I'd written the texts one after the other, without really knowing what I was in the process of doing.

JW: Your most recent book, *Childhood*, is altogether different once again. Why did you use the form of dialogue to recall these memories?

NS: That came about naturally, because I told myself, "It's not possible for you to write that." Until that point, I had always written fiction. I had a great freedom, I invented situations in which I placed things that interested me under a certain light. And in *Childhood* I would be bound to something that was fixed, that was already past. It was the opposite of everything I'd done. So I told myself, "You can't do that." I wrote down this dialogue, and it served as the start of my book. After that, all through the book I had this second conscience, which was a double of myself and which controls what I'm doing, which helps me move forward.

JW: The memories in the book often work like tropisms.

NS: I chose memories where there were tropisms, as much as possible, that's what interested me. It gives movement to the form.

Edmond Jabès

It is difficult to imagine the spoken writer behind the aphoristic intensity of his books. Edmond Jabès rarely grants interviews, preferring when he does to treat them like another text. Thus, he pays special attention that it not lapse into a routine repetition of previous questions.

Jabès encourages an informal yet respectful atmosphere. Hands animating the persistent figures of his thought, he demonstrates how thoroughly he lives his books; practically every statement sparks another observation, another analogy, so unrelenting is his own questioning.

Born in 1912 in Cairo, he grew up in a nonreligious Jewish family, which had been residents there for generations. Given his French education, he began publishing his first books of poetry in Egypt and France in the 1930s. Though he saw Nasser's later rise to power as a necessary response to English colonialism, he knew that for him as a Jew it meant he could not long remain there. Forced to leave in 1957, Jabès settled in Paris with his wife and two daughters. Two years later his book of collected poetry, Je bâtis ma demeure *(I Build My Dwelling), was published by Gallimard.*

But the break with Egypt, and the condition of exile, began to work in him. In 1963 the first volume of The Book of Questions *ap-*

peared, followed in each succeeding year by what was originally felt to be a trilogy, with The Book of Yukel *and* Return to the Book. *Within a decade of the first, the rest of the seven volumes appeared, first* Yaël *and* Elya, *then* Aely, *and finally the last, whose real title is simply a small red dot, bearing the subtitle* El, *or* The Last Book.

Through the last half of the 1970s, *the three volumes of* The Book of Resemblances *appeared:* The Book of Resemblances, Intimations The Desert, *and* The Ineffaceable The Unperceived. *They completed what Jabès realized to be a ten-volume book, which from the start has stymied critics as unclassifiable. In the* 1980s *these were followed by four books that came to be grouped as* Le livre des limites. *All of Jabès' work proceeds with a poet's sensibility, written in prose, where the primary building block is the aphorism, and where a play on words may unlock a long series of reflections. To date over two hundred essays have been devoted to his work.*

Jabès passed away at his home in Paris on January 2, 1991, *a few months before the publication of his last book,* Le livre de l'hospitalité. *He lived on a short street near the edge of the Latin Quarter, a block away from the popular market street, the rue Mouffetard. He lived with his wife in their modest apartment for more than twenty years, the walls lined with paintings done by friends. The following interview took place over two afternoons in late September* 1982. *On the bookshelves behind Jabès were the leatherbound volumes of the Talmud, given to him by his father; they were among the only books he was able to take out of Egypt.*

JW: How do you, as author of *The Book of Questions*, feel about being asked questions yourself, as in interviews?

EJ: I am always ill at ease with someone who asks me questions because I have a tendency to answer with questions. Interviews trouble me because I have the impression of never really speaking in these conditions. I have the feeling of pleasing someone who asks me questions by giving him certain responses that for me always remain very superficial. But, the interview is both disquieting and fascinating in that you are prisoner to the other's question. You yourself cannot formulate your own responses to things that may seem perhaps more important. And it's a risk for the writer because he doesn't know where it's going to lead him, in fact he never knows exactly what he would like to say. But I think he must play this game. Personally, I don't believe there are things the writer is privy to in his books, not in mine. As I accept all readings, it causes me to accept all questions as long as they have their reality for the one who asks them, as long as they are questions he asks himself in his reading of the text. But anything I can say doesn't involve the responsibility of my books; you have to read them, it's they that speak. And reading is something from deep inside, there's a complicity between the reader and the book.

JW: It was the poet Max Jacob who taught you essentially how to find your own voice. How did your encounter with him come about?

EJ: Meeting Max Jacob was extremely important to me. Not only did he teach me how to write, but he was really the most extraordinary guide. At that time I was living in Egypt, and all this poetry that was considered very modern wasn't known at all there. I was very taken with Baudelaire, Mallarmé, Rimbaud. Then all of a sudden I came upon a book by Max Jacob that completely fascinated me with its freedom, its irony, where plays on words appeared in almost every phrase. For me, it was an amazing liberation. Then, I began to examine it and to imitate it in my writings.

So I wrote to Max Jacob, I was nineteen; he replied very kindly. I published some texts in Egypt that were very close to Max Jacob's poems, and then I met him in Paris in 1935. I'd just gotten married and we came to Paris for two months. I had informed Max Jacob of my arrival, he expected me. I went to see him right away. There I arrived with a big manuscript, a hundred, a hundred and fifty pages, that took some two years to write. He received me with his great kindness, he asked about me, my life, about my wife too. Then he looked at the manuscript, and said, "Yes, I like this phrase, this one too." He read a poem. "Yes, there it seems more like you," etcetera. "But, if you like, we'll meet again tomorrow morning and we'll talk." When I arrived the next day, I was very pleased, thinking he liked this manuscript. Then, after a moment, he looked me in the eyes, to warn me, like he was going to hurt me. And he said, "All right now, I've got a lot of things to say to you, but so that this manuscript doesn't get in our way, I'm going to tear it up." He took it and threw it in his wastebasket.

For me, obviously, it was a shock, and thereupon he began to speak to me about what poetry was. He explained that it's not so simple, that the search for harmony was extremely slow and long, that one had to mature, that this wasn't mature, it was him. That he had done his time, I couldn't imitate him. He did it to force me to go more directly my own way, but also to defend himself, because Max never welcomed being imitated. He knew very well that to be imitated is to be betrayed, I understood that much later. There are some writings that are imitable and others that aren't. The writings that are, if you manage to imitate them, you freeze them. Because there are tics in the manner of writing. Well, if you imagine this multiplied to many many cases, when you get to the original it's unbearable. You feel you've read it all. There are a lot of contemporary writers like that, who are interesting in themselves, but whom we practically end up not reading anymore due to the fact that they've had lots of imitators. Not just as disciples of their thought but of their writing.

JW: But you too seem to have such imitators.

EJ: No, I don't think one can imitate my writing because it works in several registers. There's the aphorism that's very condensed, there's spacious writing, compact writing, and all that in the most classic of forms. There's no game about writing. Writing is imitable when you can grab hold of the trick. There, there is no trick. There is a total limpidity, but it's in various registers. And this too was Max's lesson, because we corresponded afterward, from 1935 to 1940, until the war, and each time I sent him a text he'd say, "No, it's not you." Or he'd say, "It's too lyrical. You should think of the classics." I'd do it more condensed, he'd say, "No, it doesn't breathe." It really wasn't until much later that I understood that both were valid. That all writing is that, real writing. There are things that must be said with a deep breath, so one can go into a great lyricism, and then things that cannot be said except in the most concise manner. Which is for me where the aphorism comes in, where everything is said in one phrase. But sometimes it's developed elsewhere. *The Book of Questions* shows all that physically. Not only within the book but from book to book. Because if in the first there's a great lyricism, in the last ones it gets more and more condensed.

Another of Max's lessons was that he saved you a tremendous amount of time, because when he judged a text, he didn't simply judge it as a text. He saw where it was going to lead you. He'd say, "Now, if you continue along this path, in two years you'll be doing Apollinaire." Or else, "You'll be doing Mallarmé." So, he put his finger on it. Above all when he'd say to me, "Now you can read Mallarmé." Huh? I can read Mallarmé? I've been reading Mallarmé for a long time. "No, after your text, you have understood Mallarmé." That is, "You have made an approach to Mallarmé through you." Because what's most important is when the author you like becomes a pretext for you, for questioning yourself. It's the way we take in a book that's important. We can only speak about it by way of ourselves. Your reading of the writer isn't mine. And yet both are true and both are false.

JW: But there's a difference between the reader who is just a reader and the one who is also a writer.

EJ: Yes, exactly. But every true reader is a writer in effect. A true reader is someone who remakes the other's book. Besides, it's the movement itself of the book. When you open a book, first of all, it's a harsh act, because you break it. You open it up, to get out what's inside. You begin your reading with the first page. You read the first page, you think you've retained it all. When you turn the page, what remains of the first in the second? One or two phrases, an emotion at the moment of an encounter. You read the second page, go on to the third; of the second that you have nonetheless read completely, few things remain. All the rest gets erased. And gradually like that until the end. At the end, the book that you've enjoyed, that you've read with the greatest attention, becomes a book that's fragmented by you, by the important pieces of your reading. It's with that that you will make your own book. And the author is always surprised when they cite a phrase of his when there were other phrases right beside it that perhaps seemed more important to him. For example, in my own experience, in the last book of *The Book of Resemblances* there are one or two phrases that were extremely important for me, phrases about myself, that revealed a lot of things. At least I thought so, that they were going to stop there and say, "Ah, look at this here." Well, even my closest friends didn't see these phrases. What does that say? That says you yourself can't transmit something through the book. It is blank each time. You can't say, on a certain page, "Here it is," because the reader doesn't understand. In the end all books either work or they don't. And when it does, it works according to the reading that you have given it. There have been the most contradictory readings of my books.

JW: According to the critics?

EJ: With critics it's different. The critics try to situate these books, to show their relationship, what they've been. The reading of a man who's very informed, especially who wants to speak about a book, often does not have the innocence of the reader who reads only for himself, who says, "Others' opinions don't interest me, the author's opinion even less, it's my opinion that counts." There have been completely amazing readings in that respect. For example, a young employee of a bookstore who didn't read any books. A young Jew, very religious, who said his prayers four times a day. He read nothing besides his prayers. One day, he was in the bookstore, there were no customers; the manager liked my books a lot, so she said to him, "Listen, there's nothing to do, why don't you read *The Book of Questions*?" And he said, "No, that doesn't interest me." She insisted he go look at the book, the first one. He began to read it, then he closed it, put it in his briefcase and was going to buy it. She said, "But I didn't say that for you to buy it. I told you simply to read it." He said, "No, no, I want it." To prove what? This young man wrote a letter, by way of this friend, to tell me that for him his prayers are incomplete now if he doesn't read a passage from *The Book of Questions* each time. This friend was so surprised and even touched by this that she went to give him the second and third, which form a trilogy, as a gift. He refused them. He said, "No, that doesn't interest me. This is the book, that's all." Well, what would you say to someone like that? You can't tell him, "Your reading is wrong. I'm not a practicing Jew, I'm not a believer." Approaches to a book assumed in such a manner are astonishing.

JW: Why do you think it's happened like that?

EJ: Because, see, it's a book of *putting* into question. A lot of young people have been very interested in these books because they don't feel at ease with themselves. So, there's an amazing questioning that has touched them, since to question is to put oneself in question each time. I allow myself to say this because it's young people especially who have taken these books in hand, in a surprising way, whether in France or elsewhere. And who assume them entirely, it's their book, they live with it.

JW: But how do these reactions affect you? How do they affect the writing?

EJ: Each time it raises questions for me, because it's a reading I wasn't expecting. At the start, when they tried to read it comparing these books to those of the Jewish tradition, for example, that annoyed me, because that wasn't at all my point of view. But later, I told myself deep down, even if I use the word "God" in all the books without believing in it, there is still a certain fascination. The word "Jew" is in all my books, it's something that haunts them, something that's important. So it's made me think. At any rate, what I've tried to do with these books is to preserve the opening by preserving the question. And the question is the opening itself. In Jewish thought, the question is very very important. There's a bringing together that's done in a natural manner.

JW: How did you start writing?

EJ: It comes from way back, I believe. In *The Book of Questions* there was a page at the beginning where I say, "When, as a child, I wrote my name for the first time, I knew I was beginning a book." And this phrase responded to something that was very true for me, very profound, which I must have experienced quite young. But I had it confirmed by one of my granddaughters, it's amazing. She was five at the time, she'd just learned how to write, and the first thing she learned to write was her name. So, she came in one day with a big sheet of white paper, where she'd written on top, Kareen, and in a very cool manner, she said, "I'm leaving you my book." I was impressed because I realized that it's true, the child, when he writes one phrase, thinks he's writing a book. At the start, when he doesn't know how to write, he puts three l's or two m's or whatever, he thinks he's mastered it all. And the disappointment for the child comes when he's really learned how to spell. Like everyone, he has to learn how to write the words, not the word he invented, the word that represented the whole world for him. They've reduced the word to what it is. And when a kid starts to write, the first thing he wants to write is his name. Naming is extremely important, I deeply believe. As soon as he's written his name, he's said it all. Kareen, that's me. It's over. What else would you have her say besides Kareen? That's the whole book. Because the book is only a name, nothing else. It's the approach of a name.

But I've digressed. In fact, I started to write quite young, at the age of nine, things that aren't very interesting. I published a book of poems at the age of seventeen, in France no less, which had a lot of success in very official, very academic circles. It was called *Les illusions sentimentales*, very Baudelairean. It was a period when I came to school wearing fancy ties sometimes. And it's funny, this book got me into the literary salons of the time, like Madame Rachilde's, where there were senators, deputies, academicians, who sent me letters. I was read at the Comédie Française by one of the great actors, and it's a detestable book! Then I wrote other books in the same vein, a false romanticism, and from there some time later I discovered Max Jacob. That was an introduction into a particular modernity, because at the time I didn't see the modernity of either Mallarmé or Baudelaire. Then, after making this necessary transition, I returned to these great writers, but after playing the game of a particular modernity. Having discovered Max Jacob, I published a book of poems in Cairo called *Les pieds en l'air* (Feet in the Air). The titles of the poems were on the bottom, and it was a whole play on words with lots of puns and such, very close to Max Jacob. After that, I wrote a book of essays, precisely on this work. I disowned all that, of course. Then I wrote this manuscript that Max tore up, and from there on I followed Max's lessons. I think really the first book where the writing is finally mine, to a certain extent, is *Chansons pour le repas de l'ogre* (Songs for the Ogre's Meal), which was written in 1942–43.

JW: And were you writing other texts at the same time you wrote the books of poetry in the 1940s and 1950s?

EJ: Until about 1951 I only wrote the poems you find in *Je bâtis ma demeure*. But I wrote a number of plays. They were performed on the radio. When I came to France, I had been in a very difficult situation financially, and one day I received a letter from the radio which said, "We are in the process of trying to bring writers to the theater. If you have a play to propose, send it to us." I said, "Why not?" So, I took out one of five plays, that I cut a little or whatever, since they were offering ten thousand francs. And it was accepted; it played on the radio several times, here, in Canada, in Francophone countries. But I haven't kept any of that.

JW: Did the theater work influence your books?

EJ: No, it was entirely different. Now, with the distance, if I could find an example—it's like the theater of Pinter. A bit harsh like that. Very stark situations. Because theater has always fascinated me. I was always performing, at the age of fifteen I had a theater troupe. Every two weeks I put on a play with friends, and half the time it was a play I wrote myself, little comedies, one act. But theater wasn't really my path. When I came to Paris, as *Je bâtis ma demeure* was going to come out with Gallimard, I showed the plays to a friend, one of the big theater critics. He found them very bad, saying they weren't worth anything. I thought at the time it was very courageous of him to say that with such frankness. It reminded me a little of the way Max acted with me, I trusted him immediately. I completely abandoned theater, and little by little *The Book of Questions* was born.

JW: What has been the value of memory in your own life and work? What has it taught you? How far back do you remember?

EJ: It's very difficult to say what is my first recollection, especially because I don't believe so much in remembrance. I believe in memory and not remembrance. Memory is something that is older than us finally, while remembrances are moments of our life we ourselves have been privileged to experience, to which we have given a certain duration that perhaps they didn't deserve. There's an old recollection which I hadn't remembered, but which I discovered in a poem from *Chansons pour le repas de l'ogre*. There was a fairly ambiguous phrase but very poetic, full of images, and I realized that I hadn't understood it. Because in fact everything I've ever written comes out of something lived. There's never been any invention on my part, there's something lived behind it. So, I questioned that phrase, not in a logical manner, but I wondered how these images could have come up, as they were so unusual. Suddenly I remembered a very strong emotion I'd had, of fright, one night. I must have been four or five, and I was coming back home with the person who accompanied me. In the neighbor's garden there was a huge wolfhound, who knew me well, and he stuck his snout out through the gate. I wasn't used to coming back in so late, and I saw him that night with his sparkling eyes. So it became that phrase, something that followed me with these lynx's eyes. That's what memories are like. On the other hand, I think what deeply affected me was the death of my sister. It was horrible, and from that moment on I felt like I was someone else, I changed.

JW: Then do those two selves come together again in your writing?

EJ: Certainly. I don't think we're made of just one piece. We're sometimes one, sometimes the other. And happy memories are sometimes as strong as sad ones. We're caught between the two, and surely childhood memories that were happy but turned sad due to the war are in the first poems of *Chansons pour le repas de l'ogre*. That collection was written during the war, and it's very strange that they're songs. It's because at the moment when the world was going up in smoke, when we were being threatened all the time, there is something like a return to childhood, as if childhood could protect us from death. And so, there were these songs that are quite surprising in comparison to what I was writing before.

JW: And you only kept the writings that went along that path?

EJ: No. Because in *Je bâtis ma demeure* there were other poems that are very different from the songs. There's work that was close to surrealism for me. And then, other work close to René Char's poetry at that time; one book is dedicated to him. It's not at all René Char, but his thinking, his aphoristic form, was important for me then. In my development there's Char, the surrealist poets, Eluard, in the first texts, which were more imagistic. But at the same time, there was Egypt and a reflection on language that wasn't elsewhere, which was utterly myself perhaps.

JW: The vocabulary in *Je bâtis ma demeure* is more extensive than in *The Book of Questions*.

EJ: Yes, but it is perhaps easier to write with a lot of images than to write in a way that's very plain. Because if you speak with many images, it sometimes seduces easily, though obviously not always. Whereas you can't be fooled with clear limpid writing. Right away you hear if it's bad.

JW: But is that one of the things you were trying to do in *The Book of Questions*, to strip down the writing?

EJ: No. The poem full of images has always frightened me, because that profusion causes one to be practically unconscious of them, thus devoid of any logic. I wanted to understand, it was a way for me to shatter the image and at the same time to rid myself of it. Gradually through my work I was able to get rid of the image by questioning it. Thus the aphorisms, especially those on the text. And that's already one of the experiences of the desert, but one which I didn't sense at the time because I was still thinking of writing poems full of images, which is the opposite of the experience of the desert. But the desert was already working around in there, unsettling things, like a subversion.

JW: Now and then you spent time in the desert. Why did you go?

EJ: The desert was a necessity that touched on a lot of things. First of all, in Cairo we were a fairly well known family, and the European colony was really quite small, in that people got to know each other along social levels. Which means that, say, if we were at the same social level in Egypt, I knew everything about you and you knew everything about me. Well, that was a big burden on me. It wasn't me inside. And I had always had a great fascination with the desert. Because the desert is at once everything and nothing. So that when you are between sky and sand you are truly in infinity. Outside of time. Time doesn't count. Not only does time not count, but the spoken word itself loses its necessity. And that was fundamental for me, who was seeking—as with the questioning of a poem—a word of truth. Because I'd always tell myself that if with the same word one can practically say the thing and its opposite, in the same manner, with the same force, then what is this word? What is this word that plays with us and that causes us to enter this game which is almost a metamorphosis? So, where is the truth there? What is the word that in the end can tell the truth, that can tell what we really are? Well, the desert teaches you first of all to get rid of everything that's useless. And in fact, if we speak, it's because we speak of things that are very close, very deep for us, and at the same time we speak of all the futility with which we live. This stream of words crowns the act of speaking. The desert teaches you to forsake that. And it's very difficult, you know. So, I went there to depersonalize myself. That is, to no longer be who I appeared to be to others in Cairo.

JW: How long were you there each time?

EJ: I went for three or four days, all alone. I could have stayed longer, but sometimes I couldn't stand it anymore. It's extremely difficult. And I'll tell you why. For the Arab nomad who lives in the desert, what counts is the space. That's his domain, his country; those are his limits, they're unlimited, he needs that. The desert for him is life almost, because he's born in this desert, which has made him in its image. So, they're close to each other. While for the rest of us, who are formed by the city, by the culture and such, the desert is something that suddenly presents the end of all that. That is, no great culture, no great thought, subsists in the desert. In that infinity it becomes almost derisory. That doesn't mean it doesn't impel you to meditation, doesn't push you very far within yourself, but you're not going to just start reciting a poem by Victor Hugo in the desert, it's not possible. You understand the desert is much more listening than anything else.

Now, in the life we lead, listening practically doesn't exist.

People speak, but they don't listen to each other. Well, the desert is listening pushed to the extreme. And to which you can't even respond with words. You're obliged to submit. Because when you arrive, at first there's an amazing silence that completely cuts you off from the noise of the city. So, at the beginning, it's very beautiful. But after a certain time, the silence becomes heavier and heavier, because it's a silence that has cut you off from speech. You don't even need to speak if there are two of you, because there's nothing to be done. You tell someone even the minimum, "I'm thirsty, I need a glass of water," you can't say it. There is no glass of water, there is no thirst, there's nothing. You are there with yourself. So, you don't speak anymore except to say one or two phrases that are the most profound and at the same time nothing in themselves. For example, "it's beautiful," and that's all. Well, "it's beautiful" doesn't mean anything, you understand. You can't develop it. If people like us can't bear the desert, it's precisely because this silence is too strong. And after three or four days, you want to hear something that's not this nothing. Anything that says, "I'm walking, I'm living, I'm dying, I'm singing." Which makes me think of people in the Middle Ages who were locked up in towers and suddenly broke out screaming; it wasn't to call for help, it was to hear their own voice, to see that they were alive, to say, "I'm still alive." Well, the desert is a language of death. Because even if there are two of you, you speak in another way. There's a way of speaking to children, for example. There's a way of speaking to those who are going to die. It's not the voice we use when we go get a pack of cigarettes. It's another voice. And one that I had experienced precisely at the age of twelve, as I was saying, when my sister died practically in my arms. I spoke to her but my voice was different. It was a voice that followed the measure of hers, beyond measure, a smile which could only say the essential, that is, the last words one says before dying. In a certain way, we had reached the last word.

JW: But what did you see in yourself, for example, when you returned from the desert each time?

EJ: Well, it did me a lot of good, because I had the feeling of having saved something that had been fatally lost. I don't know what it was, but it was something that had enriched me. Because it had lifted off of me all that was too much. In the work of writing, one recognizes it. Because what is writing? In writing one lifts away everything to get to a word that's more profound. Writing is also a pushing inside, and that's what the desert brought me. So, I really felt quite enriched and more able to put up with the rest.

JW: How did you go back to writing after the desert?

EJ: Yes, that too was something that disturbed me enormously, because I asked myself how, living in Egypt, with this experience of the desert, did I manage to write Western poems, nearly surrealist? Thus, the opposite of what I was living. I think it's because it takes a lot of time with writing to make use of what a man has lived. You cannot write, at that very instant, what you are living. You live something very intense, you can neither speak nor write about it. It's only a long long time afterward, that it comes out in the writing.

JW: And yet between those two points, it's not really memory that connects them.

EJ: No, precisely. Because we ourselves are like a very sensitive engraving plate, and we don't know what marks us. In fact, everything marks us in a way. And what marks us most deeply we cannot know at first. But we can know later, sometimes long after, because precisely this thing that has marked us the most has been at work in us, more than other things. And then suddenly, it appears in another form. Writing alone is able to preserve all the moments lived, to restore them to us, with a memory that will recapture it all, and you'll be surprised to see how it all comes out again. Because it's based on what has touched us in our lives. Which the spoken word cannot produce, because it's sometimes inexpressible. In Egypt my poems which were read in France meant for me that I was entering into the family of French literature. But that's not the desert, right? And I had only dreamed of one thing, that is, to be published, to be integrated into French literature. So for me that was more important than this experience of the desert which I felt but could not manage to define. I've never spoken about it to anyone.

JW: Did Arab culture enter into your education?

EJ: Not right away. Because at first, of course, there were the French schools. French philosophers, French writers, the history of France, and so on. But fairly quickly I became very interested in the great writings that are the masterpieces of these countries. Unfortunately, in translation. I read Arabic, but still it was an effort, and I preferred to read them in translation. So, I had a certain rapport with Arab literature and philosophy, and then I realized that in the Moslem tradition, with the Sufis, for example, there were completely amazing things, as in the questioning of language. At the same time, I was also beginning to read the great Jewish mystics, who wrote in Hebrew and Arabic. All that is a part of the East, which is a world quite apart. Even the West, which penetrated considerably, didn't deeply mark the East, didn't shake things up. For example, in the time of Romanticism, they created an East of fantasies, the men with their harems, the sad women, and so on. It's not that at all. The West has lived on this image of the East which is completely false. And the East accepted the West, because the West brought it a philosophy, a way of thinking that was entirely new but that didn't deeply affect it. There is a wisdom in the East that the West doesn't know. The wisdom of its peasants has nothing to do with the wisdom of the French peasant who is crafty, who counts his pennies. These others have an extraordinary wisdom, one would say they've traversed the centuries. And it's the landscape too that leads to that. These people have a way of thinking that's extremely deep but doesn't appear to be. The intellectuals have certainly been influenced a lot, but they've digested the West poorly. In fact, the Westerners, the European intellectuals in Egypt, lived on Western culture much more than on Arab culture there. They lived that Arab wisdom and culture, but without perceiving it, like a background.

JW: What for you is meant by "the book"? Are there particular writers or books that you think of when you use the term?

EJ: Perhaps I should speak about precisely this book, *The Book of Questions*. Because it's then, after the break with Egypt and my arrival in France, that the desert finally imposed itself on my books. How did I have the idea of the book? I really had no idea. We had spoken a lot about Mallarmé, precisely concerning his idea of the book. But it's an idea that had never really attracted me, because I had always thought that a book which presents itself as *the* book, where everything we could put there would be inside it, all knowledge, it's not eternal. It would be a very ephemeral book, because we're not made to talk or write for eternity but for the moment. And it's the accumulation of moments that makes continuity. That's part of what I wanted to show in these books, in that they work in this way: the first is in the second, that is, the second continues the first and at the same time takes its place, and the third one too, and so on to the end. So that it obliges you each time to do a double reading, a reading forward and a reading backward. And for me, that is life itself. That is the book which could have a certain duration. As I think a book is made only by what's missing in the book. You have to leave the reader room to enter. Not only room to enter but room to add his thought there. If you close him in by telling everything, it's all over, you suffocate, you die. And repetition is the most constructive thing there is, because one never repeats oneself. Even if you say the same thing twice, it's not the same thing. Because there is a second that has passed, and the repetition is linked to this new second. There has been a second more lived, which will change things. Take the case of two people who love each other, and they say to each other, often, "I love you." Why? Once is enough. They repeat themselves because they know very well that what they say today is not exactly—even if they are the same words—what was said yesterday. There has been one more day that has caused us to change each time, and everything changes with us. And that everything carries the burden of this change.

So this book has haunted me, this book that passed for being ephemeral and that confronted the desert's eternity, this duration of nothingness. Because it was like a word that wanted to go further than it could go, so that it could be heard by the surrounding infinity. A second that was making its entry into eternity. Not to assume eternity but to allow it to be, because eternity is made of all the seconds. There where the instant was continually confronted by eternity, exactly as the thought found itself constantly confronted by the unthought which obliged it to go further. So, the book had become a real place for me.

Then there was also the fact that I'd left Egypt because of my Jewish origin. As I said, I was neither practicing nor a believer. I'd always lived in this country which was mine, and one fine day, when I wasn't prepared for it, I was forced to leave because of being Jewish. So, that posed certain problems for me. I told myself that we do not escape a certain Jewish condition. At the moment we least expect it, things explode and, without knowing why, you're forced to abandon everything and to lead a life of exile, of wandering. Finally, little by little, I realized that, since the Jew has not had a real homeland for thousands of years, since he's been obliged to leave one place for another each time, what did he do? He made the book his true home, his real territory. And you find in the books of the tradition, in the Kabbalah, in the Talmud too, a questioning of the book, because it's there that the Jew's freedom was exercised, it's in the book. It's there that he could speak and there that he could hear his words. Elsewhere that was refused him. And I found that there was such a similarity between the Jew and the writer that it struck me in an amazing manner. There's a text in the tradition that says that the book, that is, the Torah, was given to us in an order that's not the right one. And that it's up to us to find the book's order again. Well, that's the writer's whole task, to find the book's order. So, when they called Jews the people of the book, it's true, they are. And little by little I told myself, "Me too." Oh, I was at home in France, but it wasn't my landscape. And the book was substituted for all that. That is, I too made the book my place, my homeland, as if I could live only in the book. And from there on, I was caught in a movement, as if the book was making and unmaking itself with me inside.

So, an entire memory arose, everything that's marked us after Auschwitz imposed itself in the form of stories that are never told, that are presented just like that, like something which everyone knows and around which a whole reflection takes place. But a reflection which each time was that of the book, the book questioning the book. They've often said these last few years that the writer doesn't exist, that there's only the text. So I wonder, first of all, how a text can exist without a writer. But if they've said that, it's because the relationship with a text, when it is very deep, causes the writer to become his word to such a degree that he *becomes* text. That doesn't mean he's done away with. He *is* his word for once. And it's that word, which is supposed to be the most profound, the word of truth, that was my constant search. In the first trilogy, it's the story of Sarah and Yukel, two lovers who are deported. She's quite young, she comes back mad and her cries are the cries of her people. He ends up committing suicide, because he knows that he can't enter Sarah's madness and that only madness could have saved him, that lucidity after Auschwitz was untenable. So he kills himself, but also because he reads on the walls, like one read everywhere, "Mort aux Juifs," and so it's that simple thing, the drop that made the vase spill over.

And that's something I myself experienced profoundly. I left Egypt—forced to leave, chased out, losing all my things—to come to France where I am welcomed. And what do I see the very day of my arrival in Paris, on the walls of the building across from where I was living? "Mort aux Juifs, Jews Go Home." It shocked me. I said to myself, how is it that no one thinks of erasing it, of saying, "I don't accept it"? And so, I picked that up again in the book finally, in a much more dramatic manner for Yukel, who had lived through the deportation, who came out of it with his reason intact, who says, "It's not possible. One cannot, after that, keep one's sanity"; who has the case of Sarah his lover who is mad and raves. It's this simple graffiti which no one takes seriously but which came at that moment. So that was a story which was never told but around which of course all the reflections revolved, questioning of language, death, life, everything. Roughly, historicity.

Then, we come to two others, *Yaël* and *Elya*, in which there is a direct questioning of the word that failed after Auschwitz. Yaël is a woman who lies to the person she lives with, and he thinks he's done her in because he was seeking a word of truth. It's here that she lies because Yaël symbolizes the word, our word, our own speech as an individual. And Elya is the silence, the stillborn child who symbolizes the silence from which the word emerges. So, Yaël invents a life for this stillborn child, she refuses death, but only to be able to continue being a word, to speak. Then, we come to *Aely*, which is a very difficult book. It's the eye, the gaze of the law, it's the one who judges and who has not participated, who doesn't participate in anything. Who judges everything. And in fact, it is the gaze of the book upon the book, in short, upon everything that the book is. And the last book is the point, the smallest circle, where I thought I'd come to the end, and where I found a reference to the Kabbalah, where it says that God to make himself known revealed himself as a point.

JW: You had already read the Kabbalah by then?

EJ: No, no. That's later. All the references that I made to Judaism, that is, to the texts of the Talmud or whatever, are transformed in my work. They hadn't aimed to simulate it, but it was like a verification for me. All at once, I said, "Okay, now that I'm that far into Judaism, what is this Judaism? Let's look a little closer." And so, I rediscovered things there that I had written long before, with such precision it was as if they had been dictated to me. But transposed, transformed.

JW: How do you explain this rapport?

EJ: I don't know. It was a complete surprise.

JW: At what point did you start reading the Talmud and the Kabbalah?

EJ: Well after the first volumes of *The Book of Questions*. I found things that had come to me as a writer and not at all as a Jew. I was first of all a writer. And I realized that to be a writer is to be a Jew in a certain way, it's to live a certain Jewish condition, separated, exiled. And that the problems that are posed to Judaism are posed regularly to the writer, because the Jew had nothing but his book, which he had to force himself to read and to understand. Whence all the commentaries of the book. Whence the obsession with what's been written. Not just with what's been written but with what conceals what's been written. What must be read. As if there was a book hiding another book from me. And there too I draw a reference to the writer, because I deeply believe that each writer carries a book in him that he will never do. All the books he writes try to approach it. And if he never does this book, it's because if he managed to, he wouldn't write anymore. Because this would be *the* book. And if it's impossible, it's because our speech is not definitive. It's a speech made up of changes. We cannot express ourselves in a total manner, only by small steps.

JW: How is it there's a book inside? Doesn't that book also change?

EJ: Ah, it changes too. Each time it's a book that we want to do and that we carry in us. It's not a fixed book. It's an idea of a book, a book which keeps reworking itself but which is blank, illegible. And we ourselves try to render it legible. It's that, listening to the book. When we say there's an order to the book, it's true. I heard the articulation of the book, exactly like in the desert where you hear before seeing. It's amazing, because when you put your ear to the sand, you hear some noises, and then an hour later you see something appear. That's what I called the listening and the speech of the book. There's a book which speaks to you but which speaks so low you don't hear it. You hear odds and ends. And then all that becomes articulated.

JW: How did you proceed with *The Book of Questions*?

EJ: This idea of aphorisms carried the thing along. Then, at times it would develop into something larger. And I'd say, "That goes there, but between that and that, something's missing." Exactly like when two people speak and you miss a word. You say, "Please, I understood, but what did you say before? I didn't hear it." There's a gap. And then, all at once, something came, and I felt that it was what I hadn't heard at that moment. So, it was a perpetual act of listening, a continual questioning of the text. And it's an immense movement. Like when you swim in the sea, you submit to the waves, you cannot just swim as you like. You are caught in the water's movement. There too, I was taken up in the book's movement. And it's very curious, when the first book appeared, there was interest right away, and then those who were interested couldn't imagine that there would be a second book and a third. And I had even said to the editor, several times, "It will be a trilogy." I didn't know why, I hadn't written a note.

When the second book appeared, there wasn't disappointment but it didn't have the impact of the first. When the third appeared, they understood that a loop had been made, and I myself was the most surprised. When you think that *The Book of Questions* and *The Book of Resemblances* is ten volumes, that makes twenty years on the same book, practically. On the same questioning, the same listening. Twenty years! If they had told me that at the start, I never would have launched into such an adventure, because it's not easy to keep up. To arrive each time at the void, always at the beginning. I never conceived of the book as something that had to be done only by me, by my will, by something premeditated. As certain novelists, for example, construct their novels.

JW: Where does the next book come from each time? Is it something interior to the work?

EJ: Interior, absolutely. And if I speak of the book that's inside the book, it's because each time there was like a book that came out of the book. That which is in parentheses, for example, in italics, is another book that emerged from this book.

JW: What you understand now about these books, did you understand it then?

EJ: No, not at all. I was in total darkness. I didn't understand what I was in the process of doing, I didn't understand the break I had made. I suffered terribly from it, because I didn't see where this adventure was going to lead me. Each time I felt myself a little more cut off from French literature, which I was so attached to; I felt that I was losing my filiation with it, that I wouldn't find again the great writers whom I relied on. And what demonstrated this to me was my correspondence with Gabriel Bounoure, who was an extraordinary man, a fantastic essayist quite a bit older than me, and who participated in the creation of these books. Because I was sending him passages I was writing, and he too entered into a questioning, "But why that, why not that," etcetera. Which shows how nothing was fixed in advance.

JW: How did you know you were on the right track?

EJ: I felt this development intimately. Something else I realized is that the question, which is fundamental in these books, unfolded in a manner that was almost outside of me. There is a passage where a young disciple asks his master, "If you never give me an answer, how shall I know that you are the master and I the disciple?" And the master responds, "By the order of the questions." When you live the questions deeply, you cannot ask certain questions before others. The questions are posed as you go along, until the last one, which remains a question. And since all the questions reap only unsatisfactory answers, to a certain extent, the question continues. If the Talmud is a book without end, it is because the questioning is without end. How does the Talmud proceed? By rigor and by questioning. And so, you find in these books, for example, a question in the first one which you find formulated differently again in the third. You have to go through two whole books before that question returns, and then it will bring a different answer. And the reason there are all these characters that I call rabbis, their voices, is to permit each one to say a thing that is sometimes in contradiction to another. Whence the flow of these characters who enter and question, question. And they question in time and outside of time.

One hears a lot about the *récit éclaté*, but this is an example for me of what is the true *récit éclaté*. It's not about bursting the story itself apart, it's to burst apart the place, by abolishing it. How can we situate these imaginary rabbis in their time when it's never stated? We see it in the long run by what they say. That is, the oldest say the simplest things, and those who are contemporary say the things that are the most developed, the most complicated, because they've inherited all that. So, they speak in and out of time, and there is no place. There is no time and there *is* an everyday. It is a time outside of time within time itself. Whence the importance of the story, because the story is situated by its details. Without fixing a date, we recognize it. It's given a dimension that it would never have if it were only a story about something just presented in that way.

All that, then, makes this sort of permanent rupture, because I don't believe in continuity. Continuity is made of ruptures, and we ourselves are this rupture. And the rupture is the broken tablets too, at the start. Because if Moses was forced to break the tablets, it is because the Hebrew people could not accept a word that came from elsewhere, a word without origin. He had to break the tablets so that they would understand, so that the human word could enter inside, after the anger. Something human passed through. So that the Hebrew people understood, they comprehended it. Otherwise, if it is a word coming from the invisible, from a God, what is it? The break was needed. And it is that break that has always haunted me with metaphors of injury and so on. Because I deeply believe that since Auschwitz, the word in general is wounded, and our speech is different. It's as if we are speaking with someone who has an injury. We cannot escape it. And if you have an ear that is very attuned to what young people or those who are not so young are able to say to each other today, you hear behind it something that has been deeply affected. And what has been deeply affected is *in* that speech. The words say the same things, obviously, but at the same time they tell of their injury, in a certain way. For me it's entirely evident, I hear it like that. In even the simplest, most ordinary speech, I hear that there is a weakness. There is a weakness. That is why we can no longer put up with moral judgments, things like that. We are fragile beings, very fragile now. And we can no longer speak like before. Because we can only speak with this fragility and from this fragility. We know that such things have been accepted that in fact it puts everything in question, even culture. As I said to Marcel Cohen, to the statement by Adorno, the German philosopher, who had said that we cannot write after Auschwitz, I say that we must write. But writing is something else entirely. We cannot write like before.

JW: But how do we read this other writing? How should we read *The Book of Questions*, are there certain ways?

EJ: Listen, I myself don't know. For me, now, it's a reading of the whole work. That is, I cannot imagine reading these books without reading all ten volumes. Because each brings something to the other. The first book could be read by itself quite well, and all the books can, somewhat. But in my opinion, one misses a lot, above all this movement of the book, how it makes itself, and then how it unmakes itself and makes itself again. And each time further on. I understand quite well that one may not be able to read all ten and that only one at a time can be translated. In each one there is the book, the essentials. But I believe they are books that call for the continuity of reading. But this said, how to enter into these books? I don't know, there are people who have begun by reading small bits. I think that's a rather good way of reading, a phrase here, a phrase there. One is not in the book, but that doesn't matter. One circles around it, at the threshold. And then, if one happens to enter it, to see again from the start how it's articulated, how one page calls to another, how one question leads to another, how the story gathers more and more pathos.

It is very difficult, in speaking of these books, to try to circumscribe them. One cannot. Perhaps that is the reading, to grasp it by fragments and then with all this baggage to enter inside. And then to participate more deeply in the book. That's one of the reasons most true readers end up by assuming these books, that is, by making it their story, their book. I know people who have gone off with it into the desert, others into the mountains—they could only read the book like that. I ask myself, "What does it do that it can work for certain people in such a way?" That's not normal for a reader with a book. There are also people who say they can't read it, who read a lot and who've had a hard time reading these books. And there are people who don't read anything and all at once say to you, "Ah, there it is." It's something else.

JW: Perhaps you've found a way where the words are not wounded.

EJ: I can't explain it myself, because with me it works in the same way as with them. Each book for me was very very difficult.

What allowed me to go to these limits in the end—which are the limits of the book but also my own limits—was the fact that I was conscious that one does not say it all, one cannot say everything, and that each time there is still something more to say, still a question. There is still a new adventure, even when one reaches total effacement. For example, this word has been taken all the way to its end for me now. The book that haunts me at the moment is a book I'll call *Le livre du dialogue*, where I ask myself the question, "Can there be a dialogue, for me, now? And what is this dialogue? What dialogue can I establish?" There is always a dialogue, because thought itself is a dialogue. Writing is a monologue, and at the same time it's a dialogue. But what else do I still have to say to another person? To one's questioning, what word shall I be able to formulate, not to respond, but to keep up this dialogue.

JW: Is *Le livre du dialogue* one book?

EJ: I don't know. I'm bringing it along like that, there are passages that come. It is already articulated to a certain extent. The first part is "L'avant-dialogue." Second part, "Carnet," reflections. Third, "Après le dialogue," the dialogue hasn't taken place. Fourth, "L'abîme." Fifth, "Le dialogue." I don't know if they're the final titles, but for me it evolved like that. It's a way of listening.

JW: Does it pick up any things from the previous books?

EJ: No. It's a bit like *Le petit livre de la subversion*, that's not part of the series but it's still a book of the same family.

JW: You've said that *Le petit livre* is a sort of key to all the other books, as in the way it speaks of subversion.

EJ: Yes, because they've talked a lot about subversion in *The Book of Questions* and *The Book of Resemblances*, and I wanted to see a little closer what subversion was. I realized that subversion is something that someone else cannot suspect as such. And if there is subversion in *The Book of Questions*, it's because we become disturbed unawares. That's where subversion works. And that led me to think that the more one is oneself, the more one is subversive in a way, in that the difference stands out. The great subversive books, for example, were not written with the aim of being subversive. As in the case of Kafka, not only did he never for a second think of being subversive, but he thought that his books were not modern. He was envious of other books, such as those of Brod. "I don't know how to write," he says. "What I've written is uninteresting." And all at once, they're revealed to be the most subversive books. His books are disturbing because he was most profoundly himself: he wrote as only Kafka could write. They became subversive after.

JW: You have written and are planning other books outside *The Book of Questions*. What are they?

EJ: Some small essays, with aphorisms and such, have been published by Fata Morgana press, with the painter Tapiés. The first book is called *Ça suit son cours*. There's a new book, *Dans la double dépendance du dit*, which is about my relationship with writing, other writers, and their thought—contemporary writers mostly. A third collection, that I haven't written, will be about Kafka and the Prophets. As these aren't essays that try to show what a certain writer is but rather my relationship to the text through him, I would like to show what in Kafka opened certain paths for me which perhaps are not in Kafka.

JW: By way of his subversion.

EJ: Right, what I experienced as entirely subversive.

JW: Have you seen any particular differences between Jewish and non-Jewish readers of your books?

EJ: Not in the reading of the true reader, who, Jewish or not, has really felt these books in quite a strong way. I think a Jew could read these books differently, but not in what he has deep inside. In what he has superficially. That is, he'll recognize certain anecdotes, rites really—a Jew recognizes them right away. But that's the exterior aspect. When one reads these books deeply, one perceives that this is a Judaism gone beyond, carried further, toward the universal. And it's through that that there is a real encounter. Precisely by being open, by questioning, by refusing everything that is fixed. So, in this sense, readers have felt that questioning deeply, and these levels have been assumed in the same way by non-Jewish as by Jewish readers.

JW: What was the reaction of Jews?

EJ: As everything in the end is Jewish for Jews, those who were the most sectarian ended up saying that perhaps the book is Jewish. But at first it was greatly disputed. There were people who attacked me saying that it had nothing to do with Judaism, that it was a fantastic Judaism, that there was no rupture in Judaism. All right, I never said it was Jewish. I said, "That's my experience as a Jew, that's how I have lived a certain Judaism." I think that Judaism is evident throughout the book, that true Judaism is there. And what's surprising now is the acceptance of this point of view, which was simply personal. And yet it's not so surprising, because there are many ways to live this Judaism. There is a religious Judaism and an atheist Judaism. And we cannot tell the difference between the two. Because never have we seen the faithful speak with such freedom in any other religion. As with the Talmud, they accept the word because it's the Bible, but at the same time they discuss it, they have to understand it. In other religions, they don't discuss, it's faith. While in Judaism, no, they must discuss it.

Also, it's very curious, if someone wants to convert, for example, never will a real rabbi ask him at the start if he believes in God. You don't see that. He'll say to him, "Why do you want to be Jewish? What madness has come over you that you want to be Jewish?" So, he has to explain himself. And it's not easy. Because Judaism is something else, it's an ethic, it's a way of living this Judaism, of questioning, of being open, of solidarity. Of memory. And that's something that annoys the Jew when he sees someone converting to Judaism. Because he says, "He cannot have this memory that we have." And it's very true. With each event the Jew puts himself in question again, as a Jew, as if he had lived a life five thousand years long. And one wonders why. The French, for example, they fight the war of 1914, they're not going to think of the Gauls. While us, that is the Jews, when anything happens, they remember. There's an unhappiness, oooh, that goes back five thousand years. They bring out a whole endless history, as if they themselves had lived it. And they do live it each time. They live an entire history with each event. Which is completely amazing.

JW: But that too recalls the writer, with memory, because each thing . . .

EJ: Each thing comes back to them. There's a weight to words, and the weight for the Jew is very heavy, you know. It's undeniable, words have the same meaning, but they don't have the same effect for each of us. When we speak of death, for example, we speak with the memory of all our dead. When we speak of love, we speak of the memories, or the experiences, of love that we have. After all, that is normal. Whence the difficulty sometimes of speaking with another. Because we speak of the same thing, with the same words, but the things are different. When you're speaking of sorrow, for example, while the other person speaks to you of theirs, you feel that there is really something between you, and then all of a sudden there is a chasm, because their pain isn't quite like yours. While, when one Jew looks at another Jew, he knows his pain. That is something that is in each Jew. He knows. When one Jew meets another Jew, he doesn't have to tell the story of his life, he doesn't need to. That too is why, in these books, I didn't want to tell these stories. I realized it was much stronger like that.

JW: Converts can't enter into that experience then.

EJ: They cannot. Because they convert for purely religious reasons, right? They don't have this lived experience, which isn't learned.

JW: At the same time, Jews who convert to Christianity can't escape it.

EJ: They can't escape it. Max Jacob, for example, and there was a group like that, who thought they had to live the experience of Christ. That is, to begin by being Jewish, in order to arrive at Christianity, which is like the fulfillment of Judaism. I have letters from Max where he says, "I have always been tormented as a Jew and as a Christian." There is a meditation by Max Jacob that I found where he says, "Thank you, my God, for having made me a Jew." That is to say, "for having made me know all the Jew's suffering." But the real Jewish experience for me is not that; it is an atheist experience.

JW: How do you understand Derrida's statement that "Jabès isn't Jewish"?

EJ: I understood it very well when he wrote it, because I don't really know what it is to be Jewish. Judaism for me is a certain lived experience that I rediscovered through the book. And I realized that what I was saying as a writer was being received as a Jewish statement.

JW: What is the significance of names for you, as in the latter volumes of *The Book of Questions*, with Yaël, Elya, Aely, El?

EJ: A name is the only way we have to make our existence known to another. If we're not named, we're nothing. So, we assume this name, we become it. And that is the power of naming, it makes you exist and at the same time it effaces you. What is important in those names is the word "El," which means God in Hebrew. But in the Kabbalah, when you invert the letters of a name, that is its death. So, Yaël, Elya, Aely, and El which remains. It is a way of showing too the effacement, by nothing but the words.

JW: I'd like to return to the question of writing and something you said to Marcel Cohen in your book of interviews with him, *From the Desert to the Book*, that "at no moment is the novelist listening to the page, listening to its whiteness and its silence." But is there not a certain compromise between the novel and the writing that you do?

EJ: Certainly. I'm convinced of it. Perhaps I said that in a way that was too direct. What I meant is that the working of the text is not the novelist's concern. First, what he wants is for his characters to be able to speak loosely, as in life, imposing on the book something he himself wants to say. So, he prepares his characters, watches them live, and then he makes them live again in his book. The book may grow to such a point, as there are some very great novels, that it becomes the story that it tells, giving a dimension that only writing can produce.

But at the start it's a way of proceeding that is contrary to my own. For me *writing* is the adventure to live. And I live it as writing. I myself become a word, I become a phrase, and what the phrases say, they say it to me too in that way. My flesh is there, you understand. While the characters that I have introduced, they themselves are only the flesh of the book. Because if there wasn't all this questioning of pain and so on in and around the book, the characters wouldn't have been able to be presented in this manner. So, everything that is their suffering, their life, isn't told but is done by this story of the book. It's the book that becomes this story at such a moment, with everything it carries as questioning. The book comes to substitute itself for the universe, in order to become the universe itself. And into which I cannot introduce something, not a star into the sky. I must let all that happen. And in general a novel is situated in a precise place, one wants to write fairly specific things, to put characters into the scene that are quite precise. I don't say that everything is premeditated with a novelist, because he lets himself be taken by the life of his characters, they live. But he uses words so he can say what he wants to make known. He doesn't let himself be taken along by the words, profoundly expressed by them. He makes use of words in order to get his story across, to give life to his characters. That is the difference. The true writer does not enter into the book, he *is* in the book, while the novelist has characters enter the book with him, they're imposed.

JW: Yes, but it seems to me that a writer can . . .

EJ: . . . do both. Certainly. On the condition that he's sensitive to that. But often they're not. Because what counts is the anecdote, after all, the story to tell, whether it's an unfortunate son, a disappointed love, or whatever. Fine, he makes beautiful things happen. When he lets himself go, all right then, there we know the writer. At that point, the story little by little makes itself a part of the book, even if it is that of a novelist.

JW: Since you say that everything in your books is lived, I wonder who is this writer who in *El, or The Last Book* jumps from the fourth story of the narrator's building, and who in *Intimations The Desert* is found dead along the desert trail.

EJ: In short, it's the image of the writer, therefore of myself. You know, writing sometimes leads to suicide, because it leads to the impossibility of speech, of the word. Many writers have written a lot about the impossibility of writing, right, which is absurd. Because if it's impossible to write, how can we write? On the contrary, there is a possibility, but we only write in this impossibility, knowing we can neither really speak nor keep silent. We want to succeed, to go all the way there, but we know we shall never be able to. Each time there's something like an innocence that makes us say, "All right, now I'm going to state . . ." It's like this thought perpetually up against the unthought, and it forces the unthought finally to let go of something.

JW: But it's an image that seems to haunt you a little.

EJ: Yes, but it's always the haunting of suicide. And it's also in *The Last Book* because in the end, as he has fallen from very high up, he constitutes nothing but a red dot. And this red dot is the title of the book. So it's to show how much this adventure of writing can lead to suicide. After all, every work is a wager with oneself. How do you explain, for example, painters who commit suicide when they're at their peak? So, who have no reason to. Who have starved all their lives, all of a sudden they're recognized, glory, one reads . . . ah, they've committed suicide. It's something between you and your conscience. And no one can do anything for someone else. It's a gamble. You see sometimes a person spends hours on a word and then changes it for another word, which represents something entirely different. Most people don't even notice this one little word. But they notice later, in the general structure of the book. Because if there hadn't been that, the book couldn't have been done that way, it wouldn't have had that force, that beauty, that harmony. But it's a wager with oneself.

JW: How do you work? You wrote much of *The Book of Questions* while riding the metro, for example, but what about now?

EJ: I don't work in a continual manner at all, it's not possible. I believe I work twenty-four hours a day, but without writing. I write very little—what I mean is, when I write one page, when it comes, that's a lot. But that page, it's been four or five days in the works or six or eight months. I write in small chunks, but without leaving the book. Like *Le livre du dialogue*, I've written other things on the side, but this book doesn't leave me. It is in my thoughts all the time.

JW: But can you hold on to more than one book at a time?

EJ: One thinks perhaps of several books, but there is only one

that's going to be done—out of all the others. And sometimes for me that is unforeseeable at the start. That is, I don't
know how this book is going to happen. All I know is that a
couple of phrases have come to me. It was very evident in the
poems. In *Je bâtis ma demeure*, I knew that when I wrote the
first line the poem was no longer lost, I could go away from
it, go to the movies, come back, I knew I was going to continue it. And I knew within a few lines how many pages it
would be. Because I would feel it in such a way.

JW: What was it about the metro that enabled you to write there?

EJ: Necessity. But it came at a point when I'd been carrying *The
Book of Questions* in me for a long time. You know, when you
do work that's completely different from your own work as a
writer, you are always a bit impatient to return to writing.
That has a double effect. It makes you suffer because you
want to write and you can't, because you're obliged to earn a
living and you have no choice. And at the same time it hastens your return to writing. As soon as you can you try to
benefit the most from this leftover time, in order to write.
But I realized something too, that in the end the writing time
is very limited, that we don't need a lot of time to write. Well,
in the metro, as the book emerged, I couldn't leave it anymore. I was really like a prisoner to something that demanded to be done. This journey between my home and
where I worked allowed me now and then to mark things
down, which remained either in the form of aphorisms, when
they had really matured, or as the beginning of a page or two
that I managed to write on Saturday or Sunday, when my
time was completely free. Consequently, I can't say the metro
was a special place for me, it was the opportunity. But I write
best at home. In general, travel cuts me off totally from
writing.

JW: And when you were working in a job?

EJ: I was thinking of the book. And that is something that really
astounded me, because perhaps it's an ability to split myself
in two. Even when I participate in seminars, when I'm speaking, whether about my books or not, when I'm answering a
question, I have the feeling of not leaving the book. There is
a continual listening. I'm not saying that all that is very

clear—it's not—but I know there is a work that continues to be done inside me. Because everything is useful to me for the book. My books are a perpetual commonplace. The most everyday things have been very important for me. To such a point that I thought of keeping a diary, not to put the things I thought most important there but the most ordinary things. I wanted to set aside everything that seemed important to me during the day in order to keep the most commonplace things, which hadn't even any significance. Because, I told myself, the important things must be left to work on their own, they shouldn't be written. We won't lose them, because one way or another we'll find them again one day, in another form.

JW: Do you have any problem with beginning to write?

EJ: Well, I always delay the moment of writing. Often I do anything—chores, arrange books, hang up a painting—all that so as not to start writing. I feel that the moment's arrived, and so at that point I'm seized with panic. I go out, I walk two or three hours, I come back and then it's as if I can't escape something. And the moment I pick up my pen, I tell myself right away that it's all over now, I can't escape anymore. I'm caught in a trap. And at the same time, there is also a certain relief. But it's not at all the pleasure of writing.

JW: Do you know what you're going to write at that point?

EJ: No. I feel there's something that's going to be expressed and I'm taken up in it. What starts it into motion suddenly is a phrase, and I know it's going to start there. As if that phrase has opened a door to you. Valéry said, for example, that the title of a book or a text is the last phrase. That the first line is the last, like a mirror effect. But it's after everything's been done that that appears.

JW: Do you have a preferred time of day for writing?

EJ: No. Perhaps now, in the last few years, it's in the morning. Before it was at night, very late.

JW: Do you see any reason for preferring the morning?

EJ: I think that during sleep things set themselves in order, that a phrase takes its real form and comes back to you the next day. As if the truth were shaped or modeled in sleep.

JW: Do you take any notes when you're working on a book?

EDMOND JABÈS 199

EJ: Never. Not a note. Each time I've always found myself at the beginning of an adventure.

JW: You've said that with *The Book of Questions* there were at least three or four versions of each book. What determined the shaping of each book? How did the versions differ?

EJ: This is the way I work: I start writing the first pages by hand. When I reach ten or fifteen pages, when I correct these pages, I absolutely have to type them out because I can't go any further. I need to have a certain lull from what has been written before. So, at that point I type out those pages. And I continue writing the rest, to then correct these other pages on the typewriter. Then I take up the whole thing again, the pages already typed out but corrected, plus the new ones that weren't in the typewriter, and I type out the whole thing. And then I correct the whole thing together again. That is, there's one correction directly with the text, and each time I add more pages there's a new correction, because it's what the other pages contribute that shows me that either there are things missing or that there is too much. And the book is done in that way. There are three or four, sometimes more.

JW: How have you known when you've reached the end with each book?

EJ: I never knew. It's never the end. It's the end of the book, that is, it's always unfinished, but it's where I feel I cannot go on anymore. I feel it.

JW: Have you, by the same token, found that the beginning wasn't the real beginning either?

EJ: Well, yes. In all these books, there is "The Fore-Book," "The Before the Fore-Book," and so on. It's always the beginning that isn't one. It's the book that is in the act of becoming but itself doesn't know how. That's why I kept them, they're like rumors of things that are coming. And then the book takes shape.

JW: What are some of the readings that have been important to you, after Baudelaire, Mallarmé, Max Jacob?

EJ: First of all, the reading of poets. But, for example, the reading of Maurice Blanchot, who is someone that is very close to me. And the writers with whom I have affinities, philosophers like Jean Grenier, Emmanuel Levinas, Derrida, writers like

Blanchot, Michel Leiris, Gabriel Bounoure, where there was also a questioning of the book inside.

JW: You've described Blanchot's attitude that certain friendships have "nothing to gain in a tête-à-tête, that the silence in which they bathe must not be broken, even in their strongest moments." What happened when you met?

EJ: I've never seen him.

JW: Still?

EJ: No, we don't know each other. For Blanchot what happens in absence is much more important than meeting, much more intense. And in effect, the correspondence that I have with him is very intense, very strong, because it is at precise moments. I have never met him personally, but he remains very close to me.

JW: You've never spoken with him on the telephone?

EJ: Never. I tried twice to see him, but he didn't want to because, well, I respect his position a great deal. I understand quite well that our meeting would only bring a momentary pleasure, after all, to see each other, to shake hands. But on the one hand, there are the books, and on the other hand, now and then a sign that takes on all its importance, because, as far as I'm concerned, I only write him at very important moments of my life. So, I know that he exists, I know that he's there. And he knows too that I'm here, on this side.

JW: There's a writer who lived his book so thoroughly that he was consumed by it: Proust. What did you find for yourself in Proust?

EJ: First of all, memory—his work about memory—and then, the great movement of Proust's books, which is very close to me. That is, there's a proximity to what is essential for me. It's not in the characters and the anecdotes, although he was saying things that coincide a great deal with what I have been able to say. But it's above all in his conception of the book, which for him was also not at all premeditated. One is swept along by these books because after all the whole pursuit is, for me too, one single book. Obviously, Proust's writing is entirely different, but it's carried along like mine by the breath. You know, we work with the heart and the soul, but we work with the body above all. The body imitates the writing. It's curious, he suffered from asthma, like me. Asthma has made me have to put in blank space sometimes, so that the phrase could breathe, because I'm suffocating and I feel that the phrase is suffocating. So, that led me to the aphorism, out of necessity. He carried the phrase on and on, until he ran out of breath.

JW: What has been the academic and critical response to your work?

EJ: Given that one of the first texts written on my books was by Derrida, in 1964 when he wasn't yet very well known, he gave these books a sort of direction. That is, when he became known, these books were mostly read by philosophers. Certain people thought that I was a theoretician too, that there wasn't this whole side of pure creation, though Derrida saw it. Besides that, there was also Blanchot's fine essay and several by Bounoure, which showed that this work was entirely apart. Many spoke about the Jewish problem as well, and there was also a lot of interest among poets. Yet, even in the universities here in France, all the doctoral theses that have been done on my books are in philosophy. At the level of the master's or beyond they are in philosophy, psychoanalysis, linguistics. There's been one single study in literature. I was a bit disappointed that they don't speak about my writing itself, of a certain poetry that is in this form. Because if I wasn't a poet, I wouldn't have been able to write these books. I listen to the text like something that sounds in my ear; if it doesn't sound right I don't accept it. That's why these aphorisms are so condensed, there is the poet's voice behind it.

Now, when they've said I was a philosopher too, I don't think so. The philosopher, when he writes a philosophical text, tries to circle the object of his thought, in making a concept perhaps, and then to develop it. While for me, this job of development is hidden, it's done inside me, and what is said is the end of all this development inside me. As if each time it was the last phrase, the last thing remaining from a long interrogation. That's how these aphorisms are presented, as in the process of thought, what has been kept, canceled, kept, canceled, and at the end one says the thing. Which is why thought itself is a dialogue, and these phrases are what is at the end of the dialogue. The theories one draws from my books are theories based on *my* practice of the text and not on a general practice. One can retrace the steps after but not before. Before is the adventure. Everything for me is based on risk. It's not worth writing if one doesn't take this risk, there is no writing. And one feels that in a book, when the author risks making a fool of himself at every page. When you think, for example, of the surrealists, who did all they did, which was interesting to a certain extent, but when Breton talked about "*le hasard objectif*," to take a revolver and go shoot it into a crowd, he never did it. But Artaud, he went all the way. They couldn't play around with Artaud. All right, Artaud was ill, but he took all the risk that was writing, he faced it in the most hazardous manner. That is what touches me deeply, it's the only thing that interests me in writing, the risk taken by the writer.

JW: Is that why you felt that each book was so difficult?

EJ: I can't say there weren't moments of joy, because at the moment one writes, or one has freed a text, one breathes. But it's not a liberation, on the contrary. Writing never liberates you, it enchains you more and more. There is a moment when one is riveted to the text, and one says, "All right, I said what I wanted to, what's written there is really me." So there is a moment of pleasure, but for me it's extremely brief, because the book has never been a continuity, it was impossible. A book always begins at each page. And the further along, the more difficult it is, because the book has carried the weight of what has been written before. That is, as it continues, the book has assumed the preceding pages. Without appropriating them.

JW: When you finished the first seven books, were you thinking right away of what followed, *The Book of Resemblances*?

EJ: No, I was completely lost. And then the resemblance that is in *The Book of Questions* began to work. I said to myself, I'm going to return to that, this questioning that wasn't over for me, but by the roundabout way of resemblance. That was the three volumes of *The Book of Resemblances*. Each book ends with a trial. The first is the trial of a soul that they condemn, because it had said that there was no Judaism, there was no book, that the book was impossible. So, they condemn him, the writer-judge says, "How can you say there is no book? Look at the books I have written that make up the whole library. You mean they are not books? You're a traitor." The judge who is a Jew says, "How can you say there is no Judaism?" etcetera. And they decapitate him. So it's a soul without a head, without anything. And he tells them, "At last I shall become this total stranger."

In the second *Book of Resemblances*, there is the second trial. The judges have begun to doubt their sentence. They say, "When you get right down to it, what is the book? How were we able to condemn in the name of the book? Which book? Who can define a book?" And then another one says, "I condemned him in the name of Judaism. What is Judaism, in a word?" And so, they say there is no possibility of judgment. They go away like that into the desert. But who remains? The public, the people, who say, "But then how shall we live without a judge, without knowing?" It ends like that, they remain in suspense. And then, the last is one of the characters who all of a sudden decides to make himself totally forgotten. He goes off all alone into the desert, believing that everything is erased behind him. And another sends him word, telling him, "Don't worry about your tracks. You alone cannot erase them." Which means that we are not in charge of leaving our mark. If today I think that by erecting a monument in the Place de l'Opéra I will be eternal, that would be crazy, because three days later they look at the monument and don't even know who it is. They see a guy on a horse or a man standing, nobody cares. But a real mark, one which remains and doesn't belong to us, it's the other who possesses it, who preserves it. It's not merely the remembrance, it's the mark that you've been able to leave on the other person. It is the other who can make you exist. Otherwise, one is nothing. So after that book I was very ill at ease. Fortunately, right away there was a trip to the United States, it took me away from this a little. And when I returned, I began the interviews with Marcel Cohen. That was an entirely different experience, it helped me a lot. It took six months, five days a week.

JW: Why did that help you? Because it was someone else's questions?

EJ: That's right. Because it was something else. And while it's troublesome to be questioned, it's also reassuring, because there is the other who is present. Exactly like when one is sad, for whatever reason, and talks to someone else. Obviously, we don't know the questions we must ask him, but because it is another who asks questions about his sorrow, we help him to bear it. Because we have entered into the sorrow. Like you, you've entered into the books, so I sense a friend, an accomplice. And a real accomplice, because to a certain extent we take almost the same risk.

JW: What led you to the trials at the end of the three books?

EJ: It's my trial. It's my own putting in question.

JW: In a traditional narrative, one retains what is read by means of the story. In these books there is no story, in that sense. How does one then retain what is read, how do you see it working?

EJ: When I wrote the first *Book of Questions*, I didn't know what it was, for the good reason that I couldn't precisely manage to fix the starting points, to tell myself, "Ah, here is what's important, I'll start from here." Well, there, no one thing takes priority over another. But that's not noticeable when you read the first book. When you read the first one, there is a story. Even if it's not told, it's upsetting. You are involved with things you feel very deeply, the story, the pain, the rapport with language in all its force, and at the same time the restlessness of the book, the obsession. It's curious, you're a bit out of your element at the start, but you believe there is a certain point you can really rely on. When you get to the second, you perceive that the points on which you thought you relied have vanished, and that by the questioning and the forward movement of the book, something else has risen to the surface. So, your reaction is: "Have I really understood, have I really seen, really read the first book? I have to go back and look." It's a movement of coming and going, from one to the other. And this movement leads you to the third book, which will also enter into that. It's a perpetual going around, around practically the same thing, which you seek to surround better each time. And since you cannot surround it, it's a deepening. I think the reader follows this movement. That doesn't mean all readers enter the book in the same manner, each has a personal way. But in the long run, they're obliged to make their way through these books in the same manner. That's why I said though one can read these books separately, for me now, with the distance of time, I think if one really wants to read them, one has to read them all. Because each one plays off of another—it's like a game of mirrors.

Bibliography of Works in English

JEAN-CLAUDE CARRIÈRE

Monsieur Hulot's Holiday. Translated by A. E. Ellis. New York: Crowell, 1959.

The Little Black Book: A Play in Two Acts. Translated by Jerome Kilty. New York: French, 1973.

The Mahabharata: A Play Based upon the Indian Epic Classic. Translated by Peter Brook. New York: Harper & Row, 1987.

E. M. CIORAN

The Temptation to Exist. Translated by Richard Howard. Chicago: Quadrangle, 1968.

The Fall into Time. Translated by Richard Howard. Chicago: Quadrangle, 1970.

The New Gods. Translated by Richard Howard. New York: Quadrangle, 1974.

A Short History of Decay. Translated by Richard Howard. New York: Viking, 1975.

The Trouble with Being Born. Translated by Richard Howard. New York: Viking, 1976.

Drawn and Quartered. Translated by Richard Howard. New York: Viking, 1983.

History and Utopia. Translated by Richard Howard. New York: Viking, 1987.

Anathemas and Admirations. Translated by Richard Howard. New York: Arcade, 1991.

JULIO CORTÁZAR

The Winners. Translated by Elaine Kerrigan. New York: Pantheon, 1965.

Hopscotch. Translated by Gregory Rabassa. New York: Pantheon, 1966.

Blow Up and Other Stories. Translated by Paul Blackburn. New York: Pantheon, 1967.

Cronopios and Famas. Translated by Paul Blackburn. New York: Pantheon, 1969.

62: A Model Kit. Translated by Gregory Rabassa. New York: Pantheon, 1972.

All Fires the Fire and Other Stories. Translated by Suzanne Jill Levine. New York: Pantheon, 1973.

A Manual for Manuel. Translated by Gregory Rabassa. New York: Pantheon, 1978.

A Change of Light and Other Stories. Translated by Gregory Rabassa. New York: Knopf, 1980.

We Love Glenda So Much and Other Tales. Translated by Gregory Rabassa. New York: Knopf, 1983.

A Certain Lucas. Translated by Gregory Rabassa. New York: Knopf, 1984.

Around the Day in Eighty Worlds. Translated by Thomas Christensen. San Francisco: North Point, 1986.

Nicaraguan Sketches. Translated by Kathleen Weaver. New York: Norton, 1989.

CARLOS FUENTES

Where the Air Is Clear. Translated by Sam Hileman. New York: Ivan Obolensky, 1960.

The Good Conscience. Translated by Sam Hileman. New York: Ivan Obolensky, 1961.

Aura. Translated by Lysander Kemp. New York: Farrar Straus & Giroux, 1964.

The Death of Artemio Cruz. Translated by Sam Hileman. New York: Farrar Straus & Giroux, 1964.

A Change of Skin. Translated by Sam Hileman. New York: Farrar Straus & Giroux, 1968.

Holy Place. Translated by Suzanne Jill Levine (in *Triple Cross*). New York: Dutton, 1972.

Terra Nostra. Translated by Margaret Sayers Peden. New York: Farrar Straus & Giroux, 1976.

The Hydra Head. Translated by Margaret Sayers Peden. New York: Farrar Straus & Giroux, 1978.

Burnt Water. Translated by Margaret Sayers Peden. New York: Farrar Straus & Giroux, 1980.

Distant Relations. Translated by Margaret Sayers Peden. New York: Farrar Straus & Giroux, 1982.

The Old Gringo. Translated by Margaret Sayers Peden and the author. New York: Farrar Straus & Giroux, 1985.

Myself with Others: Selected Essays. New York: Farrar Straus & Giroux, 1988.

Christopher Unborn. Translated by Alfred Mac Adam and the author. New York: Farrar Straus & Giroux, 1989.

Constancia and Other Stories for Virgins. Translated by Thomas Christensen. New York: Farrar Straus & Giroux, 1990.

BRION GYSIN

To Master—A Long Goodnight. New York: Creative Age Press, 1946.

The Exterminator (with William S. Burroughs). San Francisco: Auerhahn Press/Dave Haselwood Books, 1960.

Minutes to Go (with William S. Burroughs, Gregory Corso, and Sinclair Beiles). Paris: Two Cities, 1960; San Francisco: Beach Books, 1968.

The Process. Garden City: Doubleday, 1969; London: Quartet, 1985.

Brion Gysin Let the Mice In. West Glover, Vt.: Something Else Press, 1973.

The Third Mind (with William S. Burroughs). New York: Viking, 1978.

Here to Go: Planet R–101 (interviews with Terry Wilson). San
    Francisco: Re/Search, 1982; London: Quartet, 1985.
Stories. Oakland: Inkblot, 1984.
The Last Museum. New York: Grove, 1986.
Morocco Two. Oakland: Inkblot, 1986.

EUGÈNE IONESCO

Four Plays (*The Bald Soprano. The Lesson. Jack, or The Submission.
    The Chairs*). Translated by Donald M. Allen. New York:
    Grove, 1958.
Amédée. The New Tenant. Victims of Duty. Translated by Donald
    Watson. New York: Grove, 1958.
*The Killer and Other Plays (Improvisation, or The Shepherd's
    Chameleon. Maid to Marry*). Translated by Donald Watson.
    New York: Grove, 1960.
*Rhinoceros and Other Plays (The Leader. The Future Is in Eggs,
    or It Takes All Sorts to Make a World*). Translated by Derek
    Prouse. New York: Grove, 1960.
Exit the King. Translated by Donald Watson. New York: Grove,
    1963.
Notes and Counter Notes. Translated by Donald Watson. New
    York: Grove, 1964.
A Stroll in the Air and *Frenzy for Two or More*. Translated by
    Donald Watson. New York: Grove, 1965.
Fragments of a Journal. Translated by Jean Stewart. New York:
    Grove, 1968.
Hunger and Thirst and Other Plays (*The Picture. Anger.
    Salutations*). Translated by Donald Watson. New York:
    Grove, 1968.
The Colonel's Photograph. Translated by Jean Stewart. New York:
    Grove, 1969.
Present Past, Past Present. Translated by Helen R. Lane. New
    York: Grove, 1971.
Macbett. Translated by Charles Marowitz. New York: Grove,
    1973.
The Hermit. Translated by Richard Seaver. New York: Grove,
    1974.
Killing Game. Translated by Helen Gary Bishop. New York:
    Grove, 1974.

A Hell of a Mess. Translated by Helen Gary Bishop. New York: Grove, 1975.

Man with Bags. Translated by Marie-France Ionesco, adapted by Israel Horovitz. New York: Grove, 1977.

Journeys among the Dead. Translated by Barbara Wright. New York: Riverrun, 1985.

Hugoliad, or The Grotesque and Tragic Life of Victor Hugo. Translated by Yara Milos. New York: Grove, 1987.

EDMOND JABÈS

Elya. Translated by Rosmarie Waldrop. Bolinas, Calif.: Tree Books, 1973.

The Book of Questions

    I. *The Book of Questions.* Translated by Rosmarie Waldrop. Middletown, Conn.: Wesleyan University Press, 1976.

    II, III. *The Book of Yukel* and *Return to the Book.* Translated by Rosmarie Waldrop. Middletown, Conn.: Wesleyan University Press, 1977.

    IV, V, VI. *Yaël, Elya, Aely.* Translated by Rosmarie Waldrop. Middletown, Conn.: Wesleyan University Press, 1983.

    VII. *El, or The Last Book.* Translated by Rosmarie Waldrop. Middletown, Conn.: Wesleyan University Press, 1984.

A Share of Ink. Translated by Anthony Rudolf. London: Menard, 1979.

The Book of Dialogue. Translated by Rosmarie Waldrop. Middletown, Conn.: Wesleyan University Press, 1987.

If There Were Anywhere but Desert: Selected Poems. Translated by Keith Waldrop. Barrytown, N.Y.: Station Hill Press, 1988.

The Book of Shares. Translated by Rosmarie Waldrop. Chicago: University of Chicago Press, 1989.

The Book of Resemblances

    I. *The Book of Resemblances.* Translated by Rosmarie Waldrop. Middletown, Conn.: Wesleyan University Press, 1990.

    II. *Intimations   The Desert.* Translated by Rosmarie Waldrop. Middletown, Conn.: Wesleyan University Press, 1991.

    III. *The Ineffaceable   The Unperceived.* Translated by Rosmarie Waldrop. Middletown, Conn.: Wesleyan University Press, in press.

From the Book to the Book: An Edmond Jabès Reader. Translated by

Rosmarie Waldrop. Middletown, Conn.: Wesleyan University
Press, 1990.

From the Desert to the Book: Dialogues with Marcel Cohen.
Translated by Pierre Joris. Barrytown, N.Y.: Station Hill
Press, 1990.

MILAN KUNDERA

Laughable Loves. Translated by Suzanne Rappaport. New York:
Knopf, 1974.

Life Is Elsewhere. Translated by Peter Kussi. New York: Knopf,
1974.

The Farewell Party. Translated by Peter Kussi. New York: Knopf,
1976.

The Book of Laughter and Forgetting. Translated by Michael
Henry Heim. New York: Knopf, 1980.

The Joke. Translated by Michael Henry Heim. New York: Harper
& Row, 1982.

Jacques and His Master: An Homage to Diderot in Three Acts.
Translated by Michael Henry Heim. New York: Harper &
Row, 1984.

The Unbearable Lightness of Being. Translated by Michael Henry
Heim. New York: Harper & Row, 1984.

The Art of the Novel. Translated by Linda Asher. New York:
Grove, 1988.

Immortality. Translated by Peter Kussi. New York: Grove
Weidenfeld, 1991.

NATHALIE SARRAUTE

Martereau. Translated by Maria Jolas. New York: Braziller,
1953.

Portrait of a Man Unknown. Translated by Maria Jolas. New
York: Braziller, 1958.

The Planetarium. Translated by Maria Jolas. New York: Braziller,
1960.

The Age of Suspicion. Translated by Maria Jolas. New York:
Braziller, 1963.

The Golden Fruits. Translated by Maria Jolas. New York:
Braziller, 1963.

Tropisms. Translated by Maria Jolas. New York: Braziller, 1963.

Between Life and Death. Translated by Maria Jolas. New York: Braziller, 1969.

Do You Hear Them? Translated by Maria Jolas. New York: Braziller, 1973.

"Fools Say." Translated by Maria Jolas. New York: Braziller, 1977.

Collected Plays (*It Is There. It's Beautiful. Izzum. The Lie. Silence*). Translated by Maria Jolas and Barbara Wright. New York: Braziller, 1981.

The Use of Speech. Translated by Barbara Wright. New York: Braziller, 1982.

Childhood. Translated by Barbara Wright. New York: Braziller, 1983.

You Don't Love Yourself. Translated by Barbara Wright. New York: Braziller, 1990.